Claudio Monteverdi
Orfeo

Edited by

JOHN WHENHAM

CAMBRIDGE
UNIVERSITY PRESS

Published by the Press Syndicate of the University of Cambridge
The Pitt Building, Trumpington Street, Cambridge CB2 1RP
40 West 20th Street, New York, NY 10011–4211, USA
10 Stamford Road, Oakleigh, Melbourne 3166, Australia

© Cambridge University Press 1986

First published 1986
Reprinted 1991, 1994

Printed in Great Britain at the University Press, Cambridge

British Library cataloguing in publication data

Claudio Monteverdi : Orfeo. – (Cambridge opera
handbooks)
1. Monteverdi, Claudio. Orfeo
I. Whenham, John
782.1′092′4   ML410.M77

Library of Congress cataloguing in publication data

Claudio Monteverdi, Orfeo.
(Cambridge opera handbooks)
Bibliography
Discography
Includes index.
1. Monteverdi, Claudio, 1567–1643. Orfeo
I. Whenham, John. II. Title: Orfeo. II. Series.
ML410.M77C55   1985   782.1′092′4   85–9923

ISBN 0 521 28477 5 paperback

Transferred to
Digital Reprinting 1999

Printed in the
United States of America

WD

CAMBRIDGE OPERA HANDBOOKS
General preface

This is a series of studies of individual operas, written for the serious opera-goer or record-collector as well as the student or scholar. Each volume has three main concerns. The first is historical: to describe the genesis of the work, its sources or its relation to literary prototypes, the collaboration between librettist and composer, and the first perform-ance and subsequent stage history. This history is itself a record of changing attitudes towards the work, and an index of general changes of taste. The second is analytical and it is grounded in a very full synop-sis which considers the opera as a structure of musical and dramatic effects. In most volumes there is also a musical analysis of a section of the score, showing how the music serves or makes the drama. The analysis, like the history, naturally raises questions of interpretation, and the third concern of each volume is to show how critical writing about an opera, like production and performance, can direct or distort appreciation of its structural elements. Some conflict of interpretation is an inevitable part of this account; editors of the handbooks reflect this – by citing classic statements, by commissioning new essays, by taking up their own critical position. A final section gives a select bibliography, a discography and guides to other sources.

Published titles

Contents

Re-creating *Orfeo* for the modern stage

Appendixes

The text of Chapter 7 is reproduced from *Opera as Drama* by Joseph Kerman, by permission of Alfred A. Knopf, Inc.

Illustrations

Preface

Monteverdi's *Orfeo* has long been regarded as the first masterpiece in the history of opera, and it is now widely accepted as a work whose portrayal of human suffering, daring and weakness speaks directly to modern audiences without the need for historians to act as its apologists. These considerations alone would justify its inclusion in the present series of Opera Handbooks. There are, however, other reasons which prompt a new study of the opera, among them the fact that the past twenty years have seen a broadening of our knowledge of the social and musical context in which *Orfeo* was created, an increasing refinement of approach to its performance and fresh interpretations of the evidence surviving from the seventeenth-century Mantuan productions. The invitation to compile a Handbook to *Orfeo* thus offered an ideal opportunity to draw together established facts, to clear away some of the unjustifiable conclusions and speculations that have accumulated over the course of time, and to add new material. In this last respect, a request to Iain Fenlon to see whether any further information on the opera survived in the Mantuan archives bore unexpected fruit in his discovery of hitherto unpublished correspondence over the early performances, which is discussed in Chapter 1 and reproduced in Appendix 1.

The book conforms, in its broad outlines, to the general plan of the Opera Handbooks series, though in order to confine discussion to issues that are still open to debate, it contains more newly commissioned essays than reprinted material. The first section of the book is concerned with *Orfeo* in its seventeenth-century context. It includes an account of the first, Mantuan, stage of the work's theatre history, a study by F. W. Sternfeld of the sources of its libretto, and an analytical synopsis. Also included in this section is the text of Act V transmitted by the librettos printed for the performances in 1607. This text is considered by most commentators to represent the original ending of the opera, an ending which was changed at some point before the publication of the score in 1609.

The second section of the book is devoted to the rediscovery of *Orfeo* by historians, performers and critics. The performance history of the work during the twentieth century is particularly complex, since in many cases the versions of the opera heard by critics and public scarcely represented the work conceived by Monteverdi and Striggio. Nigel Fortune's essay, then, covers both performances and editions of *Orfeo*. The two other essays in this section, by Romain Rolland and Joseph Kerman, also represent stages in the rediscovery of *Orfeo*. Rolland, whose essay is ostensibly a review of the first modern performances of the opera, was in fact closely involved with Vincent d'Indy in preparing the edition used for those performances. Joseph Kerman's 'Orpheus: the neoclassic vision', slightly revised by the author and reprinted here without its complementary discussion of Gluck's *Orfeo ed Euridice*, was the first critical essay aimed at a wider opera-going public to treat Monteverdi's *Orfeo* seriously, and with real understanding, as a work of musical theatre. It remains, today, the finest short introduction to the opera.

The final section of the book contains two essays, one by a musician and one by a producer, on the processes involved in re-creating *Orfeo* for the modern stage. Jane Glover, who directed performances at Oxford in 1975, writes about the problems to be solved in editing and performing the music in a manner as close as possible to Monteverdi's original intentions. David Freeman, whose controversial production was staged by the English National Opera in 1981 and revived in 1983, writes about his approach to the opera. Now that it is generally accepted that an 'authentic' interpretation of the music is necessary to release the full expressive power of Monteverdi's score, Mr Freeman's essay raises the important question of whether 'authentic' productions are either necessary or desirable.

Since the main focus of this book is Monteverdi's *Orfeo*, discussion of the creation of opera at Florence has been kept to a minimum. Readers interested in the early history of opera are referred to the chapter 'Early Opera and Aria' in Pirrotta and Povoledo, *Music and Theatre*, pp. 237–80. Debates over terminology have been avoided by accepting the preferences of individual contributors. Thus, *Orfeo* is called both an 'opera' and, more properly, a 'favola in musica'; and both 'recitative' and 'arioso' are used as alternative terms for Monteverdi's solo writing. The term 'aria' has, however, been restricted as far as possible to designating a strophic song, its most common early-seventeenth-century musical usage. Short-title references in the text and footnotes are used for books and articles included in the Bibliography.

I should like to thank all the contributors to this book for their willing co-operation, for the free exchange of information and opinions which has made it a genuine collaboration, and for agreeing to disagree in public over contentious issues. For help of various kinds, in addition to that acknowledged elsewhere in the text, I am grateful to Tim Carter, Eric Hughes, Roger Nichols, Andrew Parrott, Harold Rosenthal O.B.E., G. W. Slowey and John C. G. Waterhouse. Dr Hans Haase of the Herzog-August-Bibliothek, Wolfenbüttel, kindly drew my attention to the existence of a second printing of Striggio's libretto. Michael Black and Rosemary Dooley of Cambridge University Press made invaluable suggestions and offered encouragement during the gestation of the book, and Eric Van Tassel lent his expertise during its final stages. Thanks are due to Ailsa Read, who typed early drafts of several sections of the book. Last, and by no means least, my gratitude goes to Jenny, Nicholas and Christopher for their patience and understanding.

Birmingham   John Whenham
Summer 1984

Abbreviations

AG	Archivio Gonzaga
AM	Archivio Mediceo
ASF	Archivio di Stato, Florence
ASL	Archivio di Stato, Lucca
ASM	Archivio di Stato, Mantua

TEXT AND CONTEXT

1 *The Mantuan 'Orfeo'*

IAIN FENLON

[Monteverdi] has shown me the words and let me hear the music of the play [*comedia*] which Your Highness had performed, and certainly both poet and musician have depicted the inclinations of the heart so skilfully that it could not have been done better. The poetry is lovely in conception, lovelier still in form, and loveliest of all in diction; and indeed no less was to be expected of a man as richly talented as Signor Striggio. The music, moreover, observing due propriety, serves the poetry so well that nothing more beautiful is to be heard anywhere.

This enthusiastic view of Monteverdi's *Orfeo* was written in August 1607 by Cherubino Ferrari, Mantuan court theologian, poet, and friend of the composer (see Appendix 1, letter 13).* Whatever Ferrari's motives for eulogy it seems likely that he, in common with other contemporary observers and listeners, was much taken by the novelty of the work. Few of those present at the first performance of *Orfeo* at Mantua on 24 February 1607 would previously have heard even the new recitative style, let alone some two hours of continuous musical theatre. As one court official, Carlo Magno, wrote the night before the performance: 'Tomorrow evening the Most Serene Lord the Prince [Francesco Gonzaga] is to sponsor a performance . . . It should be most unusual, as all the actors are to sing their parts' (Appendix 1, letter 8).[1]

Strictly speaking, of course, *Orfeo* is not the earliest opera, a distinction which belongs to the setting of Ottavio Rinuccini's *Dafne*, begun by Jacopo Corsi, completed by Jacopo Peri, and first performed at Florence in 1598.[2] The earliest operatic scores to survive in their entirety – Emilio de' Cavalieri's *Rappresentatione di Anima, et di Corpo* (first performed at the oratory of the Chiesa Nuova, Rome, in February 1600), Jacopo Peri's *Euridice* (first performed at

---

* Appendix 1 (pp. 167–72) gives the original Italian texts and English translations of some thirteen letters, in the Florentine and Mantuan archives, that are pertinent to the earliest production of *Orfeo*.

1

the Pitti Palace, Florence, on 6 October 1600, and the most important precursor of *Orfeo*) and Giulio Caccini's *Euridice* (published
1600, but not performed until 1602) – were also the products of composers associated with Florence. These works form the earliest
phase of opera, though one that has often (unjustly) been characterised as theatre monody of an experimental and amateur kind
rather than 'true' opera. According to this interpretation, Monteverdi's *Orfeo* is the first fully fledged opera, for all that Monteverdi
himself was so clearly indebted to Florentine precedent. Certainly
there can be little doubt of the impact made by *Orfeo*, which effectively heralds the spread of the new theatrical, or 'representative',
style (*stile rappresentativo*) outside Florence. Nor can there be much
question of the originality of Monteverdi's piece, particularly in
matters of formal design, or of his powers of synthesis, which forged
the language of the work from a wide range of musical resources and
expressive techniques drawn not only from the new style of theatrical recitative created by Peri, but also from the traditional forms of
madrigal and *intermedio*.

Given the importance of Monteverdi's *Orfeo* in the early history
of opera, it comes as something of a surprise to realise how little has
been discovered about the origins and first performance of the
work, and in particular how little that bears directly on attempts at
historical and musical reconstruction. Before introducing some new
evidence which throws considerable light on the first performance,
it might be useful briefly to recapitulate the known facts, the
archaeological evidence with which music historians have previously worked, and some of the problems involved in interpreting
this evidence.

Orfeo was written under the auspices of an academy (a more or
less formal gathering of gentlemen amateurs), the Accademia degli
Invaghiti, to be performed by the musicians of the Mantuan court
during the Carnival season of 1607. As such it was only one of many
essentially ephemeral works created to entertain the members of
the Mantuan aristocracy. There is, thus, no published description of
the work and its first performance such as we have for Peri's
Euridice and for Monteverdi's second opera, *Arianna*, both of
which were written for princely weddings and described in the
volumes issued to commemorate these events.[3] The only commemorative volume issued in connection with *Orfeo* was the score
of the opera itself, which was published twice during Monteverdi's
lifetime: first in 1609, two years after the first performance (with a

dedication to Francesco Gonzaga), and then again in 1615 (with no dedication).[4] The two editions were brought out by the same Venetian publisher, Ricciardo Amadino, but they differ in matters of textual detail as one might expect. Over questions of instrumentation and the allocation of voice-types to certain roles, neither is to be preferred. Both give the same list of instruments required in the prefatory matter. The list is incomplete (despite superficial appearances to the contrary), and extra instruments are called for in the course of the piece. Similarly, while in some passages the instrumentation is marked clearly, in others the indications are ambiguous, and in some cases there is no information at all (see below, Chapter 8). There is a list of characters printed at the front of the work, and the vocal lines are, for the most part, accurately labelled. But while it is evident which voice-types are required for the lower-voice roles, it is not clear for the upper ones, which could have been sung by either male or female performers.

Other than the two editions of the score, the surviving historical evidence is slight. Unlike so many of the Medici *intermedi*, for example, there are no surviving costume drawings, property lists or commemorative engravings of the sets for *Orfeo*.[5] It is not definitely known where the first performance took place, despite strong and unfounded traditions which place it either in the Galleria degli Specchi or in the Galleria dei Fiumi of the ducal palace. Equally questionable is the theory that the first performance of *Orfeo* took place earlier than 24 February 1607. This theory is based on a reading of the first phrase of Francesco Gonzaga's letter of 23 February 1607 (Appendix 1, letter 9) which would render 'Dimani si farà la favola cantata nella nostra Accademia' as 'Tomorrow there will be a performance of the play [already] sung before our Academy'. 'Favola cantata' could, however, also be taken as the equivalent of 'favola in musica' (musical fable/play), the designation which Monteverdi himself used on the title-page of the published score; and a literal translation of the letter could, thus, begin 'Tomorrow there will be a performance of the sung play before our Academy'.[6] That this is the more likely reading will become apparent in the third section of this chapter, where Francesco's letter is placed in the context of a more extensive correspondence over the opera.

With two exceptions, the names of the original performers are unknown. Eugenio Cagnani's *Lettera cronologica*, published at Mantua in 1612,[7] notes merely that the distinguished singer–composer Francesco Rasi took part: presumably he sang the title-role. In his letter of 23 February 1607, Francesco Gonzaga notes that he is satisfied with Giovanni Gualberto [Magli], who not only had learnt his part by heart in a short time, but sang it 'with much grace and a most pleasing effect' (Appendix 1, letter 9). The identity of a third singer is hinted at in a letter dated 28 October 1608 from Gabriele Bertazzuolo, the Mantuan agent at Florence, to Duke Vincenzo Gonzaga.[8] Discussing the music provided for a banquet at Florence in 1608, Bertazzuolo mentions that one of the singers was 'that little priest who performed the role of Eurydice in the Most Serene Prince's *Orfeo*' ('quel Pretino che fece da Euridice nel Orfeo del Ser.^{mo} Sr Prencipe').[9] Although the identity of the 'little priest' cannot be firmly established, this passing reference does suggest that the role of Eurydice was originally sung by a castrato, perhaps by Padre Girolamo Bacchini, a castrato known to have served at the Mantuan court at various times between 1594 and 1605.[10]

Together with Carlo Magno's letter written to his brother Giovanni, Francesco Gonzaga's letter of 23 February is the only contemporary report of the first performance of *Orfeo*. Incidentally, Francesco's letter also reveals that the literary text of the *favola* had been published so that each spectator could read the words while they were being sung. A small number of these printed librettos have survived.[11] They add no new information about musical aspects of the performance, but they do transmit a quite different ending to the final act from that given in Monteverdi's score. Whereas Striggio's libretto adheres closely to the ending employed for Poliziano's *Orfeo*, an earlier Mantuan pastoral based on the Orpheus legend, the score of 1609 substitutes a happy ending based on the *Astronomia* of Hyginus: through the intervention of a *deus ex machina*, Apollo descends to rescue Orpheus, if not from the Bacchantes then at least from his own self-pity.

The established facts are, then, few. The discussion which follows attempts to enlarge this picture first by placing *Orfeo* in the context of Monteverdi's output and of music-making at the Mantuan court, then by introducing a number of hitherto unpublished letters which relate to the preparation of the first performance, and finally by suggesting a possible reason for the substitution of a happy ending for the ending transmitted by the libretto.

*

* *

I remarked earlier that the score of *Orfeo* represents a highly original synthesis of elements drawn from the new style of theatrical recitative with elements drawn from the traditional forms of madrigal and *intermedio*. In his treatment of traditional forms Monteverdi was clearly influenced by the example of his Mantuan colleagues and by the experience of having been a member of the Mantuan court musical establishment for almost twenty years by the time he came to write *Orfeo*. He had first arrived at the Gonzaga court in 1589/90 and was taken on as 'suonatore di Vivuola': that is, as a player of either the violin or the viola da gamba. His career at Mantua not only brought him to an important musical centre with a distinguished tradition, but also began at a time when that tradition was undergoing a considerable change.

Only a few years before the composer's arrival in the city from his native Cremona, control of the Mantuan duchy had passed to Vincenzo Gonzaga, whose enthusiasm for both music and theatre was pronounced. As a young man, Vincenzo's tastes had been largely formed at the courts of Ferrara (where his sister Margherita was married to the reigning duke) and Florence (the home of his second wife, Eleonora de' Medici). It was the influence of both these courts that in turn helped to shape Vincenzo's attitude to the patronage of music at Mantua after his accession in 1587.

At the centre of musical life at Vincenzo's court were a small group of instrumentalists and an ensemble of virtuoso singers modelled on the famous Ferrarese *concerto di donne* (consort of singing ladies).[12] A description of the Ferrarese and Mantuan ensembles, written around 1628 by the Roman commentator Vincenzo Giustiniani, shows that their members not only cultivated the practice of concerted virtuoso ornamentation, but also performed madrigals in a markedly theatrical manner:

... they moderated or increased their voices, loud or soft, heavy or light, according to the demands of the piece they were singing; now slow, breaking off sometimes with a gentle sigh, now singing long passages legato or detached, now groups, now leaps, now with long trills, now with short, or again with sweet running passages sung softly, to which one sometimes heard an echo answer unexpectedly. They accompanied the music and the sentiment with appropriate facial expressions, glances and gestures, with no awkward movements of the mouth or hands or body which might not express the feeling of the song. They made the words clear in such a way that one could hear even the last syllable of every word, which was never interrupted or suppressed by passages [*passaggi*] and other embellishments.[13]

After 1598 the Mantuan ensemble also included Francesco Rasi who, as Giustiniani remarked, could sing in both the tenor and bass ranges 'with exquisite style, and passage-work, and with extraordinary feeling and a particular talent to make the words clearly heard'.[14]

Few pay documents relating to the Mantuan court during the early seventeenth century have survived. On the basis of the salary roll closest in date to 1607[15] and other documentary references, however, it is possible to gain a very approximate idea of the size of the permanent musical establishment at that time: that is, about fifteen singers, half a dozen string-players and the same number of keyboard-players, and perhaps four wind-players, all under the control of Monteverdi and his assistant, Don Bassano Casola. This permanent staff of musicians would have provided the nucleus of performers for *Orfeo*: the orchestra, the chorus, and some at least of the soloists. As we shall see, however, in 1607 Prince Francesco Gonzaga had at his disposal too few sopranos of sufficient ability to take all the leading roles in *Orfeo*.

The resources of the Mantuan *concerto*, the taste of the court for pastoral poetry and for poetry which conveyed powerful emotions, and the madrigal writing of his Mantuan colleagues (particularly the angular and declamatory writing of Giaches de Wert) exerted a strong influence on Monteverdi's own madrigalian composition, an influence that is fully evident for the first time in some of the more virtuosic pieces in his third book of madrigals (1592), such as *O come è gran martire* and *Lumi miei cari lumi*. The republication of this book in 1594 was the last collection of Monteverdi's work to appear in print until 1603, and the intervening period seems to have been substantially occupied with court duties and domestic problems. In 1595 Monteverdi was part of the ducal retinue that accompanied Duke Vincenzo on one of his three ambitious and unsuccessful forays against the Turks, and the death of the court choirmaster Giaches de Wert in 1596 may have brought additional work, for all that another man was selected to fill the post. In 1599 Monteverdi married the court singer Claudia Cattaneo. Their life together before her early death in September 1607 was evidently a hard one.

Though he had published nothing new for eight years, Monteverdi became prominent in 1600 with the appearance of the first attacks on the supposed harmonic irregularities of his music by the theorist Giovanni Maria Artusi.[16] The works discussed by Artusi had not then been published, but some are presented in the fourth and fifth madrigal books of 1603 and 1605 respectively. These volumes, which represent the integration of new elements into Monteverdi's writing, are traditionally considered to be the finest products of his early madrigalian style. By way of introduction, the fifth book includes the outline of a reply to Artusi, an outline which was elaborated by Giulio Cesare Monteverdi in the celebrated *Dichiaratione* which prefaces his brother's *Scherzi musicali* of 1607. This controversy merely quickened public interest in Monteverdi's work, and a number of madrigal books were republished. By 1607 Monteverdi was one of the ablest and most respected composers in Italy. Importantly, he was also a close friend of Alessandro Striggio the Younger, an accomplished diplomat and himself the son of a composer: that much is clear from the extensive series of letters between the two men. (Striggio was the recipient of most of Monteverdi's extant letters and, after the latter's move to Venice in 1613, became the composer's greatest ally in his dealings with the Mantuan court.) Striggio was in turn a member of the Accademia degli Invaghiti (within whose ranks he took the title 'Il Ritenuto', 'the reserved one'), and as we shall see, it was this body which, under the influence of Francesco Gonzaga, took the initiative in requiring Monteverdi to write *Orfeo* to Striggio's libretto.

While Ferrarese example of the 1580s was the principal influence on Mantuan madrigal writing of the 1590s, Vincenzo Gonzaga's enthusiasm for theatre and spectacle was largely fuelled by his contacts with Florence. Sixteenth-century Florentine traditions of musical theatre centred on the *intermedi*, interludes inserted between the acts of spoken comedies partly as a way of clarifying the division of the drama into acts. These interludes grew in size during the course of the century, not only in terms of the elaborate stage machinery required to perform them and the musical resources needed, but also in the length of time that they occupied. Although the *intermedio* tradition spread throughout Italy and beyond, it was in Florence, where the Medici cultivated the *intermedio* as a way of projecting state and dynastic propaganda, that it reached its fullest expression. The Florentine practice of commissioning elaborate *intermedi* to be performed on important Medici occasions begins with those written for the marriage of Cosimo I in 1539, includes a sequence devised to accompany a whole series of dynastic events during the 1560s, and culminates in those composed to accompany performances of Girolamo Bargagli's *La Pellegrina*, given in 1589 to celebrate the marriage of Grand Duke Ferdinando I de' Medici to Christine of Lorraine. By this time the *intermedi* had grown to overshadow the comedy that they were designed to frame, and descriptions of the complicated series of classical allusions on which the interludes were based and of the music itself were printed at the time rather in the manner of commemorative publications, as was the score of *Orfeo* itself in 1609. Although there was a large Mantuan contingent among the performers at Florence in 1589, there is no evidence to suggest that Monteverdi was present. Nevertheless, he may well have known the music of the 1589 *intermedi* through the published partbooks, and through contact with Alessandro Striggio the Elder and his son, both of whom took part. In more general terms there can be no doubt of Monteverdi's indebtedness to the Florentine *intermedi*, both through direct knowledge and through Mantuan emulation (as in Gastoldi's danced interludes for the 1598 production of Giovanni Battista Guarini's *Il pastor fido*). The influences are there in pieces such as the *moresca* which concludes *Orfeo* and in the self-contained *Ballo delle ingrate* composed in 1608. And it should be remembered that the *intermedio* tradition did not die with the advent of opera, but continued well into the seventeenth century, providing a fund of theatrical and musical expertise upon which opera continued to draw.[17]

Following the death of Alfonso II d'Este in 1597, the duchy of Ferrara was taken over by the papacy and the remnants of the court transferred their activities to Modena. Thereafter, Mantuan contacts with Florentine music became even stronger. This was a result not only of Vincenzo Gonzaga's links with the Medici court through marriage, but also of the close involvement of his younger son Ferdinando with Florentine musical life during the early years of the new century. The Gonzaga interest in Florentine music, and particularly in the new operatic forms, is strikingly demonstrated by the arrangements made by the court in 1608 to celebrate the marriage of the Gonzaga heir, Francesco, to Margherita of Savoy. The entry of the couple into the city after their wedding in Turin inaugurated a week of lavish entertainments which included Monteverdi's *Ballo delle ingrate* and his opera *Arianna* (of which only the lament now survives) to a libretto by the Florentine poet Ottavio Rinuccini. A prominent role was also played by the composer Marco da Gagliano, the founder member of the Florentine Accademia degli Elevati, which included 'the city's finest composers, instrumentalists and singers' (both Peri and Caccini were members), and which operated under the protection of Ferdinando Gonzaga. Earlier in 1608, Gagliano's *Dafne*, the setting of a revised version of Rinuccini's first operatic libretto, had been presented, and following its success Gagliano stayed on in Mantua. For the wedding celebrations he wrote the music for a *ballo*, *Il sacrificio d'Ifigenia*, and for one of the *intermedi* which accompanied the performance of Guarini's play *Idropica*.

The 1608 festivities mark a high point in Florentine involvement in Mantuan musical life, but the influence of Florence had been slowly developing for some twenty years, and had been accelerated by Ferdinando Gonzaga's strong contacts with the Medici court after 1605. Yet Monteverdi's *Orfeo* not only draws on forms rooted in older Mantuan and Florentine traditions of musical spectacle, but also, in some quite specific ways, is modelled on the first Florentine operas. It is true that the Orpheus myth, taken either directly from classical sources or from the more recent tradition stemming from Angelo Poliziano's *Orfeo*, frequently provided the action of *intermedi*. Nevertheless, Striggio's *La favola d'Orfeo*, for all its similarities with Poliziano's text, is clearly indebted to Rinuccini's libretto for Peri's *Euridice*. This is clear from details such as the close similarity between the two writers' treatments of the messenger's scene and Orpheus's lament. Similarly, Monteverdi's indebtedness to Peri's music is often evident, particularly in those cases where Striggio's text shows analogies with Rinuccini's.

*

* *

Though the established facts about the first performance of *Orfeo* are few, a series of letters between Francesco and Ferdinando Gonzaga, most of which have not previously been published, adds a good deal and helps to resolve some of the problems and discrepancies which surround the text of *Orfeo* and its first performance. It is rather surprising that the importance of this correspondence has not been commented on before, since it is in turn part of a larger group of letters between Francesco and Ferdinando Gonzaga. And while neither composer nor librettist is mentioned by name, nor the title of the opera specified, there can be no doubt about which work is being referred to.[18] Before the letters are examined in detail, however, something should be said about the two correspondents.

Prince Francesco Gonzaga (Fig. 1), first son and heir to Vincenzo Gonzaga and Eleonora de' Medici, was born in 1586. It is difficult to gain a detailed impression of his temperament. As duke he reigned briefly, from Vincenzo Gonzaga's death in February 1612

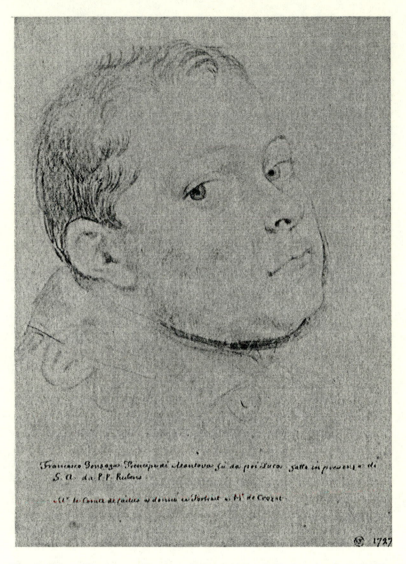

Fig. 1. Prince Francesco Gonzaga (1586–1612): chalk drawing (c. 1601) by Rubens

until his own just ten months later. According to the Venetian ambassador Pietro Gritti, writing in 1612, Francesco was of handsome appearance, grave, cautious with money, moderate in taking his pleasure; all the things in fact that his father was not.[19] Traditionally, he is thought to have had strong interests in music and theatre, but, with the exception of *Orfeo* itself, the evidence is slight. Apart from the first edition of the score of the opera, Monteverdi dedicated several other publications to him, as did a number of court composers.[20] And it seems that *Orfeo* was produced in 1607 largely at Francesco's instigation.

Rather more is known about Francesco's brother Ferdinando (born 1587) who, as second son, was destined for a career in the Church. In 1602 he was sent to study in Innsbruck, and in the same year a volume of his meditations was published in Ingolstadt.[21] Three years later he embarked upon two years' study of law, theology and philosophy at the University of Pisa. His scholarly qualities were evidently remarkable: the Venetian ambassador Giovanni da Mulla noted in a report of 1615 that he had an astonishing memory and was proficient in Latin, German, French, Spanish, Hebrew and Greek. From an early age he had taken an interest in writing poetry and composing music.[22] And while it was Francesco who seems to have had the closest contact with Mantuan musicians in general, and with Monteverdi in particular, in Pisa and Florence Ferdinando developed close relations with musicians of the Medici court during the first decade of the seventeenth century. Contact with the musicians of the Accademia degli Elevati, who included Luca Bati, Marco da Gagliano, Peri and Caccini, seems to have been particularly strong. It has been suggested that Gagliano, who dedicated his fourth book of madrigals to Ferdinando in 1606, may have taught him composition. Certainly he did a lot of it. For the Pisan Carnival of 1605/6 he devised and directed a *sbarra* (a chivalric display, often with music) on the subject of Alexander the Great, and later he supervised the Easter music in Santa Nicola, one of the city churches. For the Carnival season of the following year a comedy was staged for which Ferdinando had written both verse and music. Neither has survived, but they occupied much of his time and figure largely in the letters between Ferdinando and Francesco written in the early months of 1607.[23] It is these letters which in turn reveal new and important information about the planning and first productions of *Orfeo*.

The first letter in the series dates from the beginning of 1607, shortly after the start of the Florentine Carnival season. For this, the Medici court had moved, as traditionally it always did for the Carnival, to Pisa. In early January 1607, Ferdinando received a letter from Francesco, who was then in Mantua. From this letter it appears that Francesco had taken the initiative in organising what he calls 'una favola in musica' for the approaching Mantuan Carnival. Clearly some or all of the music had been written, or at least the characters of the drama were known, since the main point of Francesco's letter was to ask Ferdinando to request the loan of one of the castrati in the service of the Grand Duke: as Francesco remarked, 'we have very few sopranos here, and those few not good'. Francesco had heard the Grand Duke's performers on a visit to Tuscany. Ferdinando was now to select the best of those available and to take the matter up with the Grand Duke, by whom, as Francesco later remarks, he is held in great esteem (Appendix 1, letter 1; see also Fig. 2).

Ferdinando acted quickly. Within a few days he was able to reply that he had carried out Francesco's wishes and had found 'un soprano castrato', though not one of those that Francesco had previously heard. Nevertheless, this other singer had performed in comedies on two or three occasions, 'with great success'. He was a pupil of Giulio Romano (i.e. Caccini) and a salaried employee of the Grand Duke (letter 2).

Francesco's next letter, of 17 January (letter 3), is enthusiastic. It enclosed a formal letter of request to the Grand Duke, and further reveals that the *favola* was currently being composed 'nella nostra accademia'. Later in the correspondence (in letter 9) we read that the performance is to be given 'nella nostra accademia'. This can only be taken to mean 'in front of the members of the academy' rather than 'in the place where the academy holds its meetings'. The academy in question was that of the Invaghiti, founded in 1562 by Cesare Gonzaga of Guastalla. Initially, the academy met in Cesare's Mantuan *palazzo*, and his proximity to influential circles in Rome helped to acquire for it special privileges from Pope Pius IV, including the power to award various professional qualifications. Membership was open to both clergy and laity, and from its inception the Invaghiti was typical of aristocratic and courtly academies in its emphasis on chivalric ceremonial and the arts of oratory and versification. Francesco and Ferdinando were among its members; Monteverdi, it seems, was not.[24]

With the letter of 17 January, Francesco also enclosed a part for

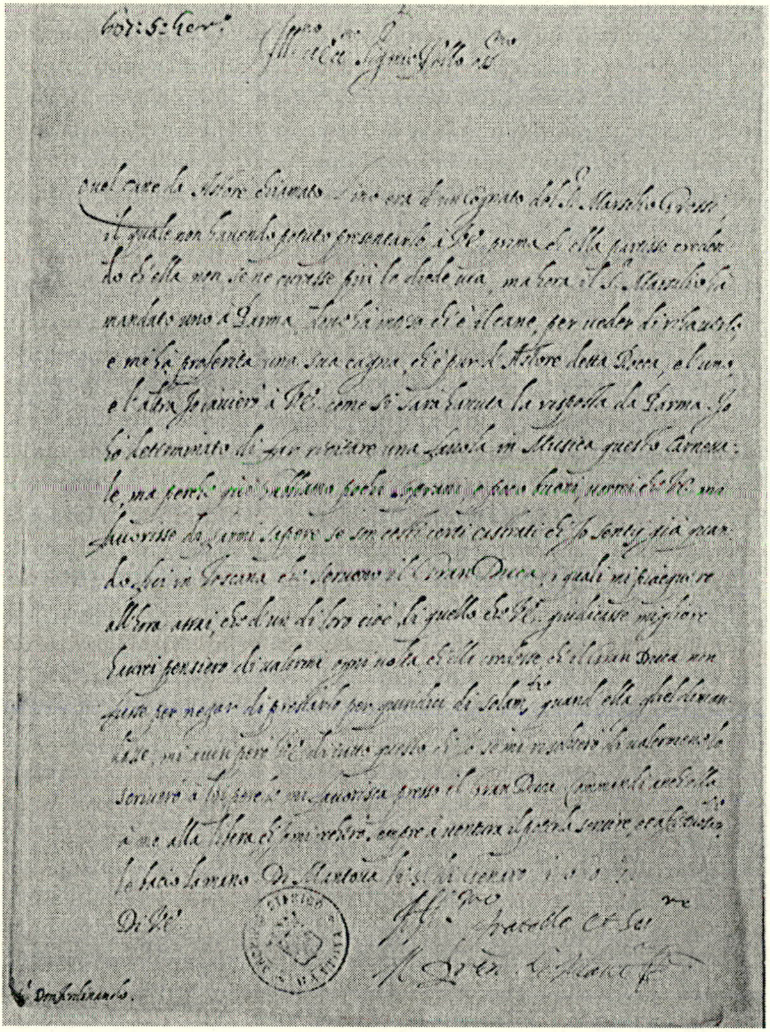

Fig. 2. Letter of 5 January 1607 from Francesco Gonzaga to his brother Ferdinando in Pisa (see Appendix 1, Letter 1)

the (still anonymous) castrato he was requesting, so that it could be studied and committed to memory should the Grand Duke accede to his request. This is the first firm indication that by now some at least of the music for what Francesco interestingly calls a 'recitazione cantata d'una favola' (thus implying a *recitativo* style) had been finished. At the beginning of February (Francesco requests), the singer should be sent on his way to Mantua with any necessary expenses for the trip provided by Ferdinando.

It is fortunate for us that the arrangements did not go smoothly. By 2 February Francesco's concern had grown considerably, and he now wrote to Ferdinando expressing the hope that by the time his letter arrived, the castrato would have reached Mantua, or would at the very least be on his way. Time was now growing short and, Francesco emphasised, without this singer the plans for the *favola* would be thrown into jeopardy: 'senza questo soprano non si potrebbe in modo veruno rappresentare' (Appendix 1, letter 4).

The next three letters in the series are of considerable interest for the light they throw upon the allocation of dramatic roles in the work. Francesco's concern for the future of the enterprise was well founded, since Ferdinando did not send the Florentine singer on his way until 5 February at the earliest. A note of that date was evidently carried by the musician as a letter of introduction. It describes him as a young castrato and for the first time gives his name – Giovanni Gualberto [Magli], who, as has long been known, sang in the first performance of *Orfeo* (letter 5).[25] Evidently Magli had experienced some difficulty in learning the music which Francesco had sent to Pisa; the prologue had been memorised but the rest required 'troppo voci'. Whatever that might mean,[26] difficulties of this sort are not surprising: from these letters it seems that Magli's roles had been composed without any precise knowledge of his vocal abilities. And here, for the first time, is some quite specific information about the vocal requirements of the piece: from the beginning, Magli had been expected to sing two roles in the work, one of them being the personification of Music who alone holds the stage for the opening prologue which announces the subject matter of what is to follow.

As Francesco's near-hysterical letter of 9 February reveals, Magli had by then still not arrived in Mantua. He should come as soon as possible; not only is he to perform the music that had been sent to him in Pisa, but Francesco would also like him to learn the role of Proserpina since the person who was originally to have sung it could no longer do so. The production was now evidently at a critical stage. As Francesco wrote: 'I am awaiting him from day to day with great eagerness, as without him the play would be a complete failure' (Appendix 1, letter 6). Clearly this was no exaggeration, as emerges from Francesco's next letter to his brother of seven days later. By now (just one week before the first performance took place), Magli had finally arrived. Francesco is grateful, but alarmed: 'he knows only the prologue, and seems to think that he will not have time to learn the other part before the Carnival; in which case I shall have no choice but to postpone the performance of the play until Easter. This morning, however, he began to study not only the music, but the words as well; and if he were able to learn the part (although it does contain too many notes [*troppo voci*], as Your Excellency says), he would at least know the melody [*l'aria*], the music could be altered to suit his needs, and we would not waste so much time ensuring that he knows it all by heart' (letter 7). This is, in itself, a remarkable and unusually detailed account of one singer's rehearsal technique. It is conceivable, if not likely, that less complicated musical lines should be learned first and the words added later, but it is difficult to imagine how this might happen in recitative sections. Even more interesting is the idea that Monteverdi would have altered the music itself to accommodate the performer.

Following this, there is a gap in the correspondence between Ferdinando and Francesco until 23 February, the day on which Carlo Magno also wrote to his brother in Rome to advise him of this extraordinary piece in which 'all the actors are to sing their parts'. Francesco's own letter speaks with enthusiasm of Magli's command of the music: 'Giovanni Gualberto has done very well in the short time he has been here. Not only has he thoroughly learned the whole of his part, he delivers it with much grace and a most pleasing effect; I am delighted with him' (Appendix 1, letter 9). Francesco's praise, as we now know, had as much to do with feelings of relief as with genuine admiration for Magli's singing abilities.

Two conclusions can be drawn immediately from this sequence of letters. First, since Magli began to learn his music in earnest only on 16 February, it seems unlikely that the first performance took place before 24 February. Secondly, Magli sang three roles, two of which were La Musica and Proserpina. His third role must have been either that of La Messaggiera (the messenger) or that of Speranza (Hope). The messenger is not, however, listed by Monteverdi as a principal role and should in any case be played by one of the nymphs attendant on Eurydice in Act I. The role of Speranza thus seems the more likely.

With these considerations in mind we can begin, if tentatively, to reconstruct the list of singers who took the principal roles in the opera.

La Musica Prologo	Giovanni Gualberto Magli (soprano castrato)
Orfeo	?Francesco Rasi (tenor)
Euridice	?Girolamo Bacchini (soprano castrato)
Speranza	?Giovanni Gualberto Magli
Caronte	(unknown)
Proserpina	Giovanni Gualberto Magli
Plutone	(unknown)

The role of Apollo probably did not exist for the first performance.

*
* *

Perhaps the most useful general conclusion to be drawn from the material presented in this chapter concerns the character of the work. Prevailing nineteenth-century notions of opera, combined with Monteverdi's own large list of instruments required, have often resulted in rather grand performances of *Orfeo* – in opera houses, on large stages, with large choruses. As we have seen, however, the work was first performed using a fairly limited number of singers and instrumentalists. It was probably played, too, in a relatively small room. Carlo Magno refers to 'a room in the apartments which the Most Serene Lady of Ferrara [i.e. Margherita Gonzaga, sister of Duke Vincenzo] had the use of', and also to the lack of space (Appendix 1, letter 8).[27] The possibility that *Orfeo* was first played in a small room may in turn help to explain the different endings given in Striggio's libretto and Monteverdi's score. The libretto must, I think, represent Monteverdi's original ending. It is known that the libretto was distributed at the first performance 'so that everyone in the audience can have a copy to follow while the performance is in progress' (letter 9); and given the size of the room in which that performance most probably took place, it would have been impossible to install the machinery required for the descent of Apollo.[28] And the verse which Monteverdi sets in the 1609 version of the ending is not sufficiently accomplished to be Striggio's work and suggests, perhaps, the hand of an amateur such as Ferdinando Gonzaga himself.[29] If all this implies that *Orfeo* was devised as an intimate chamber work, that is also indicated by Francesco Gonzaga's letters.

There is an instructive sequel to the alarms and excursions which preceded the first performance of *Orfeo* on 24 February. That was not, it seems, Magli's only intended appearance in the work. A further letter from Francesco to his brother, written one week later, reveals that the first performance had greatly impressed Duke Vincenzo Gonzaga, while Magli's singing had been particularly admired by the duchess. The duke himself had now ordered a second performance to be given on 1 March before the ladies of the city, and Magli had been kept on (Appendix 1, letter 10). Nor was this the end of the matter. From letters between Francesco and Grand Duke Ferdinando de' Medici, it appears that Duke Vincenzo again intervened to order yet a further performance, and permission was now being sought to keep Magli in Mantua even longer (letter 11). And although the reasons for this further production were not divulged to the Grand Duke, they were clearly political rather than artistic.

Throughout the period when Monteverdi's opera was being prepared and performed, negotiations were in hand to arrange a marriage between Francesco Gonzaga and Margherita, daughter of Duke Carlo Emanuele of Savoy. Discussions had begun as early as 1604, and at first the signs seemed good. Carlo Emanuele's concern about foreign involvements in Italy was no secret. The Venetian ambassador reported a characteristic expression of this concern in 1609: 'When all is said and done, I am an Italian; and it is essential that we [Italians] come to terms with one another. These foreigners offer their friendship not in our interest, but simply to take from us all that we own, and to force us to serve their purposes, so that they can rule us all the more easily.'[30] This mistrust was no doubt sharpened by Savoy's geographical position, with borders shared with France, another touched by Switzerland and (to the east) Milan, governed by Spain. When the possibility of a marriage alliance between Mantua and Savoy became known, it posed a threat to other interests, not least to the German Emperor Rudolf II, who became alarmed by union between two fiefs of the Holy Roman Empire. Another Habsburg, Philip III, was acutely conscious that his North Italian territories lay between Mantua and Savoy. Habsburg interests united and presented the somewhat bizarre proposal that the aged Rudolf himself should become Margherita's suitor, principally or solely to forestall the Mantua–

Savoy match. As his dependants, both duchies had no alternative but to allow him to press his claim: it was decided that a deadline of 31 July 1607 be set for the successful conclusion of negotiations with the Emperor.

In the spring of that year, just after the first performance of *Orfeo*, it became known that Carlo Emanuele was planning a visit to Mantua. Vincenzo Gonzaga now arranged that all steps be taken to demonstrate the suitability of Francesco as bridegroom, and the power and wealth of the Mantuan state. It was as part of these schemes that Vincenzo now ordered a third performance of Monteverdi's work, and it may not be too fanciful to suggest that the new ending might have been written for this occasion, the original having been considered unsuitable for the entertainment of a prospective father-in-law.[31] In a world where celestial and terrestrial deities were often conveniently merged, a *lieto fine* would surely seem mandatory. But delays occurred, and Magli was still in Mantua at the end of April when Francesco wrote a letter to the Grand Duke of Tuscany apologising for keeping him so long (Appendix 1, letter 12). And in the end, Carlo Emanuele altered his plans and cancelled his visit to Mantua. The third Mantuan performance of *Orfeo* seems not to have taken place.

Nor, for that matter, do any of the other early-seventeenth-century performances that have been occasionally proposed.[32] The Turin performance of 1610 rests on no more than a letter from Francesco Gonzaga asking for a copy of the newly published score, hardly an unusual request since he was both dedicatee and original promoter of the opera. Evidence of revivals elsewhere is even less secure, and the truth seems to be that *Orfeo* did not make a great impact upon contemporaries – certainly not in comparison with *Arianna*, which Monteverdi composed for Francesco's wedding celebrations in Mantua in 1608. Writing in the 1640s, Severo Bonini claimed that there was not a musical household in Italy that did not have a copy of the famous lament,[33] and for Monteverdi himself it was this which constituted the 'most fundamental part' of the work. It was a piece to which he returned; in the *Sesto libro* of 1614, where it is refashioned as a cycle of six-voice madrigals, and as late as 1640, when it was republished as a sacred *travestimento*. Performances of a revised version of the entire work were planned for Mantua in 1620, and it was with *Arianna* that the Teatro San Moisé in Venice was inaugurated in 1640. All this stands in stark contrast to *Orfeo*, which despite a second edition of 1615 (issued without a dedication) appears to have attracted little interest outside the Mantuan court.

Some insight into the rather different fortunes of his first two operas is provided by Monteverdi himself. Writing towards the end of his life, he suggested that in the *lamento* in *Arianna* he had achieved what he called 'the natural way of imitation', an intimate alliance of words and music. By implication this was something that he had striven for in *Orfeo* but had failed to realise.[34] And it seems that it is precisely this affective quality of Ariadne's lament which accounts for its contemporary popularity, a popularity which is evident from its survival as a discrete item, in both printed and manuscript form, as well as from Bonini's remarks and Monteverdi's reworkings. At the disadvantageous distance of almost four hundred years Monteverdi's own distinction rings true; the lament from *Arianna* does inhabit a different world from *Orfeo*, a world of real human emotions rather than the gilt and gesso stereotypes of the old *intermedio* tradition with its set pieces and machines. Although twentieth-century historians have elevated *Orfeo* to a position of supreme importance in the history of early opera, it is clear that for both the composer and his contemporaries the work was no more than an ephemeral entertainment for courtiers.

2 The Orpheus myth and the libretto of 'Orfeo'

F. W. STERNFELD

In the treasure house of ancient mythology the story of Orpheus survives in many variants.[1] The tale (or 'fabula' or 'mythos') concerns a Thracian singer of magic and 'divine' power. This divinity usually derives from Apollo, the Greek god of music, and in many versions of the story Orpheus is the son of Apollo and the Muse Calliope. In other versions the connection with Apollo is more mysterious, but it is only rarely that Orpheus is not at least his protégé. The divine power of Orpheus's song is able to move rocks and beasts as well as humans. Even more miraculously, it overcomes the power of Hades.

Clearly, the story of Orpheus must have appeared tailor-made for early opera, but we should remember that in the consciousness of the Western world the myth of the power of music over death has survived a time span of more than two millennia, say from Euripides to Stravinsky, and even if we were to restrict ourselves to works in which Orpheus is himself the protagonist of the plot, examples are so numerous that a mere catalogue of titles would fill several pages. Moreover, this list would need to be supplemented by works in which Orpheus is referred to only in passing, as he is in the first-century Latin tragedy *Hercules furens* by Seneca, a poet who exercised considerable influence on the dramatists of the humanist period. In *Hercules furens* the chorus speaks of the combat between Hercules and Pluto, comparing the task of Hercules with that of Orpheus, who 'had power to bend the ruthless lords of the shades by song and suppliant prayer'.[2] It is difficult to believe that Seneca would have devoted twenty-one lines within a chorus of fifty-eight lines to the analogy with Orpheus without the assumption that he was already dealing with a widely known and exemplary myth of victory over death.

The two earliest fully developed accounts of Orpheus's journey to the Underworld are those given in the fourth book of Virgil's

20

Georgics and in Books 10 and 11 of Ovid's *Metamorphoses*. Of the two authors, Ovid is the more generally important for the early history of opera. The librettos of *Dafne* and *Euridice*, as well as that of *Orfeo*, are based on material from the *Metamorphoses*, and the libretto of Monteverdi's *Arianna* develops a story from the *Heroides*. Ovid provided not only the mythological basis for these operas, but also the pastoral setting for the love story, its central lament, and the supernatural interventions and happenings which so often initiate and conclude the amorous tale.

The *Metamorphoses* formed part of the popular literature of the educated classes during the late Renaissance, and part of the pleasure for the early opera-goer must have derived from seeing an already familiar story brought to life on stage. Some members of the audiences for the early performances of *Orfeo* will have read the *Metamorphoses* in the original Latin. Others may have come to know the stories that it contains from Italian translations and reworkings of Ovid's text. Two such translations were current in the late sixteenth century. These were Lodovico Dolce's *Le trasformationi* and Giovanni Andrea Dell'Anguillara's *Le metamorfosi di Ovidio*, both of which, following a well-established tradition, include commentaries on the myths that they contain.

Dolce's allegory for the Orpheus myth points a brief moral:

Through Orpheus, who having regained Eurydice loses her through turning back, we see the state of the soul, which man loses whenever he abandons reason and turns back: that is, to pursue blameworthy and earthly concerns.[3]

The 'Annotations' provided by Gioseppe Orologgi for Dell'Anguillara's *Le metamorfosi* are much longer. Though in some respects rather inelegant, the annotations for the tenth book begin by describing the power of rhetoric in terms not unlike those used by the Florentine humanists whose thinking lay behind the creation of continuo song and operatic recitative. Orologgi's words can thus be taken as indicating, if indirectly, the significance of the Orpheus myth for the creators of opera:

The story of Orpheus shows us how much strength and vigour eloquence can have, like her who is the daughter of Apollo who is none other than wisdom. The lyre given to Orpheus by Mercury is the art of speaking properly, which, like the lyre, moves the affections with sounds, now high, now low, of the voice and of the delivery, so that the woods and the forests are moved by the pleasure that they derive from hearing the well-ordered and clear speech of a wise man.[4]

Since we do not know the full extent of Alessandro Striggio's classical learning, any attempt to trace the relationship of the libretto of *Orfeo* to its sources must, to some extent, remain speculative. Nevertheless, two things are clear: first, that Striggio's primary source for the first four acts of the opera was Ovid, the main outlines and emphases of whose account he followed as closely as the limitations of stage action would allow; secondly, that Striggio also knew Virgil's account intimately and drew from it not only specific details lacking in Ovid's version and material for Acts IV and V, but also something of the dramatic intensity of Virgil's vision.

Acts I and II of *Orfeo* are developed from the first thirteen lines of Book 10 of the *Metamorphoses*. Here we find the invocation to Hymen, god of marriage, the wedding of Orpheus and Eurydice, the death of Eurydice while wandering in the meadows with her companions, Orpheus's first response to the news of her death, and his resolve to seek her in the underworld:

Thence through the boundless air Hymen, clad in a saffron mantle, departed and took his way to the country of the Ciconians, and was summoned by the voice of Orpheus, though all in vain. He was present, it is true; but he brought neither the hallowed words, nor joyous faces, nor lucky omen. The torch also which he held kept sputtering and filled the eyes with smoke, nor would it catch fire for any brandishing. The outcome of the wedding was worse than the beginning; for while the bride was strolling through the grass with a group of naiads in attendance, she fell dead, smitten in the ankle by a serpent's tooth. When the bard of Rhodope had mourned her to the full in the upper world, that he might try the shades as well he dared to go down to the Stygian world through the gate of Taenarus.[5]

Ovid's rather flat reference to Orpheus's mourning for Eurydice is amplified by Virgil, who also provides a classical precedent for the general chorus of mourning, 'Ahi, caso acerbo,' with which Act II ends:

But the band of her Dryad comrades [chorus aequalis Dryadum] filled with their cries the mountain-peaks; the towers of Rhodope wept, and the Pangaean heights, and the martial land of Rhesus, the Getae and Hebrus and Orithyia, child of Acte. But he, solacing love's anguish with his hollow shell, sang of thee, sweet wife – of thee, to himself on the lonely shore; of thee as day drew nigh, of thee as day declined.[6]

It is Virgil, too, who provides the description of the approaches to the Underworld which informs Speranza's speech at the beginning of Act III (see below, p. 66). Ovid gives scarcely any detail of Orpheus's journey, saying only that he travelled 'through the unsubstantial throngs and the ghosts who had received burial'[7] before treating his arrival before Pluto and Proserpine. This is because Ovid's main concern is to recreate Orpheus's prayer to the gods of the Underworld, to which he devotes no fewer than twenty-three lines. The actual words that Ovid puts into Orpheus's mouth bear little relation to Striggio's version, the Act III aria 'Possente spirto', though his reference to Pluto's own love for Proserpine is developed in Act IV into a short dialogue between the two deities (see below, p. 72). The importance of Orpheus's prayer in Ovid's account is, however, reflected in the opera, for Striggio places 'Possente spirto' (addressed to Charon rather than to Pluto and Proserpine) almost exactly at the centre of the five-act structure, reinforcing its centrality by the near-symmetrical placing round it of the two other arias in the main body of the opera: 'Vi ricorda o bosch'ombrosi' (near the beginning of Act II) and 'Qual honor di te fia degno' (near the end of Act IV).

After describing the profound effect produced by Orpheus's prayer, Ovid treats the granting of Eurydice, the condition laid upon Orpheus, and Eurydice's second death, events which form the substance of Act IV of *Orfeo*:

. . . nor could the queen nor he who rules the lower world refuse the suppliant. They called Eurydice. She was among the new shades and came with steps halting from her wound. Orpheus, the Thracian, then received his wife and with her this condition, that he should not turn his eyes backward until he had gone forth from the valley of Avernus, or else the gift would be in vain. They took the up-sloping path through places of utter silence, a steep path, indistinct and clouded in pitchy darkness. And now they were nearing the margin of the upper earth, when he, afraid that she might fail him, eager for the sight of her, turned back his longing eyes; and instantly she slipped into the depths. He stretched out his arms, eager to catch her or to feel her clasp; but, unhappy one, he clasped nothing but the yielding air. And now, dying a second time, she made no complaint against her husband; for of what could she complain save that she was beloved? She spake one last 'farewell' which scarcely reached her husband's ears, and fell back again to the place whence she had come.[8]

The dialogue that Striggio invented for the journey of Orpheus and Eurydice from the Underworld contains recognisable features of Ovid's account, in particular the idea that it is a lack of faith which makes Orpheus turn round. Nevertheless, if we look closely at the dialogue we can see that much of its material clearly does not come from the *Metamorphoses*:

SPIRIT: Here is the gentle singer
Who leads his wife to the skies above.
ORPHEUS: What honour is worthy of you,
My all-powerful lyre,
For in the Tartarean kingdom
You have been able to bend each obdurate will.
[remainder of aria 'Qual honor' omitted]
But while I sing (alas) who will assure me
That she is following? Alas, who hides from me
The sweet light of her beloved eyes?
Could it be that the gods of Avernus,
Spurred by envy,
Wish to deny me complete happiness here below
By preventing me from seeing you,
Blessed eyes and joyful,
You who can make others happy simply with your glance?
But what do you fear, my heart?
That which Pluto forbids, Love [Cupid] commands.
I would do well to obey
The more powerful deity
Who conquers both men and gods.
(*Here a noise is made behind the scenes*)
But what do I hear, alas?
Perhaps the enamoured Furies
Are arming themselves with rage against me
To carry off my beloved; and shall I consent?
(*Here Orpheus turns round*)
O sweetest eyes, I see you,
I . . . but what darkness eclipses you?
SPIRIT: You have broken the law and are unworthy of grace.
EURYDICE: Ah! glance too sweet and too bitter:
Would you thus lose me through loving me too much?
And I, unhappy, lose
My chance to enjoy again
Both light and life; and with it
I lose you, my consort, the most dear of all dear things.
SPIRIT: Return to the shadows of death,
Unhappy Eurydice,
Nor hope again to see the stars,
For henceforth the Inferno will be deaf to your prayers.
ORPHEUS: Where are you going, my life? Behold, I follow you.
But who prevents me, alas: do I dream, do I rave?
What secret power of these grim shades
Draws me from these beloved shades against my will
And leads me to the hateful light?

In fact, it is at this point in the opera that we find the most interesting fusion of Ovid and Virgil in Striggio's dramatisation. Both classical authors agree on the general outline of the narrative, and on the mysterious way in which Eurydice is taken back by the powers of the Underworld, but it was Virgil who provided Striggio with by far the more vivid verbal picture of this crucial episode and its aftermath. The thunderous crash which, in Virgil's account, marks the breaking of Pluto's and Proserpine's stern decree becomes, in *Orfeo*, the unnerving noise which finally causes Orpheus to turn round. It is Virgil, too, who suggests the images of light and darkness which Striggio develops and the notion that Orpheus loses Eurydice through allowing love to overcome reason. Finally, from Virgil comes Orpheus's sudden translation back to the upper world and his lament for Eurydice, the elements used for the beginning of Act V. At the same juncture in the story, Ovid has Orpheus remaining on the banks of the Styx for another week, lamenting the cruelty of the gods and repulsed by Charon in his further attempts to cross the river. He then travels to 'high Rhodope and wind-swept Haemus', where he spends the years before his death. Here, then, is the ending of Virgil's account, from the second loss of Eurydice through to Orpheus's death at the hands of the Bacchantes:

And now as he retraced his steps he had escaped every mischance, and the regained Eurydice was nearing the upper world, following behind . . . when a sudden frenzy seized Orpheus, unwary in his love, frenzy meet for pardon, did Hell know how to pardon! He stopped, and on the very verge of light, unmindful, alas! and vanquished in purpose, on Eurydice, now his own, looked back! In that moment all his toil was spent, the ruthless tyrant's pact was broken, and thrice a crash was heard amid the pools of Avernus. She cried: 'What madness Orpheus, what dreadful madness hath ruined my unhappy self and thee? Lo, again the cruel Fates call me back and sleep veils my swimming eyes. And now farewell! I am swept off, wrapped in uttermost night, and stretching out to thee strengthless hands, thine, alas! no more.' She spake, and straightway from his sight, like smoke mingling with thin air, vanished afar, and, vainly as he clutched at the shadows and yearned to say much, never saw him more; nor did the warden of Orchus [i.e. Charon] suffer him again to pass that barrier of the marsh. What could he do? Whither turn himself, twice robbed of his wife? With what tears move Hell, with what prayers its powers? She, alas! even now death-cold, was afloat in the Stygian barque. Month in, month out, seven whole months men say, beneath a skyey cliff by lonely Strymon's wave, he wept, and, deep in icy caverns, unfolded this his tale, charming the tigers, and making the oaks attend his strain . . . Alone he would roam the northern ice, the snowy Tanais, and the fields ever wedded to Rhipaean frosts, wailing Eurydice lost, and the gift of Dis annulled. But the Ciconian dames, scorned by such devotion, in the midst of their sacred rites and the midnight orgies of Bacchus, tore the youth limb from limb and strewed him broadcast over the fields. Even then, while Oeagrian Hebrus swept and rolled in mid-current that head, plucked from its marble neck, the bare voice and death-cold tongue, with fleeting breath, called Eurydice – ah hapless Eurydice! 'Eurydice' the banks re-echoed, all adown the stream.[9]

The death and dismemberment of Orpheus at the hands of the Bacchantes forms the conclusion of both Virgil's and Ovid's accounts. A stylised version of this ending appears in Striggio's 1607 libretto, in which the finale of the opera is a Bacchanalian chorus. Virgil's concluding vision of Orpheus's head borne away by the River Hebrus does not, of course, appear in the opera, but two of its elements are used: the idea of the echoing of Orpheus's voice (also present in Ovid's account) is employed in the echo section of Orpheus's Act V lament; and his dying invocation of Eurydice's name, transferred in the opera to the lips of the dying Eurydice, forms the climax of the messenger's narrative of Act II.

Ovid and Virgil, then, provided Striggio with the basic material for his *favola*, but they furnished no model for the ways in which this material could be developed and shaped into a play suitable for musical setting. This aspect of the background to the libretto is particularly complex, and only a few points can be touched on in a discussion of this length. It is important, however, to realise that the early operas were not isolated literary phenomena, and that opera was not created in a naive and ill-informed attempt to revive classical tragedy.

The idea that opera was created by the so-called Florentine 'Camerata' of Count Giovanni de' Bardi has now largely been superseded by a more refined (and much more interesting) picture of Florentine intellectual life and courtly intrigue at the end of the sixteenth century. Bardi's informal salon, which must have ceased meeting in 1592 when Bardi left Florence for Rome, may be credited with having done much to inspire the new type of rhetorical solo song with continuo accompaniment cultivated by the singer–composer Giulio Caccini and published in his *Le nuove musiche* (Florence, 1602); but the creation of opera and a specifically operatic style of declamation must be attributed to another, distinct, circle of Florentines, working under the patronage of Jacopo Corsi and including the poet Ottavio Rinuccini and another singer–composer, Jacopo Peri, Caccini's rival at the Florentine court.[10]

Peri's and Rinuccini's *Euridice*, performed at Florence on 6 October 1600 for the wedding celebrations of Maria de' Medici and Henry IV of France, provided the most immediate model for the subject matter, the structure and the musical and literary language of *Orfeo*. The two operas have in common a pastoral setting, the division of the action into five sections, a happy ending and a 'Greek' chorus which both participates in and comments on the action. In these respects, though, they reveal affinities not only with classical tragedy, but also with the much more recent precedents provided by the pastoral plays of Torquato Tasso and Giovanni Battista Guarini.

Guarini's five-act play *Il pastor fido* (The Faithful Shepherd) is of particular importance here. Guarini called this Arcadian pastoral a 'tragicomedy'. Its text was first published in 1589, but even before publication its fusion of the elements of tragedy and comedy had been the subject of intense debate in academic circles. The laments and prayers uttered by its characters formed the basis of many madrigal settings, notably the settings published by Monteverdi in his fourth and fifth books of madrigals (1603 and 1605 respectively). More important, the play was performed in its entirety at Mantua in 1598 and was evidently much admired by Duke Vincenzo Gonzaga.

The early opera librettos, which graft a happy ending on to an action cast in the general mould of classical tragedy, also qualify for the designation 'pastoral tragicomedy', though they differ from Guarini's play in their shorter length and in the choice of heroic rather than Arcadian subject matter. One further, and rather interesting, difference is that where Guarini employs the chorus only as a body, both Rinuccini and Striggio allow individuals from the chorus (the unnamed shepherds and nymphs of Acts I and II of *Orfeo*) to speak on behalf of the chorus as a whole. This technique was certainly sanctioned in late-sixteenth-century dramatic theory;[11] but in the context of court opera it also served the eminently practical purpose of extending the number of solo roles available to members of the expert resident ensemble.

It is clear that Monteverdi and Striggio had access to a copy of the score of Peri's and Rinuccini's *Euridice* and that Striggio tried to improve upon certain aspects of its dramatisation of the Orpheus story. In the messenger scene, for example, Rinuccini presents the entire narrative of Eurydice's death before Orpheus is allowed to react to the news. In *Orfeo*, on the other hand, the messenger, after some hesitation, tells Orpheus quite bluntly that Eurydice is dead. Orpheus reacts briefly and then lapses into stunned silence while the full circumstances of Eurydice's death are related.

Despite the more obvious parallels between the two operas, however, Rinuccini's *Euridice* differs radically from *Orfeo* in its treatment of the ending of the story. Rinuccini made two bold alterations to the plot which simplify the entire action: Orpheus does not lose his Eurydice a second time, and he does not die; rather, his happy reunion with Eurydice is celebrated by a festive final chorus. In the dedication to his libretto Rinuccini gave as a major reason for his radical changes to the traditional story the general rejoicing elicited by the Medici wedding. At the same time, he was aware of the fact that he might well be censured for having acted too audaciously:

> To some I may seem to have been too bold in altering the conclusion of the fable of Orpheus, but so it seemed fitting to me at a time of such great rejoicing, having as my justification the example of the Greek poets in other fables.[12]

Alessandro Striggio, unconstrained by the practical (one might say political) considerations of writing for a court celebration, was able to follow the precedent set by a more distant model, Angelo Poliziano's *La favola di Orfeo* of 1480. This play was one of the most important precursors of the early opera librettos. We know from archival evidence that Poliziano's achievement was still admired in Florence more than a century after his death, and we can detect echoes of his verse and of his elaboration of the Orpheus story both in Rinuccini's *Euridice* and in Striggio's *Orfeo*. This is not surprising. Poliziano was, after all, a great poet, and his *Orfeo* is chronologically the first secular Italian vernacular drama. More important, his play shows considerable musical imagination, containing quite a few musical 'numbers': a serenade, several laments and a choral finale. In fact, more than half of the 406 lines of his drama were sung, not spoken. The musical 'numbers' are cast in regular stanzas and are sometimes set apart by virtue of their use of contrasting metres. In this they anticipate the use of strophic texts for the set-piece arias in early opera. There are, for example, four strophic arias in Striggio's libretto: the prologue (five 4-line stanzas of 11-syllable lines), 'Vi ricorda o bosch'ombrosi' in Act II (four 4-line stanzas of 8-syllable lines), 'Possente spirto' in Act III (six stanzas of *terza rima*: 3-line stanzas of 11-syllable lines) and 'Qual honor di te fia degno' in Act IV (three 4-line stanzas with the unusual metrical scheme 8:7:7:11). These contrast with the prevailing mixture of 7- and 11-syllable lines which supports Monteverdi's use of a freer arioso declamation.

Of equal importance for his successors is Poliziano's treatment of the myth of Orpheus. As a teacher Poliziano was one of the most distinguished interpreters of Greek and Latin literature among the earliest humanists; but as a poet and dramatist he followed his classical sources in a far from slavish manner. Among the most important alterations to the tale of Orpheus that he made are the treatment of the laments and prayers in the centre of the story, and the emotions implied and aroused by its Bacchanalian conclusion.

For Poliziano, as for Striggio, the main sources were Ovid's *Metamorphoses* and Virgil's *Georgics*. In both of these works pastoral happiness acts as a foil for poignant laments. The same is true of Poliziano's tale, except that the number of laments and passionate pleas is greatly increased. After a messenger has related the news of Eurydice's death, for example, Orpheus moans and pleads in no fewer than thirteen 8-line stanzas (*ottave rime*), occupying 104 lines out of a passage of 156 which carries the drama through from the death of Eurydice to Orpheus's own death.

The parallels between Poliziano's and Striggio's versions of *Orfeo* are particularly close in relation to Acts IV and V of the opera. In Poliziano's play, for example, it is Proserpine who is first softened by Orpheus's prayer; and as Eurydice is once more taken from Orpheus she says 'Oimè, che 'l troppo amore n'ha disfatti ambedua' ('Alas, through too much love we are undone'). Even more interesting are the lines of triumph (which Poliziano quotes in Latin from Ovid's *Amores* (II, 12) uttered by Orpheus as he leads Eurydice from the Underworld: lines which may have suggested to Striggio the composition of the aria 'Qual honor di te fia degno' near the end of Act IV:

> Ite triumphales circum mea tempora lauri!
> Vicimus Eurydicen, reddita vita mihi est.
> Haec est praecipuo victoria digna triumpho;
> Huc ades, o cura parte triumphe mea!

Come, lie triumphant about my forehead, oh laurels. We have achieved victory, bringing Eurydice back, and life has been restored to me. Here is a victory, deserving of a special triumph. Come hither, Triumph, won by my concern.[13]

Though he follows the original ending of the story given by Ovid and Virgil, Poliziano does not conclude his play on a doleful note. Orpheus is, it is true, killed and dismembered (off stage) and his head borne back by one of the Bacchantes; but mindful of the festive occasion for which the play was written – a banquet given at Mantua in 1480 – Poliziano concludes with a drinking song of the Bacchic women, striking a tone of Dionysian revelry. The content of this choral finale prefigures the ending used in Striggio's libretto. Its form – four stanzas sung by a solo voice interspersed with a refrain for full chorus, giving an interplay of tutti and concertino – exercised considerable influence not only on the librettos of Striggio and Rinuccini, but also, at a further remove, on Calzabigi's great libretto of 1762 set by Gluck.

A number of questions remain. Why, after the apparent success of *Orfeo*, should Monteverdi have turned away from his Mantuan colleague and friend Alessandro Striggio to seek the libretto for his next opera from the Florentine Rinuccini? For after Striggio's *Orfeo* in 1607 he set Rinuccini's *Arianna* for Mantua in 1608, and later in the same year of 1608 he was seriously considering Rinuccini's *Narciso* for some Florentine festivities. Why did he set *Arianna* but not *Narciso*? Finally, why are there two finales for *Orfeo*, one preserved in Striggio's libretto of 1607 and one in Monteverdi's score of 1609?

In none of the early operas are the lovers whose emotions dominate the plot united at the end of the work. Orpheus loses Eurydice, Apollo Daphne, Ariadne Theseus, Echo Narcissus. As we have seen, this does not necessarily imply a tragic or a sad ending. The obligatory *lieto fine* may be arrived at in a variety of ways: by apotheosis, transporting the sufferer from the vale of tears and transforming him into a constellation; by the metamorphosis of the beloved into a brook or a plant; or by the substitution of a divine lover for his terrestrial predecessor. For a happy finale was *de rigueur*, be it a chorus or an ensemble of soloists. This situation continued until Venetian operas, with their love duets, took over in the 1640s. With their joyous affirmation of life these finales provided a welcome relief from the solo laments in the earlier stages of the plot which intrigued and impressed audiences both vocally and harmonically.

The length of the finale, and of the libretto as a whole, rarely fell below certain minimum standards which we can measure approximately by the number of lines allotted to them. The plot itself consists of a fairly simple outline: a development from pastoral joy to tragic reversal and lament, and on to a ceremonious conclusion. Poliziano's *Orfeo* had some 400 lines, and more than a century later Rinuccini's *Dafne* had only 440. These are miniature dramas that could not fill an evening or an afternoon. But after the success of *Dafne* in 1598 Rinuccini moved quickly to expand the structure: *Euridice* has 790 lines, *Arianna* some 1100, *Narciso* 1200. Venetian opera continued in the same vein. Monteverdi's *Ulisse* of 1640 consists of about 1200 lines, his *Poppea* of 1642 about 1600, and Cavalli's *Xerse* of 1654 some 2500. Clearly, in this sort of perspective, Striggio's libretto for *Orfeo*, at 678 lines, is very short – too short, one is inclined to say – and one of Rinuccini's assets was that he provided the composer with a large canvas, a more varied and extended framework.

The finale, too, rarely fell below a certain minimum length. It was usually scored for an ensemble of five to eight parts (mostly choral parts in Florence and Mantua, and solo parts in later Roman opera), and these ensembles were often punctuated by episodes for one, two or three soloists. Organisation by stanza usually assures a minimum of some 30 lines, extending at times to longer structures. Good examples are Poliziano's *Orfeo* (34 lines), the Florentine *intermedi* of 1589 (68), *Euridice* (48), *Arianna* (47), *Narciso* (146). The 62-line finale of Striggio's *Orfeo* (as printed in the libretto) seems to fit into this pattern. But the plot as told in Monteverdi's score differs radically from the libretto. Some 118 lines of chorus have been cut from the five acts, notably the entire choral finale from Act V (62 lines of chorus, punctuated by concertino episodes). The Apollo–Orpheus scene has been substituted, concluding with an extraordinarily brief chorus: two stanzas of six lines each. Since Monteverdi published this version in 1609 and again in 1615 we must assume that he approved of the change if, indeed, he did not make it himself. The answer lies, I suspect, in his firm belief that festive and not tragic strains were required to conclude an opera. In a letter to Striggio, written twenty years after the performance of *Orfeo*, Monteverdi explained why he refused to set to music Rinuccini's libretto of *Narciso* (1608). The composer noted as its main defect the want of variety and its lack of *lieto fine*: 'non altro di variazione, e più con fine tragico e mesto . . .'[14] Opinion is divided on the chronology of the two versions of the ending of *Orfeo*. Most scholars hold that Striggio presented the composer with a *mesto fine* which Monteverdi changed some time before the score was printed in 1609. But a minority opinion advances another hypothesis, namely that the *lieto fine* with its concluding moralising chorus was, in fact, the original finale; but that the hall at Mantua where the opera was first presented proved too small to accommodate a cloud machine in which Apollo and Orpheus ascend to Heaven. The finale of the Bacchic women, according to this theory, was a second thought, an accommodation to the small stage of the first performance. Later on, Monteverdi, unhampered by local conditions, published the original finale. This is an interesting thought, but my own

Fig. 3. The Orpheus Myth: woodcut from Ovid, *Le trasformationi*, trans. Lodovico Dolce (6th edn, Venice, 1561)

opinion favours the generally accepted chronology according to which Monteverdi changed Striggio's sad finale some time before 1609.

The use of a happy ending is found in other operas by Monteverdi: Ariadne is happy in the famous opera of 1608, Penelope in that of 1640, Poppea in 1642. Only in Striggio's libretto of 1607 is Orpheus not consoled, and the notion of happiness restricted to the revels of the Bacchic women. It seems to me that Monteverdi's dissatisfaction with Striggio's plot was a major factor in this revision. But, whatever the dramatic merits of the *lieto fine*, the surgical operation performed on Striggio's original text produced a curiously shaped opera with an undersized fifth act and an even more severely condensed final chorus. The result does not seem to have appealed to seventeenth-century audiences, judging from the lack of reliably documented revivals. It is interesting, too, that after he moved to Venice the composer revived *Arianna* at the Teatro San Moisé, but not *Orfeo*. Even in the twentieth century, when Monteverdi's undisputed musical genius has assured him a hearing, the brevity and emotional stance of the finale produces a letdown that has been noted by several conductors and singers of post-war revivals. Orpheus's happiness at being able to view Eurydice's lovely 'semblance' in the stars instead of beholding her personally is a faithful reflection of Neoplatonist views, but Orpheus's expression of contentment at accepting Apollo's counsel is too short to balance his magnificent lament, which dominates the fifth act in its only extant musical version. It required a poet of Rinuccini's dramatic and musical imagination to change Ovid's classical plot radically, eliminating the second loss of Eurydice entirely to produce a dramatic framework such as *Euridice* of 1600. Here the *lieto fine* is built into the structure which the poet presented to the composer, and no after-thoughts, practical or artistic, interfere with the emotional balance of the work.

3 'Orfeo', Act V: Alessandro Striggio's original ending

JOHN WHENHAM

Several references have been made in the preceding chapters to the original ending of *Orfeo*: that is, to the ending transmitted by the libretto. The text of Act V, with Striggio's original ending, is reprinted below with a parallel English translation.

Four copies of the libretto have been available to the editor – they are located in Genoa, Biblioteca universitaria [source A], in Wolfenbüttel, Herzog-August-Bibliothek, shelfmarks 174 Hist. [source B] and 549 Quodl. [source C], and in Bologna, Biblioteca comunale dell'Archiginnasio [source D]. Sources A and B agree in their readings of Act V and appear to derive from a single printing. Sources C and D are printed in a different typeface and occupy 35 instead of 45 pages. Their title-page exhibits typographical differences from that of sources A and B and employs a different block for the coat of arms. They also incorporate several minor corrections to the text transmitted by the other sources. The text of Act V reproduced below is transcribed from source C and retains its original spelling, punctuation and use of accents.

35

ATTO QUINTO

ORFEO.

Questi i campi di Tracia, e questo è il loco
  Dove passommi il core
  Per l'amara novella il mio dolore.
Poiche non hò più spene
  Di ricovrar pregando
  Piagnendo e sospirando
  Il perduto mio bene,
  Che poss'io più? se non volgermi à voi
  Selve soave un tempo
  Conforto a' miei martir, mentre à Dio piacque,
  Per farvi per pietà meco languire
  Al mio languire.
Voi vi doleste ò Monti, e lagrimaste
  Voi sassi al disparir del nostro sole,
  Et io con voi lagrimerò mai sempre,
  E mai sempre dorròmmi, ahi doglia, ahi pianto. **Eco.** Hai pianto.

Cortese Eco amorosa
  Che sconsolata sei
  E consolar mi vuoi ne' dolor miei,
  Benche queste mie luci
  Sien già per lagrimar fatte due fonti.
  In così grave mia fiera sventura
  Non hò pianto però tanto che basti. **Ec.** Basti.
Se gli occhi d'Argo havessi,
  E spandessero tutti un Mar di pianto,
  Non fora il duol conforme à tanti guai. **Ec.** Ahi.

S'hai del mio mal pietade, io ti ringrazio
  Di tua benignitate.
  Ma mentre io mi querelo
  Deh perche mi rispondi
  Sol con gli ultimi accenti?
  Rendimi tutti integri i miei lamenti.
Ma tu anima mia se mai ritorna
  La tua fredd'ombra à queste amiche piagge,
  Prendi hor da me queste tue lodi estreme
  C'hor à te sacro la mia cetra e 'l canto
  Come à te già sopra l'altar del core
  Lo spirto acceso in sacrifizio offersi.
Tu bella fusti e saggia, e in te ripose
  Tutte le grazie sue cortese il Cielo
  Mentre ad ogni altra de suoi don fù scarso,
  D'ogni lingua ogni lode à te conviensi
  Ch'albergasti in bel corpo alma più bella,
  Fastosa men quanto d'honor più degna.

ACT V

ORPHEUS.
These are the fields of Thrace, and this is the place
    Where my heart was transfixed with grief
    At the bitter news.
Since I no longer have any hope
    Of recovering, by prayer,
    Weeping and sighing,
    My lost beloved,
    What more can I do? except to turn to you,
    Sweet woods, once
    The consolation of my torments, while it pleased God,
    Through pity, to make you languish with me
    At my languishing.
You complained, O mountains, and you wept,
    O stones, at the departure of our sun,
    And I with you will weep for ever,
    And for ever I shall grieve, Ah, pain! Ah, weeping! [ECHO:] You have
      wept.
Kind, loving Echo,
    How disconsolate you are,
    And you wish to console me in my sorrow,
    Although my eyes
    Have already become two fountains through weeping.
    At my grave misfortune
    I have not wept, however, nearly enough. [ECHO:] Enough!
If I had the eyes of Argus
    And they had all shed a sea of tears,
    Such lamentation would still not match my grief. [ECHO:]
      Ah!
If you have pity for my suffering, I thank you
    For your kindness.
    But while I lament,
    Ah, why do you answer me
    Only with my final accents?
    Render back to me my laments in their entirety.
But you, my soul, if ever
    Your cold shade returns to these beloved shores,
    Then accept from me the highest praises,
    For now I consecrate to you my lyre and my song
    As to you already, on the altar of my heart,
    My ardent soul has been offered in sacrifice.
You were beautiful and wise, and in you Heaven hid
    All its enchanting graces,
    While to all others it was sparing with its gifts.
    The praises of every tongue are yours,
    For you harboured in a beautiful body a soul even more beautiful,
    The less proud the more worthy of honour.

Hor l'altre Donne son superbe e perfide
Ver chi le adora, dispietate instabili,
Prive di senno e d'ogni pensier nobile,
Ond'à ragione opra di lor non lodansi:
Quinci non fia giamai che per vil femina
Amor con aureo strale il cor trafiggami.
Ma ecco stuol nemico
Di Donne amiche à l'ubbriaco Nume,
Sottrar mi voglio à l'odiosa vista
Che fuggon gli occhi ciò che l'alma aborre.

CHORO DI BACCANTI.
Evohe padre Lieo
    Bassareo
    Te chiamiam con chiari accenti,
    Evohe liete e ridenti
    Te lodiam padre Leneo
    Hor c'habbiam colmo il core
    Del tuo divin furore.

BACCANTE.
Fuggito è pur da questa destra ultrice
    L'empio nostro avversario il Trace ORFEO
    Disprezzator de' nostri pregi alteri.

UN'ALTRA BACCANTE.
Non fuggirà, che grave
    Suol esser più quanto più tarda scende
    Sovra nocente capo ira celeste.

DUE BACCANTI.
Cantiam di Bacco intanto, e in varij modi
    Sua Deità si benedica e lodi.

CHORO DI BACCANTI.
Evohe padre Lieo
    Bassareo
    Te chiamiam con chiari accenti,
    Evohe liete e ridenti
    Te lodiam padre Leneo
    Hor c'habbiam colmo il core
    Del tuo divin furore.

BACCANTE.
Tu pria trovasti la felice pianta
    Onde nasce il licore
    Che sgombra ogni dolore,

Other women are proud and perfidious
Toward those who adore them, pitiless and fickle,
Devoid of reason and of all noble thoughts,
Whence it is right that their works should not be praised.
Hence let it never be that for vile womankind
Cupid should transfix my heart with his golden dart.
But behold the hostile troop
Of women, friends to the drunken deity.
I shall withdraw at the hateful sight,
For the eyes flee that which the soul abhors.

CHORUS OF BACCHANTES.
Evoe! Father Lyaeus,*
  Bassareus,*
  We call you in accents clear;
  Evoe! Merry and laughing
  We praise you, father Lenaeus,*
  Now that our hearts are brimful
  Of your divine fury.

A BACCHANTE.
Flown from this avenging arm
  Is our impious adversary, the Thracian Orpheus,
  Despiser of our high worth.

ANOTHER BACCHANTE.
He will not escape, for heavenly anger
  Is wont to be all the more severe the later it descends
  On his guilty head.

TWO BACCHANTES.
Let us sing, meanwhile, of Bacchus, and in various ways
  Let his deity be blessed and praised.

CHORUS OF BACCHANTES.
Evoe! Father Lyaeus,
  Bassareus,
  We call you in accents clear;
  Evoe! Merry and laughing
  We praise you, father Lenaeus,
  Now that our hearts are brimful
  Of your divine fury.

A BACCHANTE.
You were the first to find the happy plant
  Whence is born the liquor
  Which washes away all sorrow

* All names for Bacchus.

Et à gli egri mortali
Del sonno è padre e dolce oblio de i mali.

CHORO.
Evohe padre Lieo
   Bassareo
   Te chiamiam con chiari accenti,
   Evohe liete e ridenti
   Te lodiam padre Leneo,
   Hor c'habbiam colmo il core
   Del tuo divin furore.

BACCANTE.
Te domator del lucido Oriente
   Vide di spoglie alteramente adorno
   Sopr'aureo carro il portator del giorno.

BACCANTE.
Tu qual Leon possente
   Con forte destra e con invitto core
   Spargesti & abbattesti
   Le Gigantee falangi, & al furore
   De le lor braccia ferreo fren ponesti.
   Allhor che l'empia guerra
   Mosse co' suoi gran figli al Ciel la Terra.

CHORO.
Evohe padre Lieo
   Bassareo
   Te chiamiam con chiari accenti,
   Evohe liete e ridenti
   Te lodiam padre Leneo,
   Hor c'habbiam colmo il core
   Del tuo divin furore.

BACCANTE.
Senza te l'alma Dea che Cipro honora
   Fredda e insipida fora
   O d'ogni human piacer gran condimento
   E d'ogni afflitto cor dolce contento.

CHORO.
Evohe padre Lieo
   Bassareo
   Te chiamiam con chiari accenti,
   Evohe liete e ridenti
   Te lodiam padre Leneo
   Hor c'habbiam colmo il core
   Del tuo divin furore.   Il Fine del Quinto Atto.

And is, to sick mortals,
The father of sleep and sweet forgetfulness of all ills.

CHORUS.
Evoe! Father Lyaeus,
    Bassareus,
    We call you in accents clear;
    Evoe! Merry and laughing
    We praise you, father Lenaeus,
    Now that our hearts are brimful
    Of your divine fury.

A BACCHANTE.
You, the tamer of the brilliant East,
    Proudly adorned with spoils, were seen
    By the bringer of day on his golden chariot.

BACCHANTE.
Like a powerful lion,
    With strong right arm and unconquered heart,
    You scattered and threw down
    The phalanxes of giants, and curbed
    The fury of their arms
    When, in impious war,
    Earth moved to Heaven with her great sons.

CHORUS.
Evoe! Father Lyaeus,
    Bassareus,
    We call you in accents clear;
    Evoe! Merry and laughing
    We praise you, father Lenaeus,
    Now that our hearts are brimful
    Of your divine fury.

BACCHANTE.
Without you, the divine goddess [Venus] whom Cyprus honours
    Would be cold and insipid,
    She the seasoning of every human pleasure
    And the sweet contentment of every afflicted heart.

CHORUS.
Evoe! Father Lyaeus,
    Bassareus,
    We call you in accents clear;
    Evoe! Merry and laughing
    We praise you, father Lenaeus,
    Now that our hearts are brimful
    Of your divine fury.   The end of the fifth act.

4   Five acts: one action

JOHN WHENHAM

The explicit five-act structure of *Orfeo* is unique among the operas performed at Florence and Mantua between 1598 and 1608. The librettos which Ottavio Rinuccini provided for *Dafne* (both the original version and the revised version of 1608), *Euridice* and *Arianna* are each clearly shaped into what might be called 'episodes', but they contain no explicit act or scene divisions. There seems, therefore, every reason to believe that these operas were originally performed from beginning to end without breaks. We know, too, that Monteverdi's setting of *Arianna*, performed at Mantua in 1608, lasted two and a half hours.[1] This, for a drama of 1114 lines (as compared with the 678 of *Orfeo*, which lasts almost two hours in performance), would scarcely have allowed time for an interval.

If *Orfeo* is unique in this respect, then how did Striggio and Monteverdi intend that it should be played? The answer seems obvious, and has been tacitly accepted as such by most commentators: *Orfeo* was intended to be played in five discrete acts separated by intervals, or at least by the descent of the curtain. In all probability, however, the obvious answer is not the correct one. The evidence of Monteverdi's score and the surviving librettos, supported by a close reading of Striggio's text, suggests very strongly that *Orfeo*, too, was originally played as a single, continuous action, without intervals or curtains between the acts. In this respect it conforms to the normal stage practice for court entertainments of the period, and to the theory that continuity of performance represented the Aristotelian concept of 'unity of action'.[2] This conclusion, first advanced in 1968 by Nino Pirrotta,[3] has not yet achieved general currency, but it is crucial to an understanding of the way in which the action of *Orfeo* is shaped, and to a critical evaluation of the work. Some of its implications are explored in the synopsis presented later in this chapter.

The Renaissance tradition of continuous stage action is amply documented in the surviving descriptions of comedies played with *intermedi* in late-sixteenth- and early-seventeenth-century Italy. These show that each *intermedio* followed on directly from the act of the comedy that preceded it, the action being interrupted only for any necessary changes of scenery, which took place before the eyes of the audience, not behind a closed curtain. The feats of stage engineering required to effect rapid and sometimes spectacular changes of scene were, in fact, one of the main attractions of the entertainment.

A description of the fourth *intermedio* for Girolamo Bargagli's comedy *La Pellegrina*, performed at Florence in 1589 for the wedding of Ferdinando I de' Medici and Christine of Lorraine, will serve to illustrate this point and to show some of the stage effects employed in large-scale *intermedi*. This example is chosen not at random, but because it may have influenced Alessandro Striggio (who took part in the Florentine performance) in his conception of the Underworld scenes of *Orfeo*.

The fourth *intermedio* contrasted a vision of the Golden Age which was to follow the marriage of Ferdinando and Christine with a chilling vision of souls suffering torments in the Inferno. Its action began against the scenery used for the third act of the comedy: a view of the city of Pisa. A sorceress appeared in a golden chariot drawn by winged dragons. When the chariot reached mid stage it halted, and the sorceress sang a solo madrigal while conjuring up fire demons. Following her exit a ball of fire appeared in the sky and opened to reveal a choir of spirits who sang a madrigal prophesying the new Golden Age. When the madrigal ended, the ball of fire closed again. Suddenly the stage was covered with fiery rocks, chasms and caves. The earth opened, revealing an Inferno from which emerged a giant statue of Lucifer and two groups of actors representing Furies and demons.

At the entrance to the Inferno we saw the aged Charon, with his boat, as Dante depicted him, with a long white beard; around his eyes, resembling fire, some wheels of flame; and his boat was filling with souls who competed to go on board, while he, with a burning oar, beat those who held back. Through all the Inferno [were] endless ranks of ugly demons and tormented souls, and especially around Lucifer, who stood in a lake like a circle, all of ice . . .
When the demons who were sitting on the rocks had finished their mournful song, they plunged [into the abyss] with plaintive howls and shrieks; Lucifer, too, was swallowed up, and the Inferno closed, and the rocks and caves and fiery caverns disappeared; the scene returned to its

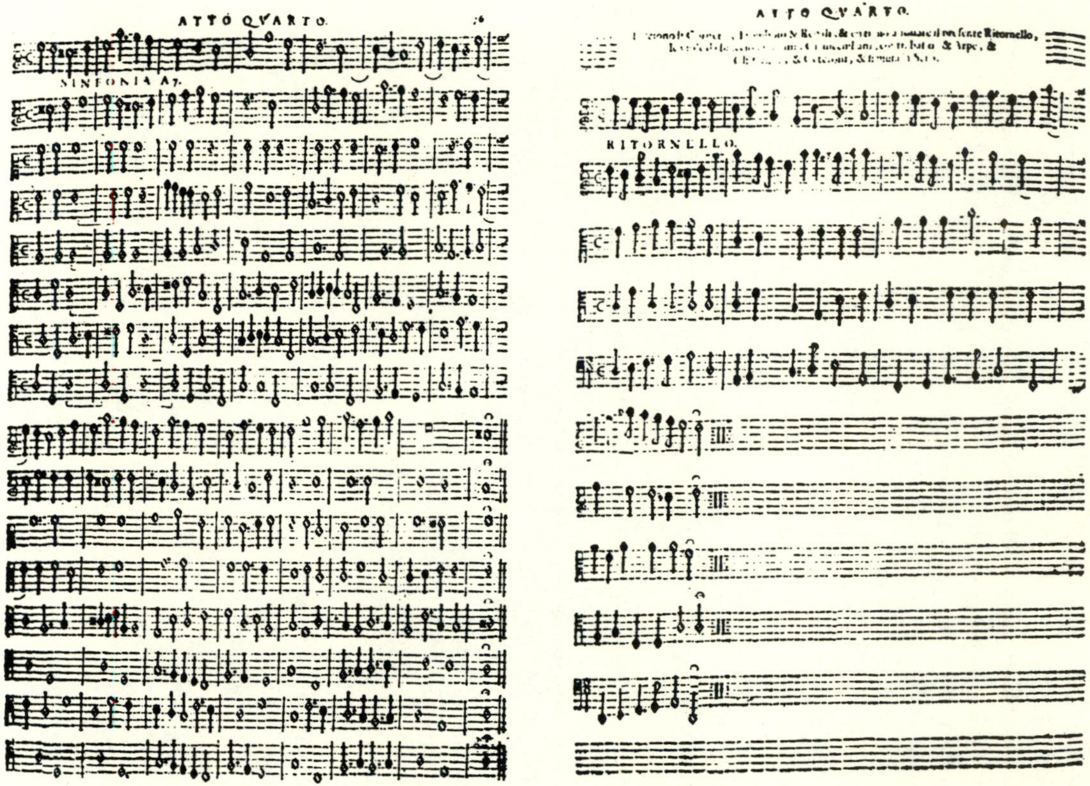

Fig. 4. Monteverdi, *Orfeo*: the transition from Act IV to Act V (1609 edition)

former beauty, and the *intermedio* ended, and the fourth act of the comedy began.[4]

Performances of comedies with lavish *intermedi* of this kind lasted for several hours without a break. No timing seems to be available for the Florentine entertainment, but the performance of Guarini's *Idropica* which was given at Mantua in 1608 with a prologue and *intermedi* by Monteverdi and others is reported to have lasted between five and six hours.[5] In comparison with these huge spectacles, which remained the standard form of court entertainment for many years after the birth of opera, the early Florentine and Mantuan operas must have seemed fairly short-breathed affairs. They were staged without *intermedi* (unlike their relatives, the pastoral plays of Tasso and Guarini) and with only modest stage effects.

The key to the conclusion that *Orfeo* was played without breaks between the acts lies in the fact that it was customary for scene changes to take place before the eyes of the audience. With this in mind we can see that Monteverdi conceived a simple but telling dramatic effect to mark the changes of location in the opera. The two points at which the scenes are to be changed are indicated quite clearly by rubrics in the 1609 and 1615 scores and in the surviving librettos: they occur between Acts II and III and between Acts IV and V. At the end of Act II we hear a five-part ritornello scored for strings, harpsichord(s), and organs with wooden pipes. This was first heard at the beginning of the opera as part of the prologue, sung by Music (La Musica). Immediately following its playing at the end of Act II the scene is changed and we hear the first of the Underworld sinfonias, an eight-part piece scored for trombones, cornetts and reed organ, and Act III follows without a pause. At the end of Act IV the process is reversed: an eight-part 'Underworld' sinfonia scored for wind instruments precedes the scene change, and Music's ritornello follows or covers it, leading directly into Act V (see Fig. 4).[6] Monteverdi's idea was to highlight the sudden change of scene with a dramatic change of instrumentation, from a string ensemble representing the upper world to the wind ensemble of the Underworld and vice versa (incidentally framing Acts III and IV with symmetrically placed statements of Music's ritornello). The dramatic point intended by the composer is lost if there is a break between the acts and the scene change takes place behind curtains.

The dramatic point would also be diluted if the process were to take too long. Even in the relatively small room in which *Orfeo* was probably first performed, however, simple mechanical devices such as sliding frames and back shutters could have been used to effect a rapid change of scene.[7]

Of the instrumental movements at the points where the scenes change, all but one (the sinfonia ending Act IV) are printed with repeat marks. I should guess that the repeats in Music's ritornello at the end of Act II covered the exit of the chorus at this point, while those marked into the first of the Underworld sinfonias covered the scene change and allowed the audience to settle and to admire the new set before the action of the opera recommenced. The sinfonia at the end of Act IV is sufficiently long to cover exits, but Music's ritornello at the beginning of Act V needs to be repeated in order to cover the change of scene and Orpheus's entrance.

At the junctures between the other acts only one (unrepeated) sinfonia is provided because there are no scene changes at these points. In the original scores (and in Malipiero's 1930 edition) these sinfonias appear to be wrongly placed. The sinfonia which begins Act II, for example, and which is clearly the instrumental introduction to Orpheus's arioso 'Ecco pur ch'a voi ritorno', is printed before the heading 'Atto Secondo'. In fact, though, there is nothing wrong here. The sinfonia simply marks the uninterrupted transition from Act I to Act II, and the heading 'Atto Secondo' appears, as in a play, just before the first words of the new act.

If we accept that the evidence of the score and the libretto indicates that the transitions from Act II to Act III and from Act IV to Act V were intended to be played without breaks, then the likelihood of breaks between the other acts is slight. Moreover, as we shall see in considering the action of the work, Acts I and II are linked dramatically, as are Acts III and IV; and to separate them would make nonsense of Striggio's concept, for he planned the action in the knowledge that the opera would be played continuously.

Although the five-act structure of *Orfeo* does not imply its mode of performance, it did provide the librettist with a means of shaping his material clearly and economically. Each act develops one main element of the story, and each ends with a chorus. Act I depicts Orpheus and Eurydice on their wedding day; Act II deals with the death of Eurydice and Orpheus's resolve to seek her in the Underworld; in Act III Orpheus encounters Charon and gains entry to the Inferno; in Act IV Eurydice is released, but Orpheus loses her for the second time; in Act V Orpheus laments the second loss of

Eurydice and (in the published score) is transported to the heavens by Apollo. This simple outline remains clearly perceptible even in a continuous performance, just as the five 'episodes' of Peri and Rinuccini's *Euridice*, each ending with a chorus, are perceptible even though composer and poet did not draw attention to them by calling them 'acts' or 'scenes'.

For reasons which will become apparent from a synopsis of the opera, I believe that *Orfeo* was originally performed using only two stage sets. The first, representing the fields of Thrace, was a pastoral woodland scene, perhaps showing the banks of a stream. This was used for Acts I, II and V. The second set showed the approaches to the Inferno, with some representation of the Stygian marshes, the river Styx itself, and the gateway to the Inferno. This Underworld setting was used for Acts III and IV.[8]

In its use of two stage sets only, *Orfeo* resembles Peri's *Euridice*; and the published description of the earlier opera may be taken as indicative of the type of staging used for Monteverdi's work, though there were no doubt many differences of detail. Only one 'episode' of *Euridice* is set in the Underworld, but it is interesting to note that in it Orpheus encounters Pluto and Proserpine, as well as Charon, before the entrance to the Inferno and not within the Inferno itself (cf. below, p. 71).

. . . Signor Jacopo Corsi, having arranged that *Euridice*, a touching and most amiable fable by Signor Ottavio Rinuccini, should be set to music with much care, and that costumes of the richest and most beautiful kind should be prepared for the actors [*personaggi*], offered the work to Their Highnesses. It was accepted, and a noble setting made ready in the Pitti Palace; and on the evening following the royal wedding the work was performed . . .

The magnificent setting, in a worthy room, appeared thus: after the curtains, and within the prospect [*aspetto*] of a great arch, with a niche at either side in which were statues of Poetry and Painting (a fine invention of the designer), appeared the most beautiful woods, both painted and in relief, arranged with good design and, through the clever disposition of the lighting, seeming to be full of daylight.

But when it became necessary that the Inferno should be seen, everything changed, and we saw fearful and horrible rocks which seemed real; and above them appeared leafless stumps and ashen grass. And yonder, through a crack in a large rock, we perceived that the city of Dis burned, pulsating tongues of flame [visible] through the openings of its towers, the air around blazing with a colour like that of copper. After this single change of scenery the first returned and no more changes were seen . . .[9]

SYNOPSIS

Since the score and libretto of *Orfeo* contain almost no stage directions *per se*, the synopsis offered here is itself an interpretation of the stage action as conveyed by the text and the musical setting. I have attempted to show that a careful reading of Striggio's text offers much information about the staging of the first performance and its intended shaping into episodes, one of which overlaps the division between Acts I and II. I have also tried to suggest some of the resonances that the text might have evoked in the minds of a literate seventeenth-century court audience (particularly important in relation to the staging of Acts III and IV), and to follow through the implications of the continuous manner of performance that Monteverdi and Striggio envisaged for their work.

Monteverdi's experience of writing emotionally powerful and quasi-dramatic madrigals for performance before the Mantuan court served him well in the new medium of opera. The devices that he uses – rising lines and quickening rhythms to suggest agitation, for example, dissonances to suggest anguish, sudden changes in harmonic direction to signal a change of direction in the discourse – are in many cases prefigured in his madrigals. Their implications, for movement and gesture as well as for attack, timbre and dynamics, would have been readily understood by the singers of the Mantuan ensemble (see above, p. 5), and are also taken into account in the synopsis.

All this has inevitably led to rather more asides than might reasonably be expected in a simple account of the action of *Orfeo*. I can only hope that what emerges from this rather lengthy process is a view of the opera which shows it to be even more elegantly shaped and certainly less static than has sometimes been supposed. For *Orfeo* is not only powerful in musical terms, but also very effective theatre.

Toccata

The opera is prefaced by a five-part Toccata (the English equivalent is 'Tucket' – 'a flourish on a trumpet'), which is marked 'to be played three times, with all the instruments, before the curtain is raised'.[10] Its musical material consists of a drone for the two lowest parts, above which three instruments (or groups of instruments) play a series of flourishes which may be derived from authentic military signals. The Toccata functions as a call-to-attention, a sign to members of the audience that the opera is about to begin and that they should take their places. The trumpets of the instrumental ensemble are to be muted. This has the effect of raising their pitch by a whole tone, and the tonality of the Toccata from written C to sounding D, the tonality of the prologue.

Prologue

After the third sounding of the Toccata, the curtain rises to reveal the pastoral setting for Acts I and II. A five-part ritornello for strings, which acquires considerable significance during the course of the opera, introduces the figure of Music personified, who sings the prologue. The choice of Music as the singer of the prologue, rather than Ovid (*Dafne*) or Tragedy (*Euridice*), indicates that one of the main themes of the opera is to be the power of music, thus providing an intellectual justification, if one were needed, for a drama that is to be sung throughout.

The prologue is cast in five regular stanzas, set as variations over a consistent harmonic framework (strophic variations) and separated by a shortened version of the ritornello. Its text reveals a carefully structured sequence of ideas. In stanza 1 Music pays tribute to the Gonzaga family assembled before her, saying that she has come to them from her beloved Permessus[11] and describing them as 'Incliti eroi' – 'famous heroes, the gentle blood of kings, whose high virtues are proclaimed by Fame'. By implication, then, she associates the Gonzagas with the heroic action that is to follow. In stanza 2 she introduces herself as the power which is able 'to soothe each troubled heart and to inflame the coldest minds [an icy dissonance here] now with noble anger, now with love'. This is, of course, a reference to the ancient Greek concept of the ethical virtues of music, a concept which lay behind the creation of Florentine rhetorical song and operatic recitative; and this classical allusion is developed in stanza 3 with a reference to the music of the spheres. The ethical power of music gives way in stanza 4 to the mythical power of Orpheus's singing, as Music introduces the hero of the action to follow: 'Hence desire spurs me to tell you of Orpheus [i.e. the play is to be sung], of Orpheus who held the wild beasts with his song, and who made a servant of the Inferno with his prayer [in this case the third-act aria 'Possente spirto'], the immortal glory of Pindus[12] and Helicon.'[13]

The last stanza of the prologue gives us a picture of the scenery used for the first two acts, and provides us with the first evidence of a gentle humour which is also evident in Orpheus's encounter with Charon in Act III:

Hor mentre i canti alterno hor lieti, hor mesti	Now while I alternate my songs, now happy, now sad,
Non si mova Augellin fra queste piante,	Let no bird move among these trees,
Nè s'oda in queste rive onda sonante,	Nor let there be heard a wave sounding on these banks,
Et ogni Auretta in suo cammin s'arresti.	And let every breeze halt in its journey.

The humour (if I interpret it correctly) arises from Monteverdi's use of notated silence after the words 'Nè s'oda' ('Nor let there be heard'). At one level this can be read simply as word-painting; but the sudden silence might also be interpreted in theatrical terms as a trick to catch out any members of the audience who might be talking and to remind them that they, too, should be attentive. The last word of the stanza – 's'arresti' ('let it halt') – is left hanging in the air. Instead of the expected cadence on A minor, the phrase halts on an E major harmony and is followed by another notated silence. And instead of then resolving on to the harmony of A minor which began the shortened form of the ritornello, the music progresses to the unexpected D minor of the ritornello's full version, an indication that the prologue has ended and Act I is about to begin.

Act I

Orpheus and Eurydice enter in the company of a chorus of nymphs and shepherds. A shepherd of the chorus sets the general mood of rejoicing in an arioso whose ABA shape follows a similar structure in Striggio's verse. The shepherd tells us that this is the day on which Eurydice will put an end to Orpheus's 'amorous anguish', and in the second section of the song, which is less lyrical than the first, gives us to understand that Eurydice had long spurned Orpheus's advances and that for her sake he had often gone 'sighing and weeping through these woods' (another reference to the *mise-en-scène*). With the return of the A section of the song the shepherd urges his companions to sing in accents worthy of Orpheus. They join in singing 'Vieni Imeneo, deh vieni', a five-part choral invocation to Hymen, god of marriage. Hymen's torch is compared with the light of the rising sun, which brings days of serenity to the lovers and dispels the shadows of suffering. This is only the first of many images which involve or imply the sun (i.e. Apollo, Orpheus's father in the version of the myth followed by Striggio).

The dignified strains of the invocation cadence on G minor, and the tonality then sinks a tone as a nymph of the chorus initiates a new choral action. She calls on the Muses to tune their 'cetre' (either kitharas or lyres)[14] to the sound of the chorus's song. Then follows a five-part *balletto*, 'Lasciate i monti', a choral dance with an extended and lively instrumental ritornello in triple metre. The text that Striggio provided for this is in three stanzas. Monteverdi sets the first in duple metre and then underlays both the second and third stanzas to the same triple-metre setting before reaching the ritornello. Although repeat marks are lacking in the original score, the order of performance that Monteverdi seems to have intended is stanza 1 - stanza 2 - ritornello - stanza 1 - stanza 3 - ritornello, making a lengthy and varied dance sequence.

After the choral invocation and celebratory dance we are introduced to the protagonist as a shepherd invites Orpheus, 'whose laments [at being spurned by Eurydice] have already made the countryside weep', to sing 'a happy song that speaks of love'. Orpheus responds not with the light-hearted song that we might expect, but with a passionate arioso worthy of a great singer. The main cadences of his song – on G, B flat and D – suggest the (transposed) Dorian mode, a mode which, according to the sixteenth-century theorist Zarlino, had 'a certain intermediate effect between sadness and joy'.[15] Orpheus begins by invoking the sun in a line replete with minor thirds above a static G minor harmony: 'Rosa del Ciel, vita del mondo, e degna / Prole di lui che l'universo affrena' ('Rose of the heaven, life of the world, and worthy offspring of him who steers the universe'). While this is clearly a reference to Apollo, son of Jupiter,[16] Striggio carefully couches it in terms which could also be interpreted as referring to the sun as the creation of a Christian God, a cultural ambiguity which is exploited throughout the opera until the final (1609) chorus, which is explicitly Christian in tone (perhaps a further indication that the new ending was written by someone other than Striggio). After the opening phrases, Orpheus's arioso moves to an F major harmony, leading to a cadence centre of B flat as he continues, 'Tell me, did you ever see a happier and more fortunate lover than I?' He then turns to Eurydice and blesses the day on which he first saw and sighed for her. His expressions of pleasure lead to further cadences on F and B flat before arriving at another extended passage over G minor harmony which gives way to a final cadence on D, Eurydice's tonal level, as it were inviting her to speak. She replies, pledging her heart to him, in a simple but affecting arioso.

The speeches of Orpheus and Eurydice form the centre point of the first structural unit, the first 'episode' of the opera, which is now rounded off symmetrically by a shortened repeat of the *balletto* 'Lasciate i monti' and the invocation to Hymen, 'Vieni Imeneo, deh vieni'. The second 'episode' begins with the next speech, 'Ma se il nostro gioir', for a shepherd of the chorus,[17] and lasts until the end of the duet 'E dopo l'aspro gel'[18] just before the end of Act I. This has been one of the most consistently misunderstood passages of the opera, and the misunderstanding has led to a perception of Act I and the beginning of Act II as being shapeless and repetitive.

Here, as elsewhere in the opera, a careful reading of the score and libretto shows quite clearly what were Monteverdi's and Striggio's intentions, and even suggests that they changed their mind during the preparation of the work. The shepherd's speech which follows the repeat of 'Vieni Imeneo' is crucial:

Ma se il nostro gioir dal Ciel deriva	But if our joy derives from Heaven
Com'è dal Ciel ciò che quà giù n'incontra	As does everything else that we encounter on Earth,
Giusto è ben che divoti	It is indeed right that, devoutly,
Gli offriamo incensi e voti.	We should offer to Heaven incense and prayers.
Dunque al Tempio ciascun rivolga i passi	Then let each one turn his steps to the temple
A pregar lui ne la cui destra è il Mondo,	To pray of him who holds the world in his right hand
Che lungamente il nostro ben conservi.	That he may long preserve our wellbeing.

Since Acts I and II are to be played continuously, some device must be found to take Eurydice off stage so that her death can be reported in Act II. This speech clearly provides the motivation for her exit. The temple must be located off stage, and Orpheus, Eurydice and most of their companions process there to the accompaniment of the stately instrumental polyphony which follows the shepherd's speech.[19] A small ensemble is left on stage to sing the ensuing chorus, which serves, among other things, the function of suggesting the passage of time during which the marriage of Orpheus and Eurydice is consecrated at the temple.

The words sung by the small choral ensemble are addressed directly to the audience and point the moral to be drawn from the first act: 'Alcun non sia che disperato in preda . . . ' ('Let no one fall prey to despair [as Orpheus did] . . . for after the dark cloud . . . the sun displays its bright rays all the more clearly. And after the bitter cold of bare winter, spring clothes the field with flowers'). In Striggio's libretto, the eight lines of this chorus are printed as a continuum, the whole of which is simply headed 'Choro'. Monteverdi, however, divides the lines into three 'stanzas' of three, three and two lines, which he sets as a group of strophic variations, for two, three and two voices respectively, using the 'exit' music as a ritornello.

The final stanza of the strophic variations is not followed by the ritornello. Instead its G major cadence leads immediately to a C major harmony which begins a new five-part ensemble. The change of harmony, simple though it is, seems to strike a new direction in the action, as though the choral ensemble were turning to welcome Orpheus (but not, of course, Eurydice) back on to the stage with their words 'Ecco Orfeo, cui pur dianzi . . . ' ('Behold Orpheus, for whom not long ago sighs were food and tears drink'). This interpretation seems to be confirmed by the fact that the word 'Ecco' ('Behold') does not appear in the libretto: Striggio's original line was 'Orfeo di cui pur dianzi'.[20] I suspect that Striggio had originally intended that Orpheus should re-enter immediately before the words 'Ecco pur ch'a voi ritorno' which he sings at the beginning of Act II. But at some stage in the preparation of the opera Monteverdi, or Monteverdi and Striggio in collaboration, must have decided that it would be more effective to bring Orpheus back at a slightly earlier stage and to draw attention to his return. The word 'Ecco' was added, and the remainder of Striggio's chorus cut from nineteen lines to four, lending point to the first line of Act II, 'Ecco *pur* ch'a voi ritorno' ('Behold, *indeed*, I return to you'). The decision to have Orpheus return during the short final ensemble of Act I is inconceivable if the intention had been to lower the curtain at the end of the act.

One problem remains. When do the remainder of the chorus come back on to the stage? There are several possible answers. They could enter with Orpheus: the words 'Behold Orpheus' would be as appropriate for them to sing as for the ensemble which has remained on stage. Or they could enter at some point in Act II, perhaps with the messenger who brings the news of Eurydice's death. Even more intriguing, however, is the possibility that they might remain off stage for the whole of Act II, changing costumes in order to reappear as infernal spirits at the beginning of Act III. This would present no technical problems. When Monteverdi wrote the choral strophic variations 'Alcun non sia che disperato in preda' at the end of Act I, he was careful to keep on stage a full five-part ensemble consisting of soprano, three tenors (the alto clef probably indicates a high tenor voice) and bass. This ensemble is adequate for all the choruses of Act II.

Act II

Act II follows immediately with the introductory sinfonia to Orpheus's arioso 'Ecco pur ch'a voi ritorno, / Care selve e piaggie amate' ('Behold, indeed, I return to you, dear woods and beloved shores' – yet another reference to the *mise-en-scène* of the first two acts). Like the arioso with which Act I began, this is cast in ABA form, though this time Monteverdi has superimposed the form on a text which contains no repetition. Like 'Rosa del Ciel', this arioso begins with G minor harmony, but its regular rhythmic pulse conveys none of the introspection of the earlier piece.

This prompts a general consideration of the function of the first section of Act II and the reason for the decision to blur the division between the first two acts, creating a third 'episode' which ends with the entrance of the messenger. At first glance, the beginning of Act II seems simply to continue the mood of rejoicing set by Act I, though on a more personal level (another good reason for keeping the main body of the chorus off stage during this act). In fact, though, there is a qualitative difference. The personal utterances of Act I were serious in nature, and tinged with melancholy at the remembrance of Orpheus's former suffering. From the final ensemble of Act I onwards, however, this sense of melancholy almost entirely disappears, and the music that Monteverdi supplies, culminating in Orpheus's aria 'Vi ricorda o bosch' ombrosi'[21] and the shepherd's arioso 'Mira, deh mira Orfeo', is based entirely on regular rhythmic patterns. The idea seems to have been to build a sense of unaffected joy cumulatively from the final choral ensemble of Act I through to the point where the messenger enters, making her news and the tragic reversal of Orpheus's fortune the more devastating by contrast with the sense of joy that precedes it.

The progression towards Orpheus's aria is provided in the libretto by six four-line stanzas – by another strophic aria text, in fact – in which shepherds of the chorus express their pleasure in the countryside which surrounds them, before calling on Orpheus to 'make worthy with the sound of your lyre ['lira' in this case] these fields where blows the breeze with Sheban perfume'. The libretto indicates that the first two stanzas are to be sung by a single shepherd, the third and fourth by two shepherds, the fifth by two shepherds, and the last by a choral ensemble – exactly the pattern that Monteverdi follows, though instead of writing a single melody which would serve for all six stanzas he creates a musical feast by writing three 'arias', each of which serves for two stanzas of the text. And for each 'aria' he provides a new and differently orchestrated ritornello, the first and third of which are marked to be played behind the scenes. The last of the 'arias', sung first by two shepherds and then in a five-part version by the full ensemble, contains a melodic figure already used in the final ensemble of Act I, emphasising the organic link between the two acts.

The climax of this third 'episode' is reached in the strophic aria 'Vi ricorda o bosch'ombrosi', which is prefaced and punctuated by a ritornello whose apparent simplicity of sound belies the complexity of its notation, which has caused the spilling of more scholarly ink than any other single movement in the opera. The lively hemiola rhythm of the aria is in keeping with the mood already established in the second act. Its text and harmonies, however, encapsulate the ambivalent emotions expressed in Acts I and II: past melancholy and present happiness. The first stanza is concerned entirely with the remembrance of things past:

Vi ricorda o bosch'ombrosi	Do you remember, O shady woods,
De' miei lungh'aspri tormenti	My long, bitter torments,
Quando i sassi ai miei lamenti	When the stones responded
Rispondean fatti pietosi?	In pity to my laments?

In each of the remaining three stanzas, however, this mood is contrasted with Orpheus's present state of mind; and it is this contrast which is reflected in Monteverdi's setting, which begins with two minor harmonies – E and A – and a first cadence on A minor, but progresses immediately in sequence to cadence on G major, which is also the harmony on which the aria ends. This contrast is summed up in the final stanza:

Sol per te bella Euridice	Only through you, fair Eurydice,
Benedico il mio tormento,	Do I bless my torment;
Dopo 'l duol vi è più contento,	After grief one is the more glad,
Dopo il mal vi è più felice.	After pain the more happy.

The scene which follows, in which Eurydice's death is announced to Orpheus and his shepherd companions, has long been regarded as one of the most powerful and moving in the opera. It is also one of the most interesting as regards Monteverdi's use of tonality, since its action is articulated on a large scale by the use of two contrasting modes – the Hypoionian, with cadence centres on C and G major, and the Hypoaeolian, with cadences on A minor, C major and E major/minor. The first of these, a 'cheerful mode' according to Zarlino,[22] is used to suggest a state of blissful unawareness of the tragedy that has occurred off stage; the second, a mode apt for 'tears, sadness, solicitude, calamities, and every kind of misery',[23] is employed for emotions associated with full knowledge of the tragedy. In order to demonstrate Monteverdi's tonal usage here, the first part of the scene is given as an extended music example.

During the aria 'Vi ricorda o bosch'ombrosi', the mythical power of Orpheus's singing to stir inanimate nature has woven its magic, and Orpheus is now urged by one of his shepherd companions to continue in the same vein (bars 1–14). The shepherd's arioso serves to establish the cadence centres of G and C and to associate them with emotions of pleasure and wellbeing. It also serves to heighten our expectation of yet another set-piece. Instead, after a twist from C to C sharp in the bass line, we hear the messenger's first words – words that are to become a refrain throughout the remainder of the act:

Ahi caso acerbo, ahi fat'empio e crudele,	Ah! bitter chance, Ah! Fate pitiless and cruel,
Ahi stelle ingiuriose, ahi ciel avaro.	Ah! fateful stars, Ah! avaricious Heaven.

The messenger's first phrase cadences on A minor (bar 17), and our attention is focused on the new, darker tonality by the declamatory nature of the line, which interrupts the rhythmic regularity of the preceding music, and by the acrid dissonance on the second syllable of 'acerbo'. Startled by the messenger's interruption, a shepherd asks 'What is this doleful sound that disturbs the happy day?' (bars 27–29). His musical line is introduced by an F major har-

PASTORE

Mi - ra, deh mi-ra Or - feo, che d'o-gni in-tor - no

Ri - de il bo-sco e ri - de il pra - to, Se - gui

pur co'l plet - tr'au - ra - to D'ad-dol - cir l'a - ria in sì be -

MESSAGGIERA. Un organo di legno & un Chit.

- a - to gior - no. Ahi, _____ ca - so a -

-so - la, Con le pa-ro - le mie pas-sar - gli_il co - re?

PASTORE

Que - sta_è Sil - via gen - ti - le, Dol-cis - si - ma com-pa

-gna De la bel-l'Eu-ri - di - ce: O quan-to_è_in vi - sta Do-lo - ro -

-sa: hor — che fia? deh som-mi De - i Non tor-ce -

mony. It begins on a dissonance against the bass F and rises to a chromatic E flat before both line and harmony are wrenched round to an abrupt cadence on C and a notated silence. The messenger, tormented by the news that she bears, pays no heed to the shepherd's question (bars 30–41). The harmonies that accompany her line are those of A minor, but the first cadence, at the word 'consola', is an unexpected progression from D to C major, perhaps because the text here refers to an Orpheus as yet unaware of

Eurydice's death. As the messenger's thoughts turn to the pain that she must inflict on Orpheus, however, A minor inexorably returns.

In a gesture towards the audience, another shepherd introduces the messenger as Sylvia, one of Eurydice's companions (C major; bars 42–48). He, too, is troubled by the signs of grief in Sylvia's face. His concern and his re-entry into the action are signalled by an unexpected shift of tonality to D (bars 49–52). His thoughts turn inwards (bars 53–58) as he appeals to the gods not to turn away their kindly glance (C major).

Sylvia now begins to face the task that she has to perform (bars 59–66). She tells the shepherd to abandon his song (cadence on G major), 'for all our happiness is turned to pain' (cadence on A minor). The action now moves swiftly towards the first climax of the scene. Orpheus breaks in, urging Sylvia to give her news (bars 67–71). His growing anxiety is matched by a vocal line which moves with increasing speed until it steps ahead of the harmonies implied by the bass. His realisation of the import of Sylvia's demeanour is suggested by a rapid transition from F major to a cadence on E major, expecting an answer beginning on A minor. Sylvia, however, still hesitating to answer directly, at first avoids the expected harmony and once more declares her unhappiness at being the bearer of sad tidings (bars 72–78). Then, on an E major harmony (bars 78–80), she utters the words 'your fair Eurydice . . . '. Orpheus, struck to the heart by her words, interjects the phrase 'Alas, what do I hear?', before Sylvia continues, finally arriving at the long-awaited A minor harmony (bar 85) with the words 'Your beloved wife is dead'. Orpheus reacts by uttering the single word 'Alas!' before falling silent, 'like a mute stone, so grieved that he cannot express his grief', as a shepherd later describes him.

The first of Orpheus's two responses (bars 80–82), with its sudden return to Dorian G minor harmony (employed in Act I for 'Rosa del Ciel') and its subsequent progression to E flat, represents a complete disruption of the prevailing tonalities, suggesting both the personal nature of Orpheus's grief and the shattering of his world. The second of his responses (bars 86–87), cadencing on D major and expecting a progression to G minor, also presupposes a return to the transposed Dorian mode, but, since Orpheus is too shocked to continue, this mode is not re-established until the beginning of his arioso 'Tu se' morta'. Instead, the F sharp is flattened to a minor third above D as, after a full bar's silence, Sylvia begins to relate the circumstances of Eurydice's death. Her narration begins at an emotionally neutral level as she paints a picture of Eurydice and her companions gathering flowers in the meadow to make a garland for Orpheus's hair,[24] but it gathers speed both rhythmically and harmonically as she leads to the moment when Eurydice was bitten by the snake hidden in the grass. After a sudden change from E major to G minor (a device learned from Jacopo Peri, but given new significance in the present context) Sylvia offers a vivid and moving description of Eurydice, life draining from her, sinking to the ground.

The narration returns to a less emotional level as we hear of the other nymphs rushing to Eurydice's aid and attempting to revive her. It halts at Sylvia's exclamation 'Alas!' and we return to the picture of Eurydice, dying. Her drooping eyelids open, and with her dying breath she utters Orpheus's name twice, her last cry rising to the highest note of Sylvia's narration. Another change from E major to G minor saves us from the anticlimax which might have followed as Sylvia rounds off her story:

Dopo un grave sospiro	After a deep sigh
Spirò fra queste braccia, ed io rimasi	She died in these arms [notated silence], and I remained,
Piena il cor di pietade e di spavento.	My heart full of pity and of terror.

Had convention allowed that Eurydice's death could have taken place on stage, the event itself and the emotions that it arouses could scarcely have been conveyed as vividly or as economically as they are through the pen-pictures created by Striggio and Monteverdi.

. Now that the full horror of the story is known, and thus the reason for the words uttered by Sylvia at her entrance, a shepherd's echoing of both the words and the music (and thus the A minor harmonies) of 'Ahi, caso acerbo' seems a natural reaction at this point, rather than a structural device to link the various parts of the scene. As the shepherd finishes, a second shepherd draws our attention to Orpheus, who has so far remained silent. The shepherd's speech – 'A l'amara novella'[25] ('At the bitter news the unhappy one seems like a mute stone, so grieved that he cannot express his grief') – parallels musically the one beginning at bar 28 of the music example, suggesting that both should be allotted to a single singer. This time, though, there is no return to the 'innocence' of a C major harmony. The prominent use of E flat here reflects Orpheus's descent to an E flat harmony in his first reaction to the news of

Eurydice's death. After a cadence on B flat the shepherd's music sinks to A minor as he paraphrases the messenger's initial melodic line to the words 'Ahi, ben havrebbe un cor di Tigre o d'Orsa . . . ' ('Ah! he must have the heart of a tiger or a bear who does not feel pity for your sad state').

Orpheus now rouses himself. His first phrases, beginning over G minor and expressing a numbed reaction to the finality of death, are slow-paced, coloured by acute dissonances, and broken by long rests. This is not, however, to be a lament for Eurydice (the lament is reserved for the last act). Within a few bars, though apparently longer, his music quickens. He resolves to follow Eurydice 'to the deepest abysses', to lead her back 'to see the stars again' ('a riveder le stelle' – an echo of the final line of Dante's *Inferno*) or to remain with her 'in the company of death'. As he exits he sings one of the most memorable lines of the opera:

A dio terra, a dio Cielo, e Sole a dio.	Farewell Earth, farewell Heaven, and farewell, O Sun.

Orpheus's departure seems to signal the beginning of the choral finale to the act. The ensemble takes up the messenger's tonality of A minor and her words 'Ahi, caso acerbo' (the original musical phrase is now in the bass line) as an expression of their own sorrow. Then, with a change from A minor to F major which distances them from the action, the chorus assumes the persona of commentator, reversing the moral presented at the end of the first act:

Non si fidi huom mortale Di ben caduco e frale Che tosto fugge, e spesso A gran salita il precipizio è presso.	Mortal man should not trust In wellbeing, frail and fleeting, Which quickly flies, and often In a great ascent the precipice is near.

This is not the end of the action, however, for Striggio evidently felt the need to round off his portrayal of the messenger, Sylvia. In narrating the death of Eurydice, Sylvia had revealed herself as a genuine personality, torn between the necessity of presenting her news, her own response to Eurydice's death, and the thought of the effect that her words would have on Orpheus. Now, consumed with self-disgust and imagining herself shunned by her former companions, she resolves to spend the remainder of her days in solitary exile. As her speech rises to its final climax, the conflict between her resolution to leave and her reluctance to do so is vividly suggested by the bass line of her music, which drags 'reluctantly' behind the vocal line.

As Sylvia exits we hear a doleful sinfonia which introduces the choral finale proper. Having already pointed the 'moral' to be drawn from the act, Striggio and Monteverdi are now free to concentrate on the personal reaction of the chorus to the events which have just passed. In two duets of great emotional power, punctuated by the refrain 'Ahi, caso acerbo', two shepherds first mourn the loss of Eurydice and Orpheus and then invite their companions to go with them to find Eurydice's body and to mourn over it. As the chorus leaves the stage Music's ritornello returns, suggesting the power that music has to provide consolation in grief and, since we are already familiar with the story, the power that music will have to move the spirits of the Underworld.

Act III

As the sound of Music's ritornello dies away, the scene changes and we hear the first of the Underworld sinfonias, a grand eight-part piece which serves to introduce the new scene and to suggest the awe-inspiring nature of Pluto's kingdom. Orpheus enters, accompanied by Hope (Speranza), whose encouragement has led him thus far. His opening speech introduces the scene – the 'sad and shadowy kingdom which no ray of sunlight ever pierces'. At the beginning of this speech, and at his description of the scene, the harmony is C minor, a tonal level also touched on by the messenger, Sylvia, in Act II, when she described herself as an 'ill-omened bird of night' ('notola infausta').[26]

Hope, too, describes the scene:

Ecco l'atra palude, ecco il nocchiero	Behold the horrid marsh, behold the boatman [Charon]
Che trahe gli ignudi spirti a l'altra riva	Who ferries the naked spirits to the other bank
Dove ha Pluton de l'ombr'il vasto impero.	Where Pluto holds sway over the vast empire of the shades.
Oltre quel nero stagn'oltre quel fiume,	Beyond this black mere [Cocytus], beyond this river [Styx],

| In quei campi di pianto e di dolore, | In those fields of weeping and of grief, |
| Destin crudele ogni tuo ben t'asconde. | Cruel Destiny hides all your wellbeing. |

Hope, however, can travel no further with Orpheus, for over the gateway to Pluto's kingdom are inscribed the words 'Lasciate ogni speranza voi ch'entrate' ('Abandon all hope, ye who enter').

This, of course, is one of the lines inscribed over the entrance to Dante's Inferno,[27] and its quotation in this context could be seen as a learned witticism on Striggio's part. Alternatively, the whole episode could be seen as an archaic device for externalising an inner process: Orpheus enters the Underworld full of hope, but hope deserts him as he sees the entrance to the Inferno. In fact, though, the quotation from Dante, to which Hope specifically draws our attention by singing the phrase twice, provides us with the key to Striggio's vision of the Underworld and suggests one reason for his having made Charon so important a character in the opera.

In their retelling of the Orpheus myth, both Ovid and Virgil conjure up pictures of the approach to the Underworld, though they are less specific about the Underworld itself. Ovid's account is the shorter:

When the bard of Rhodope had mourned her [Eurydice] to the full in the upper world, that he might try the shades as well he dared to go down to the Stygian world through the gate of Taenarus.[28] And through the unsubstantial throngs and the ghosts who had received burial, he came to Persephone [Proserpine] and him who rules those unlovely realms, lord of the shades.[29]

Virgil is more evocative, and thus of more use to Striggio as librettist:

Even the jaws of Taenarus, the lofty portals of Dis, he entered, and the grove that is murky with black terror, and came to the dead, and the king of terrors, and the hearts that know not how to soften at human prayers. Startled by the strain [of Orpheus's song] there came from the lowest depths of Erebus[30] the bodiless shadows and the phantoms of those bereft of light . . . But round them are the black ooze and unsightly reeds of Cocytus,[31] the unlovely mere enchaining them with its sluggish water, and Styx holding them fast within its ninefold circles.[32]

Virgil's description of Cocytus and the Styx are carried over into *Orfeo* in the speech of Hope quoted above; and 'the hearts that know not how to soften at human prayers' are later exemplified in the character of Charon. Nevertheless, neither account tells us how Orpheus managed to gain entry to Hades, and in both Charon appears only after Orpheus has lost Eurydice for the second time. To supply himself with a stage picture of the entry into the Under-world, then, Striggio may have turned first to Virgil's account of Aeneas's journey to Hades (*Aeneid*, Book VI), in which Charon is an important figure, or perhaps to Seneca's *Hercules Oetaeus* (lines 1072–4), in which the effect of Orpheus's song on Charon is men-tioned; but it is clear that the librettist wanted to go beyond a classi-cal vision of Hell to one that would hold real terrors for his audi-ence. His quotation from Dante achieves this. Its implications for the setting of Act III would have been readily understood by a seventeenth-century audience, and their mental picture of Dante's description of the approaches to the Inferno would have been con-firmed by the sight of Charon as Dante had depicted him (just as in the fourth Florentine *intermedio* of 1589):

I kept from speaking until we reached the river. And lo, coming towards us in a boat, an old man, his hair white with age, crying: 'Woe to you, wicked souls, hope not ever to see the sky. I come to bring you to the other bank, into the eternal shades, into fire and frost; and thou there that art a living soul [Dante], take thyself apart from these that are dead.' But when he saw that I did not go, he said: 'By another way, by other ports, not here, thou shalt come to the shore and pass. A lighter vessel must carry thee.'
  And my Leader [Virgil]: 'Charon, do not torment thyself. It is so willed where will and power are one, and ask no more.'
  On that the shaggy jaws of the pilot of the livid marsh, about whose eyes were wheels of flame, were quiet. But those souls, which were weary and naked, changed colour and gnashed their teeth as soon as they heard his cruel words; they blasphemed God and their parents, the human kind, the place, the time, and the seed of their begetting and of their birth, then weeping bitterly, they drew all together to the accursed shore which awaits every man that fears not God. The demon Charon, with eyes of burning coal, beckons to them and gathers them all in, smiting with the oar any that linger.[33]

Striggio's evocation of Dante's vision, wholly appropriate in stage terms for a seventeenth-century audience, also accords well with the cultural ambivalence – the mixture of classical and Christian terms of reference – evident elsewhere in the libretto of *Orfeo*: in Orpheus's 'Rosa del Ciel', for example. And doubtless it did not escape Striggio that Dante (a Florentine poet) developed his description from that of Virgil (a Mantuan poet).

  If we accept, then, that the stage picture that Striggio envisaged for Act III of *Orfeo* was intended to prompt a vision of Dante's Inferno in the minds of the audience, then Charon's prominence in the action becomes readily explicable. It also follows, though, that

Charon is intended to be a figure inspiring awe and terror – a fitting opponent for Orpheus – and not the humorous character depicted in other seventeenth-century sources, and in a later opera like Lully's *Alceste*. Such humour as Monteverdi and Striggio manage to derive from Orpheus's encounter with Charon is incidental to the primary conception of the character.

After the departure of Hope, then, Orpheus is confronted by the awesome figure of Charon, who bars his path and refuses to ferry him, a mortal, across the Styx. Singing in suitably cavernous tones to the accompaniment of a regal (reed organ), Charon voices his suspicion of Orpheus's motives and alludes to 'old outrages' which he has not forgotten: his encounter with Theseus and Pirithous, who had attempted to abduct Proserpine, and with Hercules, who had stolen the dog Cerberus.

Orpheus's response to Charon is the major test of his powers as a singer, the great central aria 'Possente spirto e formidabil nume' ('Powerful spirit and dreadful deity'). Since Orpheus is depicted as a great singer, the attributes that he displays in this aria are those of the early-seventeenth-century virtuoso: a singer schooled both in the older art of complex ornamented song and in the newer Florentine art of passionate rhetorical declamation. The first four stanzas of the aria, in which Orpheus introduces himself and the reason for his journey to the Underworld, represent the art of florid song. They are cast in the form of variations over a slow-moving bass, accompanied by a chitarrone and an organ with wooden pipes, and punctuated by phrases for obbligato instruments – two violins (stanzas 1 and 4), two cornetts (stanza 2) and double harp (stanza 3). The symbolism of these obbligato instruments is not entirely clear. The violins and harp can be related to the Renaissance iconography of Orpheus and his lyre; the cornetts cannot. On balance, I am inclined to believe that Orpheus's 'lyre' is represented by the chitarrone which accompanies his song, while the obbligato instruments, representing the three main classes of late-Renaissance instruments – bowed string instruments, wind/brass instruments,[34] and plucked string instruments – are intended to suggest that Orpheus conjured up all the available forces of music to aid his plea to Charon.

The vocal line of the aria is itself interesting. Monteverdi provided two alternatives: one line with written-out ornamentation (the line usually adopted in present-day performance), and one with no ornamentation. The plain line was provided for the performer who wished to devise his own ornamentation, and it exists simply as the framework around which an ornamented version can be built.[35] The florid version provided by Monteverdi indicated to the singer that the aria was one that required ornamentation, and furnished a model, though one which the singer was by no means bound to follow.

The main part of the variation sequence of 'Possente sprirto' culminates in stanza 4 as Orpheus reveals his identity ('Orfeo son io'). Stanza 5 interrupts the sequence. As Orpheus thinks fondly of Eurydice's eyes, of the glance that could return him to life, Monteverdi abandons the variation bass and turns to a simpler melodic style, rather in the manner of the solo songs of Giulio Caccini. In stanza 6, as Orpheus makes his appeal to Charon, the variation bass returns, though Monteverdi retains the simpler, more direct, melodic style. Now, however, he surrounds the voice with a halo of bowed strings, representing the sound of Orpheus's lyre.

Charon answers. He asserts that he has been both flattered and pleased by Orpheus's song, though since his own music is substantially the same as that of his first speech it is clear that he remains totally unmoved. His refusal to help provokes a passionate outburst from Orpheus. Abandoning the 'arts' of the singer, Orpheus expresses his frustration, and his fear that he will never again see Eurydice, in a line which unleashes the full emotional power of the new recitative style. And he concludes with a direct and forceful appeal:

Rendetemi il mio ben,	Give me back my beloved,
Tartarei Numi.	deities of Tartarus.

Though he has run the full gamut of early-seventeenth-century song-styles, Orpheus has still failed to affect Charon. Now it is time to try the power of his lyre, represented by a five-part sinfonia which, Monteverdi states, was played 'very quietly, by *viole da braccio*, an organ with wooden pipes and a *contrabasso de Viola da gamba*'. (Incidentally, the same sinfonia precedes 'Possente spirto' and, because of its connotations, should in my view be played by the same string ensemble with organ continuo.)[36] The sound of the lyre lulls Charon to sleep, leaving Orpheus to observe wryly:

Ei dorme, e la mia cetra	He sleeps, and though my lyre
Se pietà non impetra	Awakens no pity
Nel indurato core, almen il sonno	In his hard heart, at least his eyes
Fuggir al mio cantar gl'occhi non ponno.	Cannot escape sleep at my singing.

Orpheus seizes the opportunity thus presented. Uttering the words 'Let boldness prevail if prayers are in vain', he steals Charon's boat; and as he crosses the Styx he sings once again 'Rendetemi il mio ben, Tartarei Numi'. As he disembarks and enters the mouth of the Inferno we hear again the sinfonia with which the act began.

The chorus of spirits, which has so far been silent, though presumably on stage throughout the act as part of the re-creation of Dante's vision, now assumes the role of commentator. Unlike the choruses of Acts I and II, which include duets and trios, the final chorus of Act III is set for five voices throughout. It is the more forceful for being clearly detached from the preceding action. The message that the chorus delivers is unequivocally humanist in tone:

Nulla impresa per huom si tenta invano	No enterprise is undertaken by man in vain,
Nè contr'a lui più sa natura armarse,	Nor does Nature know any longer how to arm herself against him,
. . .	. . .
Ch'ei pose freno al Mar con fragil legno	For he has tamed the sea with fragile wood
Che sprezzò d'Austro e d'Aquilon lo sdegno.	Which scorned the wrath of Aquilo [a north wind] and Auster [a south wind].

Act IV

The introduction of the Charon episode as Act III solved some problems for Striggio, but created others. The appearance of Charon confirmed the Dantesque vision of the act and presented an element of opposition to Orpheus's entry into the Underworld; and it also provided a necessary fifth action for the five-act structure. At the same time, having sung his showpiece aria to Charon, Orpheus could not repeat this in an encounter with Pluto and Proserpine; and if the aria itself had produced no effect on Charon, then what price Orpheus's mythical powers as a singer?

The key to this apparent weakness in the opera is found in the unity of action that Striggio intended between Acts III and IV. The two acts are to be played without a break. The chorus at the end of Act III stands outside the action and should not be perceived as interrupting it. The action, therefore, proceeds directly from Orpheus's exit through the gateway to the Inferno to the entrance of

Pluto and Proserpine; and it is clea r from Proserpine's first words that both she and Pluto have heard Orpheus's aria, and that she, unlike Charon, has been moved to pity:

Signor, quell'infelice	My lord, that unhappy man
Che per queste di morte ampie campagne	Who through these broad fields of death
Va chiamando Euridice,	Goes calling 'Eurydice',
Ch'udito hai tu pur dianzi	W'.,om you have just now heard
Così soavemente lamentarsi,	So sweetly lamenting,
Moss'ha tanta pietà dentro al mio core	Has so moved my heart to pity
Ch'un altra volta io torno a porger prieghi	That I return once more to entreat
Perchè il tuo nume al suo pregar si pieghi.	That you will soften your judgment at his prayer.

Act IV must have been played before the same stage set as Act III, presumably with Charon remaining on stage, asleep. No scene change is indicated in either the libretto or the score, and to have introduced one would have destroyed the concept of unity of action which is crucial to the credibility of Striggio's Orpheus. Moreover, when Striggio evoked Dante's *Inferno* in Act III, he must have intended to raise a question in the minds of the audience as to just what kind of hell lay beyond the gateway to the Inferno. Any attempt to change scene for Act IV would force an answer to this question (by no means easy to find) and destroy the uncomfortable ambiguity so carefully created in Act III.

The transition from Act III to Act IV is marked by the sinfonia which opened Act III. Pluto and Proserpine enter, and Proserpine addresses her husband with the words just quoted. She goes on to remind him of their own love for each other and to plead for Eurydice's release. Pluto, whose thoughts have already been turned to those of love by Orpheus's singing, makes no more than a passing reference to the 'immutable law' which forbids his consort's wishes before consenting, though he immediately imposes the condition that Orpheus should not turn round to look at Eurydice as he leads her from the Underworld. He commands his servants to go and proclaim the decision throughout his kingdom:

Sì che l'intenda Orfeo	So that Orpheus should under- stand it
E l'intenda Euridice,	And so that Eurydice should understand it,
Nè di cangiarlo altrui sperar più lice.	Nor should others hope to change it.

One of his servants, though clearly puzzled by this whim of Pluto's, goes to do his bidding. Another spirit, addressing the audience, poses the crucial question:

Trarrà da quest'orribili caverne	Will Orpheus lead his wife
Sua sposa Orfeo, s'adoprerà suo ingegno	From these horrible caverns? Will he employ reason
Sì che nol vinca giovenil desio,	And not let it be conquered by youthful desire,
Nè i gravi imperi suoi sparga d'oblio?	Nor forget the stern conditions laid on him?

While Pluto's commands are being carried to Orpheus and Eurydice, the characters of Pluto and Proserpine are developed in a short love scene in which both allude to their own mythical story, itself almost a mirror image of the fate of Orpheus and Eurydice. Where Orpheus seeks to lead Eurydice back to the upper world and is prevented from doing so, Pluto abducted Proserpine from Earth and carried her to the Underworld, but was prevented by Ceres from keeping her there permanently.[37] Striggio underscores the tragedy of Orpheus's impending second loss by making the release of Eurydice a reason for Proserpine's happily reconciling herself to her union with Pluto; and the chorus respond 'Pity and love triumph today in the Inferno'.

Orpheus is now seen returning. As he emerges from the gateway to the Inferno, leading Eurydice, he sings an aria, another set of strophic variations, though this time over a faster-moving bass suggesting a sense of joy and triumph. He sings in praise of his lyre, which has overcome the stony hearts of the infernal deities and is thus worthy of a place in the heavens, where the stars will dance to its music (cf. the imagery of stanza 3 of the prologue). He has sung only three stanzas, however, before doubt assails him. Who will assure him that Eurydice is following? (A written-out silence while he listens.) Who keeps the sweet light of her beloved eyes hidden from him? (Another silence.) Perhaps the envious deities of the Inferno have prevented him from looking at Eurydice so that his happiness will not be complete. Why should he be afraid? What Pluto forbids, Cupid commands. (Another silence.) He must obey the more powerful of the two gods.

At this point a great noise is heard off stage ('Qui si fa strepito dietro la tela'). Orpheus, imagining that the Furies are carrying off Eurydice, turns and catches a glimpse of her eyes before the vision is abruptly cut off and one of the infernal spirits pronounces judgment: 'You have broken the law and are unworthy of grace'. Eurydice's voice is heard for the last time as she laments Orpheus's losing her 'for too much love', and her own loss of life and husband. She is ordered to return once more to the shades of the dead, with no hope of ever seeing the stars again (another echo of Dante). Orpheus tries to follow her, but is held back by a force invisible to him which also drags him back towards the upper world. As he is pulled away, a new sinfonia is heard, introducing a five-part chorus which parallels the one heard at the end of Act III:

E la virtute un raggio	Virtue is a ray
Di celeste bellezza	Of heavenly beauty
. . .	. . .
Orfeo vinse l'Inferno e vinto poi	Orpheus conquered Hell and was then conquered
Fu da gl'affetti suoi.	By his own passions.
Degno d'eterna gloria	Worthy alone of eternal glory
Fia sol colui ch'avrà di sè vittoria.	Is he who has victory over himself.

The sinfonia is heard again, concluding the act, and the scene is changed.

The second death of Eurydice is one of the most difficult episodes of the opera to stage. Its details, however, seem to have been developed from Virgil, and Virgil's account (see above, pp. 25–6) suggests the sort of stage picture that Striggio might have intended – even to the extent of offering an idea of the part that Charon might play in this act, a final appearance that would reinforce the symmetry of Acts III and IV.

Act V

As Act V begins, Music's ritornello is heard again, as it was at the end of Act II, offering consolation, though no longer any hope of recovering Eurydice. Once more the scene is set in Thrace, the stage setting the same as that used for Acts I and II, as we learn from the first words that Orpheus utters:

Questi i campi di Tracia, e quest'è il loco	These are the fields of Thrace, and this is the place
Dove passomm'il core	Where my heart was pierced
Per l'amara novella il mio dolore.	By grief at the bitter news.

Orpheus, transported back to Thrace (could his journey to the Underworld simply have been a dream?), is alone, and most of the act is devoted to his solitary lamenting for Eurydice. His long soliloquy is a sequence of six paragraphs, articulated by abrupt changes of harmony. The first comprises the first three lines of text, as Orpheus looks about him at the scene in which he first heard the news of Eurydice's death. The relatively slow movement of his vocal line, sung almost entirely over a single sustained G minor harmony, suggests his inner desolation or, perhaps, numbness after his sudden translation back to the upper world. The longer second paragraph, set over a series of sustained harmonies and concluding with a more poignant version of the cadence which ended paragraph 1, makes the sense of desolation explicit: Orpheus no longer has any hope of recovering his lost beloved and can now only seek consolation among the woodlands where he first languished for Eurydice.

The third paragraph ('Voi vi doleste, o monti'), based on the hallowed tradition of the echo lament, moves away from a G minor cadence centre towards one of A minor, embracing a poignant E flat harmony *en route* and thus paralleling the tonal symbolism of the messenger scene in Act II. The harmonies move faster here, as Orpheus pours out his sorrow and moves the mountains and stones to pity. As he reaches the end of each sentence, the echo gives back the last syllable or two of his utterance, subtly changing its meaning so that, for example, Orpheus's 'guai' ('woes') becomes the echo's 'Ahi!' ('Ah!').

The echo ceases, and paragraphs four and five ('Ma tu, anima mia') form a hymn of praise to Eurydice's beauty, a last, profoundly felt expression of Orpheus's love for her. This cadences on G minor. With a change to G major at 'Hor l'altre donne', preserving a sense of continuity, we move into the final phase of the soliloquy, in which Orpheus declares his rejection of all other women. Unlike the earlier part of the soliloquy, these lines are cast in *versi sdruccioli* – that is, in lines in which the accent falls on the antepenultimate syllable instead of the more usual penultimate. This type of line, often used by poets as a 'rustic' metre, is employed here to suggest scorn, climaxing in the phrase 'vil femmina' ('vile womankind').

In the libretto, and in the original ending of the opera, it is this scornful rejection of women which provokes the eruption on to the stage of the Bacchantes, at whose approach Orpheus withdraws (see above, p. 38). In the version of the opera transmitted by the score, however, this outburst – which hints at, but does not make

explicit, Orpheus's turn to homosexuality[38] – is immediately
followed by the sinfonia used in Act III to represent Orpheus playing his lyre.

The lyre represented here could be either that of Orpheus or that
of Apollo, for it is at this point that Apollo appears, descending to
Earth in a cloud. He chides his son for abandoning himself to sorrow
and disdain. He has seen the 'blame and peril' ('biasmo e periglio')
which hangs over Orpheus and has come to aid him. (Whether the
'peril' that Apollo mentions derives from the Bacchantes or from
Orpheus's failure to master his emotions is not clear.) Orpheus
expresses his grief, but stands as a dutiful son, awaiting his father's
advice. Apollo, a god associated not only with the sun and with
music but also with reason and intellect, points the moral:

Troppo, troppo gioisti	Too much you rejoiced
Di tua lieta ventura:	At your happy lot:
Hor troppo piagni	Now you weep too much
Tua sorte acerba e dura.	At your hard and bitter fate.
Ancor non sai	Do you still not know
Come nulla quà giù diletta e dura?	That nothing here below delights and lasts?

and invites Orpheus to enjoy immortal life in the heavens. Orpheus
asks whether he will never again see Eurydice, and is told that he
will recognise her 'fair semblance' ('le sue sembianze belle') in the
sun and the stars. Orpheus declares that he would be an unworthy
son of Apollo if he did not follow such good counsel, and the two
ascend to the skies singing, as befits the god and demigod of song,
a florid duet:

Saliam cantando al cielo	We ascend, singing, to the heavens
Dove ha virtù verace	Where true virtue has
Degno premio di sè, diletto e pace.	A prize worthy of itself: delight and peace.

A lively ritornello initiates the perfunctory choral finale of the
1609 score, a chorus sung by shepherds, who rejoice in Orpheus's
translation to the heavens and conclude with an explicitly Biblical
moral which seems curiously at odds with the earlier part of the
opera:

Così gratia in ciel impetra	Thus he entreats for grace in the heavens
Che qua giù provò l'inferno	Who experienced the Inferno here below.

| E chi semina fra doglie | And he who sows in tears |
| D'ogni gratia il frutto coglie.[39] | Shall reap the fruit of grace. |

The opera ends on a note of rejoicing, with a *moresca* (literally a 'Moorish' dance)[40] performed by the shepherds. It is worth noting, though, that the *moresca* was usually performed by two groups of dancers and depicted a stylised fight between Christians and Muslims, and one is left with the suspicion that Monteverdi may simply have employed here, despite the change of context, a battle dance which had formed part of the Bacchanalian orgy with which the opera originally ended.

Although, as far as we know, neither Striggio nor Monteverdi had any experience of writing theatrical works prior to *Orfeo*, both men evidently had a sophisticated appreciation of stage practice and of the ways in which the realities of time and place can be manipulated in the theatre. If we accept that it was Striggio's intention that *Orfeo* should be played without breaks between the acts, then we can see how he used the larger framework thus provided to solve some of the problems inherent in a five-act structure. This is apparent, for example, in his handling of Act I and the beginning of Act II. By dividing the action into three structural units, articulated by the exit to the temple and the re-entry of Orpheus at the end of Act I, Striggio manages not only to compress the passage of time, but also to introduce stage movement into an otherwise static section of the drama. Similarly, one of the apparent weaknesses of *Orfeo* – the failure of 'Possente spirto' to move Charon – becomes explicable when we understand that Acts III and IV form a single unit and that the aria is also heard by Pluto and Proserpine.

It is also apparent that very little of the instrumental music of the opera is introduced for purely musical reasons. Sinfonias and ritornellos are used to mark exits, to cover scene changes and the use of machinery, as well as to represent changes of location, the power of music and Orpheus's lyre. Since much of this music serves a dramatic function, relatively little is available for dancing. Only two items in the opera – the *balletto* 'Lasciate i monti' and the concluding *moresca* – are in fact marked as dance movements.

The exit to the temple in Act I helps to throw the concluding chorus into greater relief, thus marking more clearly the end of the act. This, in turn, helps to make more readily appreciable the symmetrical shaping of *Orfeo*, in which 'Possente spirto' is placed almost exactly at the centre of the five-act structure. In performance, though, the most striking correspondence is between the choruses which end Acts III and IV. That this should be the case is not surprising, since these choruses contain Alessandro Striggio's interpretation of the significance of the Orpheus myth. The first expresses the self-confidence of Renaissance man. The second concludes that Orpheus's ultimate failure was due to his inability to let reason control his emotions.

Monteverdi's response to the story resides in the powerful way in which he communicates Orpheus's reactions to the unfolding of events. That Monteverdi saw *Orfeo* as an essentially human drama is confirmed by his letter to Alessandro Striggio of 9 December, 1616. In discussing the maritime fable *Le nozze di Tetide*, which he had been asked to set for Mantua, he stated:

In addition, I have noticed that the interlocutors are winds, Cupids, little Zephyrs and Sirens: consequently many sopranos will be needed, and it can also be said that the winds have to sing – that is, the Zephyrs and the Boreals. How, dear Sir, can I imitate the speech of the winds, if they do not speak? And how can I, by such means, move the passions? Ariadne moved us because she was a woman, and similarly Orpheus because he was a man, not a wind . . . And as to the story as a whole – as far as my no little ignorance is concerned – I do not feel that it moves me at all (moreover I find it hard to understand), nor do I feel that it carries me in a natural manner to an end that moves me. *Arianna* led me to a just lament, and *Orfeo* to a righteous prayer, but this fable leads me I don't know to what end.[41]

5   *The rediscovery of 'Orfeo'*

NIGEL FORTUNE

Introduction

Monteverdi's music was soon forgotten after his death in 1643 and generally remained so until about a hundred years ago. In the intervening centuries the only references to it are those of pioneer music historians. Among the earliest of these were the Englishmen Charles Burney and John Hawkins in the later eighteenth century. They were clearly puzzled, yet also fascinated, by some, at least, of what they unearthed. In his account of the earliest operas, Burney wrote: 'I am unable to discover Monteverdi's superiority';[1] while Hawkins, discussing *Orfeo*, reported that 'the structure of this drama is so very unlike that of the modern opera, as to render it a subject of curious speculation'.[2] Both men were struck by two other features of the opera – certain bold harmonic progressions, and the size of the orchestra (in Burney's words, 'greatly superior to that of [Peri's] Euridice',[3] if only for the quantity of instruments required) – and they illustrated their accounts of the work with several music examples.

In Germany in the nineteenth century, Monteverdi was taken ever more seriously by the founding fathers of modern musical scholarship: by Carl von Winterfeld, who in 1834 devoted much space to him, including half a dozen pages on *Orfeo*, in a pioneering study centring on Giovanni Gabrieli,[4] and later by men such as August Wilhelm Ambros and Hugo Riemann and above all Emil Vogel, who in 1887 at the age of twenty-eight completed a doctoral dissertation on Monteverdi at Berlin University and had it published in a scholarly journal.[5] This was the first major independent work on Monteverdi, but since it is primarily a biographical study *Orfeo* is naturally mentioned only briefly. Such historians as these can certainly be said to have 'rediscovered' Monteverdi, but they wrote mainly for academics and connoisseurs, and the music itself can scarcely have been known at all, even to this restricted audience.

Interest in *Orfeo* and early opera in general broadened at the end of the nineteenth century and in the early twentieth century with the advent of two other types of publication. One of these was the book devoted wholly to such operas or to a relatively restricted period of early music. A distinguished example was a two-volume study of seventeenth-century Italian opera by another fine German scholar, Hugo Goldschmidt,[6] though this too was probably read in the main by a relatively small circle. Two other books, at least, were probably of wider appeal and must have done much to make Monteverdi known in France and Britain respectively. One, by the young Romain Rolland,[7] more famous later in life as a novelist and man of letters than as a writer on music, started out, like Vogel's study, as a doctoral dissertation. It is a lively, enthusiastic book, which achieved a fourth edition by 1936, but it is vitiated, like so much writing of this period, by the author's susceptibility to and excessive reverence for the music of Wagner. Its pages on Monteverdi – duly invoking the example of Wagner (not for the last time in the literature) – must have introduced him to many new readers; there is, however, no specific discussion of *Orfeo*. Hubert Parry could start his history of seventeenth-century music by lamenting the likely state of his readers' knowledge – not, as has sometimes been alleged, stating his own view of the music: 'the seventeenth century is, musically, a blank, even to those who take more than an average interest in the Art . . . '[8] In this book he wrote warmly of *Orfeo*: 'considering the elementary state of the musical dramatic art when it was written, it is one of the most astonishing products of genius in the whole range of music'.[9] In a later paper, read to a specialist audience, however, he was inclined to take a loftier view, particularly of Monteverdi's instrumental writing:

The musical material [of the ritornellos and sinfonias] is almost without significance, and has little or no relevance to the context . . . there does seem to have been some vague idea of relevance of colour to situation; . . . when Orpheus returns to the familiar earth the brass instruments cease, and the accompaniment of strings and lutes and 'organo di legno' is resumed; which undoubtedly would throw the colour used for the nether regions into strong and effective relief. But the procedure does not amount to much more than simple adaptation of crude resources such as any child might have attempted, with a birthday party of mouth-organs and tooth-combs and banjos and kitchen furniture.[10]

General histories of music or opera and studies of Monteverdi did of course continue to treat *Orfeo* increasingly fully in the light of experience of it in performance and from study of the score – in however unauthentic a form – and with developing awareness and understanding of the opera's musical and social contexts. Detailed articles on specific aspects of *Orfeo* began in 1902–3 with Alfred Heuss's exhaustive examination of the instrumental movements[11] – again originating as a thesis, and an excellent example of the distinguished scholarship applied to the work, especially in Germany, at an early date – and have appeared from time to time ever since; the instrumental music has attracted particular attention. As early as 1910 a leading Italian scholar, Gaetano Cesari, could refer to *Orfeo* as 'certainly the least forgotten of the earliest operas'.[12]

The other important new factor in the re-emergence of the work was the publication of the music. A major pioneer here was another eminent German musicologist, Robert Eitner (1832–1905), who published an edition of *Orfeo* in 1881.[13] As is explained below, this edition, like most of the publications mentioned so far, would be known only to a restricted public; but at least those interested in consulting the music of *Orfeo* could now do so much more conveniently than hitherto, when they would have had to track down (with almost no help from bibliographers) one of the handful of surviving copies of the 1609 and 1615 editions, and read it in the library housing it. Eitner's edition is thus a landmark in the developing interest in *Orfeo*.

Eitner's score appeared in one of a series of volumes running from 1873 to 1905 in which he made available a wide range of early music and theoretical writings, complementing the scholarly histories, monographs and articles now being produced with increasing frequency by himself and others. It was at this period that the complete works of past composers already recognised as great masters were being intensively published, especially in Germany. As well as those devoted to such obvious candidates as Bach, Beethoven and Mozart, German complete editions included those devoted to Monteverdi's non-German predecessors Palestrina (from 1862) and Lassus (from 1894), and even in England the Purcell Society Edition began to appear as early as 1878; yet Monteverdi was barely represented in modern prints at all, which suggests how far he still was from being thought of as a great composer. Such comparative neglect may have had something to do with the veneration of sacred polyphony in certain influential scholarly circles and the complementary suspicion of Italian opera and other early secular music.

Eitner's edition of *Orfeo* was clearly intended for the scholar in his study, and no performance of it was envisaged. The text is given only in Italian, and original clefs and bar-lines are retained. But there is a realisation of the bass for piano, relatively plain by some later standards but nevertheless fussy and stodgy. Yet when considering this feature here and in subsequent editions we ought to remember how little research had been done on the methods of performance of early music, not least the realisation of continuo parts. Then and for years to come, realisations invariably imitated the keyboard textures of current compositions: Alfred Moffat's editions of music for violin and keyboard (still dying hard in some circles) are typical examples. Unless he was simply making room for as much as possible of the other early operatic music in his volume, it is curious, given the aim of his edition, that Eitner should have made two arbitrary cuts, totalling 41 systems: calculating from the 1609 edition, the first three and a half pages of Act III – meaning that the act virtually starts with 'Possente spirto' – and a comparable amount at the start of Act IV, omitting the dialogue between Pluto and Proserpine. The gratuitous alterations are equally curious, as a later editor pointed out:[14] for all his distinction as scholar and bibliographer, Eitner clearly did not understand aspects of the style of the work or simply could not believe that Monteverdi intended some of his bolder harmonic progressions.[15]

More than twenty years elapsed before another edition of *Orfeo* appeared, and it is now that the editing of it for performance effectively begins. The fact that the new edition came not from a musicologist but from a composer, Vincent d'Indy (1851–1931), prompts general consideration, before discussing it and its successors, of the wide variety of musicians who have been drawn to *Orfeo* in the twentieth century to the extent of preparing editions of it. The high proportion of composers among them, over a period of some eighty years, is striking: it is to be doubted whether any other work in the history of music has attracted so many. Few of their editions seem to have been commissioned. They seem to have been paying tribute to the power of music, responding as creative artists to the archetypal theme of a masterpiece that, however much it may perpetuate sixteenth-century traditions – a fact that in any case was not fully understood in the earlier decades of the century – comes from the very dawn of one of the most potent of all art forms. As we shall see, their individual decisions to turn to *Orfeo*, and their approaches to it, could also have been influenced by the artistic, social and political climates in which they worked and by their personal orientations within them. Besides d'Indy, the composers, more or less prominent, who have produced versions of *Orfeo* – six Italians and two Germans – are (in chronological order) Gian Francesco Malipiero, Carl Orff, Ottorino Respighi, Vito Frazzi, Paul Hindemith, Valentino Bucchi, Bruno Maderna and Luciano Berio. With them may be classed two lesser Italians who also composed: Giacomo Orefice, who was a critic, pianist and editor too, and Giacomo Benvenuti, who was best known as an editor. The first non-composer after Eitner to edit the work was Hans Erdmann-Guckel over thirty years later; the first to have an edition published was August Wenzinger, as late as 1955.

Mention of Wenzinger introduces to this survey the comparatively recent figure of the specialist scholar–performer, who has dominated the field, at the expense of the composer, ever since. Versions by two composers – Bucchi and Maderna – and the recent version conceived by Luciano Berio are the only ones to postdate Wenzinger's, whereas several specialists, most of them responding to commissions to perform *Orfeo*, have found enough that is challenging in the work – and no doubt enough that dissatisfied them in the details of the previous versions available to them – to insist on producing their own editions: for example, those of Denis Stevens (published in 1967 on the occasion of the quatercentenary of Monteverdi's birth), Jane Glover (marking the fiftieth anniversary, in 1975, of the performances of J. A. Westrup's edition and the founding of the Oxford University Opera Club), Roger Norrington (a commission from Kent Opera first performed in 1976) and John Eliot Gardiner (a commission from the English National Opera first performed in 1981 and replacing an earlier, superseded version by Raymond Leppard), as well as those of Nikolaus Harnoncourt, Jürgen Jürgens, and Edward H. Tarr (all presumably prepared for gramophone recordings), bear witness to this decisive recent trend, which is likely to remain much the dominant one in future performances and editions.

Henceforward, it will be appropriate for this survey to concentrate on various versions of the opera that have been produced and on performances of them. There are at least forty (published and unpublished) editions, about a fifth of them prompted by anniversaries, notably those of Monteverdi's birth and death in 1967 and 1943 respectively. The quantity is so great that several of the earlier scores that I have been unable to consult (manuscript ones in the main) have to be treated rather summarily. The same applies to the numerous recent editions, dating from after the point at which the work can really be said to have been 'rediscovered', which I would see as 1967.

Free adaptations of *Orfeo*

In studying the fortunes of *Orfeo* during the present century I consider first what might be called the 'impure' or 're-creative' versions – free adaptations or arrangements of the original, most of them the work of composers. I then turn to the products of 'pure' attitudes towards the work in which scholarly considerations are paramount; almost all of these have come from non-composers, though two composers, Malipiero and Hindemith, also figure here.

The first modern performances of *Orfeo* were given at the Schola Cantorum, Paris, under Vincent d'Indy, on 25 February and 2 March 1904 (the dates corresponding almost exactly with those of the two Mantuan performances of 1607). These were concert performances, using d'Indy's edition of the opera sung in his own French translation. The Schola Cantorum, which d'Indy had co-founded in 1894 and now directed, had soon established itself as one of the two leading musical academies in Paris. Its courses included the study of music of the more distant past such as Gregorian chant and Renaissance polyphony. The associated performances of *Orfeo* and other early music therefore had an essentially educational role. It is clear, however, from an article that d'Indy wrote in 1902 on Debussy's *Pelléas et Mélisande* that his interest in Monteverdi's music was not merely academic and that he saw in it an analogy with developments in French music of his own day:

The same system of expressive recitative heightened by the ambient harmony; so similar, indeed, that one could apply to Debussy himself the maxim that Monteverdi applied to Marenzio: *L'orazione padrona dell'armonia e non serva* (the discourse must govern the harmony, not serve it). The same preoccupation with painting the emotions through a general tint in the instrumentation and not through detail. The same audacity of harmonic writing; and I do not believe that I go too far in saying that the audacities of Monteverdi would seem, to the eyes of critics and the makers of treatises – if they knew them – even more astounding than those of the composer of the *Nocturnes* and the *Damoiselle élue*.[16]

As teacher and performer, d'Indy can be seen as a practical counterpart to the scholarly Eitner. As well as having a dig at

Eitner, he spoke for the ethos of the Schola Cantorum and for all his fellow composer–editors when he declared in the preface to the published score of his version of *Orfeo* (1905): 'it has been my intention to produce a work of art, not of archaeology'. He clearly felt that he could realise this aim only by radically altering the work. It was plausible to present the text only in French (involving not unreasonable adjustments to note values), but his cuts seem far less defensible. His 203 missing systems make Eitner's omission of 41 seem innocuous indeed. The shape of the opera is seriously damaged: the whole of Act V disappears, allegedly because the drama is over before then, and so does the whole of Act I, presumably because it has not yet begun (the act 'consists only of pastoral songs and dances'). D'Indy's other cuts include the two that Eitner made in Acts III and IV, and he even extended the former to include the first three strophes of 'Possente spirto', so that the aria begins with the words 'Orfeo son'io'. In a letter to Gaetano Cesari, d'Indy disarmingly explained that he had to omit *'Orpheus's admirable entry* in the third act . . . only because it was impossible to translate into French' (his italics).[17] No doubt the over-elaborate continuo realisation was also meant, paradoxically, to play a part in creating a lively impact: sometimes a voice is doubled at the tenth above; two-part vocal writing may be duplicated, without further notes added; and so on. But d'Indy took Monteverdi's bolder harmonic progressions in his stride, and his orchestra at the 1904 performances included organ, harpsichord, harp and harp–lute (a guitar-like hybrid instrument).

Both d'Indy's score and his performances at the Schola Cantorum were well received. Another prominent composer interested in the past responded admiringly to this exhumation of a masterpiece, however dismembered. This was Paul Dukas, who, in a review of the score,[18] saw Monteverdi as a dramatic innovator to be classed with Lully, Rameau, Gluck and – again – Wagner; moreover, 'the boldness and novelty of his style reappear to us in all their brilliance and force our admiration', and he was yet another to be particularly struck by the scoring: the 'prodigality of instruments [*agents sonores*] has been surpassed only by the most modern dramatic composers'.[19]

If d'Indy did intend his performance of *Orfeo* to be, at least in part, a contribution to the polemic surrounding Debussy's work, then the point was certainly not lost on the critic René de Castéra, who quoted d'Indy's analogy between Monteverdi and Debussy in his own review of the Schola Cantorum performance.[20] Nor was the relevance of *Orfeo* to the younger generation of French composers overlooked by Romain Rolland, who, apparently abandoning his former respect for German music, included in his review an onslaught on the tyranny of the Italian and German musical traditions of the nineteenth century (see below, Chapter 6).

The idea that *Orfeo* could be related to contemporary issues in French music may go some way to account for the sympathetic reception accorded to d'Indy's performances. Nevertheless, the impression that emerges most clearly from reviews is that *Orfeo* itself proved to be of much more than mere historical interest. This much is clear from Rolland's review, though we should remember that Rolland was not a dispassionate commentator, for he had helped d'Indy to prepare his edition.[21] His review is, rather, an eloquent expression of the excitement that he felt in hearing for the first time a work with which he had long been familiar. His judgment that the musical highlight of the evening was the messenger scene of Act II is confirmed by Julien Tiersot, who wrote in the weekly musical journal *Le ménestrel* (6 March 1904):

There is a scene in *Orfeo* which was, for all of us who heard it the other evening, a revelation: the scene in which, in the middle of the shepherds' festivities, a messenger arrives to announce the death of Eurydice. It is a page of great beauty in its own right, but quite astounding if one looks back to the period in which it was written. The declamation and the harmony form a compact and indissoluble whole. The tone is intense, the inflections occasionally of an unexpected modernity, and the *coups de théâtre* are expressed by successions of harmonies both bold and apposite.

In the years before the First World War, d'Indy's edition was also given in a concert performance under Sylvain Dupuis at the 'Concerts populaires' at Brussels on 21 January 1910. More important, it formed the basis of the first modern stage performance of the opera, given at the Théâtre Réjane, Paris, on 2 May 1911 under Marcel Labey, a professor at the Schola Cantorum since 1903. Clearly, Labey and his colleagues did not wish to risk presenting *Orfeo* as a commercial venture. Their solution, to give the production as a single charity matinée in aid of the Orphélinat des Arts, was a shrewd one, doubtless intended to ensure an audience and to disarm potential criticism. It also allowed them to call upon the services of singers from a number of established companies, including Claire Croiza from the Théâtre de la Monnaie in Brussels for the crucial role of the Messenger. The cast list was as follows:

La Musique	Mme Mellot-Joubert
La Messagère	Mme Claire Croiza
Une Bergère	Mme B. Mendès (of the Opéra)
Un Berger	Mme Duvernax (of the Opéra-Comique)
Orphée	M. Robert Le Lubez
Caron	M. Tarquini d'Or (of the Trianon Lyrique)[22]

The disadvantage of giving only one performance was that the opera had to be played against a set from the play currently being given at the Théâtre Réjane – Maeterlinck's *L'oiseau bleu* – a fact which prompted the critic F. Guérillot to remark:

Out of all this it should be remembered that an Italian work of 1607 was able to excite a Parisian public of 1911 in the scenery created by Russians for a work by Maeterlinck! [The sets for this production of *L'oiseau bleu* were designed by Vladimir Egoroff.] Here is a state of affairs which will, perhaps, disturb the defenders of a sense of history, but one which argues in favour of the eternal life of Art. This production is a step towards a genuine restoration of *Orfeo*, and it is to be hoped that it will encourage M. d'Indy to issue a score of the whole work.[23]

As a charitable venture, the production seems to have been a success, and it was revived, again as a charity matinée and with an almost identical cast, on 11 April 1913. On this occasion, however, the opera was given its own set, described by a critic as 'a Botticellian framework'.[24]

Despite the pioneering efforts of such men as Oscar Chilesotti, Angelo Solerti and Luigi Torchi and of a number of local historians, scholarly research into early music moved at a slower tempo in Italy than in Germany or France, and it is not until the next edition that we begin to chart the rediscovery of *Orfeo* in its own country. There was, however, talk of performing it at the Bologna exhibition of 1888, but it came to nothing.[25] In the 1890s the celebrated writer Gabriele d'Annunzio undoubtedly played a part in directing interest towards Monteverdi, whom he was later to cite, with Dante, Michelangelo and Palestrina, as one of four great Italian artists. His novel *Il fuoco*, begun in 1896, may be an empty and feverish document, but it is extraordinary to find in a novel of this period, alongside ritual reverence for the 'godlike' Wagner, a discussion of the 'purity' of the Florentine Camerata and an important, ecstatic episode featuring a performance of the lament from Monteverdi's *Arianna* (among English novelists of the time, for example, only George Moore seems to have attempted anything comparable, in the exactly contemporary *Evelyn Innes*, where early music, and Wagner, likewise feature prominently).[26] Eventually, on 30 November 1909, perhaps to mark the tercentenary of the first publication of the opera, the Associazione Italiana di Amici della Musica put on, in concert form, at the Conservatorio di Musica 'Giuseppe Verdi', Milan, a version of *Orfeo* requested from their founder, Giacomo Orefice (1865–1922). The performance was directed by Amilcare Zanella. In the same year, the Association published both the libretto of this version and a vocal score, the latter including five facsimiles from the 1609 print. This edition was heard again at Mantua on 5 April 1910 and shortly afterwards in other Italian cities and at Monte Carlo. It is interesting – and perhaps not surprising – to find the English critic Claude Trevor referring to Orefice's version and earnestly hoping for a performance in England, not on the stage but 'by one of the many Choral Societies'.[27]

In the preface to their publications, the Association followed d'Indy in dismissing Eitner's version as purely for musicologists. They also pointed out how incomplete d'Indy's was, while conceding that theirs too amounted only to 'a selection, but such as to give a complete idea of the original work'. Yet 197 systems were cut – only six fewer than in d'Indy's version – and three-quarters of them are the same ones. Act V again disappears, as well as over half of Act I and even more of 'Possente spirto', which, like the little else that remains in Act III, becomes almost meaningless. As Cesari pointed out,[28] Orefice appeared to have made his selections for their dramatic importance – again like d'Indy – and according to subjective criteria of musical value. The result may not seriously misrepresent the dramatic action, but for the architecture of the work it is a catastrophe, which is compounded by the egregiously unstylish realisation of the continuo and the addition of modern dynamic and expression marks – Orpheus's 'Dove t'en vai' in Act IV, here marked 'agitato', looks superficially like a song by Brahms – and above all by wilful recomposition that makes flexible vocal lines square and rigid. The article by Cesari already referred to, a magisterial study of nearly fifty pages that ranges more widely than its title suggests, includes a sustained critique of Orefice's efforts[29] and chides him for ignoring the important work of German scholars such as Alfred Heuss and Theodor Kroyer, which would have helped him produce a more persuasive edition. We see here the typical conflict between two fundamentally opposed views of the editing and performance of early music that was to be much in evidence over the next sixty years, not least in connection with the operas of Monteverdi and Cavalli: on the one side, broadly speaking, the well-meaning composer or conductor innocent – or even disdainful – of the findings of scholarship and convinced that, by whatever methods, the music needed to be made more palatable in order to appeal to audiences unfamiliar with, and thus supposedly hostile to, the conventions governing it; on the other, the musicologist or scholarly conductor impatient of what he would consider presumptuous maltreatment and subscribing only to the tenets of historical authenticity. Although the latter view has now prevailed, it was by no means certain in 1910 that it would do so.

Despite Cesari's strictures, Orefice's edition was widely performed in the years before the Second World War. It was given at Buenos Aires in 1920 and in a stage performance at Cairo in 1928; it was probably the edition used in 1933 for the performance in the Sala Manto of the ducal palace at Mantua, when Amilcare Zanella again conducted the work; and it was certainly the edition used for the first Italian stage performance in modern times, at the Teatro Morlacchi, Perugia, on 19 September 1934. (This production used the scenery and costumes designed by Emanuele and Cito Filomarino for the 1928 Cairo performance, which had been produced by Vincenzo Sorelli and sung by Spartaco Marchi, Isora Rinolfi, Matelda Ceccherini and Sergio Cocciubei.[30] It was also used for the first (concert) performances in the United States, at New York in 1912 and Chicago in 1913. The first of these, a Sunday evening concert at the Metropolitan Opera House on 14 April, proved that even so radical a modernisation of the opera as Orefice's could not guarantee success, as the review in the *New York Times* (15 April 1912), published under the headline 'A Primitive Opera Heard', shows:

The audience last evening, who did not, presumably, come in a historical frame of mind, was considerably nonplused by the work, which of course is the most archaic music ever heard in the Metropolitan Opera House. A historical frame of mind, however, is not absolutely indispensable for obtaining enjoyment even from this music. Much of it is monotonous, and the obsolete forms of cadence sometimes become wearisome. But there are passages that give an impression of beauty and musical characterization to listeners of this day. Most of the instrumental preludes and interludes have melodious charm, simple though it be; and so have the choruses. The solos are largely kept in the form of a rich recitative or declamatory arioso. This verges on the modern conception of melody, occasionally, as in the first solo of Orpheus in the third act and in several passages of the fourth act

. . . The piece was sung in English with a very diverse measure of success in making the words understood. Mr. Weil's singing and diction as Orpheus left much to be desired: so did Mme. Duchene's in three characters. The chorus sang well and Mr. Pasternack conducted with zeal. The audience listened with amazement and with only the faintest attempts at applause.

The Chicago performance, reviewed sympathetically by Glenn Dillard Gunn (*Chicago Daily Tribune*, 6 January 1913), was given on 5 January 1913 at one of the Sunday afternoon Campanini Concerts, with soloists, chorus and orchestra of the Chicago Opera conducted by Cleofonte Campanini. Gunn's review, however, reveals how easy it was for a critic working without access to a reasonable edition of the opera to be deceived into praising an orchestration which was not Monteverdi's at all:

none has sounded a note of tragedy more searching, more profound than may be heard in the portentous utterance of the cellos, basses and muted horns that accompanies the contralto aria, 'O bitter lot and cruel' . . .

There is an almost audible sigh of relief in the review when the critic was able to report that

in the concert's second division Mr. Campanini scored a hit with a tarantella by Martucci which derived its most effective accent from the circumstances that he conducted it with his hands in his pockets.

Two versions of *Orfeo* emanating from Germany again treated the opera very freely. The first of them, prepared by the young music historian Hans Erdmann-Guckel, was given in a stage performance at the Stadttheater, Breslau [Wrocław], on the afternoon of Sunday 8 June 1913, after the end of the main opera season. Erdmann-Guckel himself directed the performance, which was sung in his German translation by soloists from the Breslau State Opera (among them the baritone Hecker as Orpheus and Fräulein Zuska as the Messenger) and an amateur chorus trained by Theodor Paul. The performance was produced by the pseudonymous Dr Otto Erhardt, *Dramaturg* of the Breslau Opera, who was praised by the critic Adolf Aber (*Berliner Tageblatt*, 9 June 1913) for his handling of the Underworld scenes and for overcoming the static nature of the beginning of the opera through the use of dance.

Erdmann-Guckel's performance was well received both by the critics and by the select audience that attended the production, an audience drawn mainly from university circles and including two of the doyens of German musicology, Hermann Kretzschmar and Max Friedländer from Berlin. Two critics – Adolf Aber and Ernst

Neufeld, the latter writing in *Signale für das musikalische Welt* (1913, pp. 1090–3) – hailed the production as the first stage performance of *Orfeo* in modern times, a reflection of the scant notice accorded the French productions at the Théâtre Réjane in 1911 and 1913. Like the French productions, Erdmann-Guckel's was a severely cut version of *Orfeo*. Act V had again disappeared, and only a little of Act I survived, merged with Act II, so that a three-act structure resulted.[31] The continuo group used by Erdmann-Guckel – piano, harmonium and guitar – was rather less faithful to Monteverdi's intentions than that employed by d'Indy.

Erdmann-Guckel's edition was not published, but to coincide with the production the libretto was published at Breslau with an introductory essay by the American musicologist Otto Kinkeldey, then lecturer in music history at Breslau, a member of the directorate of the Opera and (according to Paul Riesenfeld, writing in the *Allgemeine Musik-Zeitung* (1913), p. 998) the supervisor of the whole project.

In some respects the second of these German versions, prepared by Carl Orff (1895–1982), departs even further from Monteverdi's original than any considered so far. Outside his educational music, Orff composed almost entirely for the stage, preoccupied by a desire to fuse words, music and dance in a way that can already be experienced in his first original (and still best-known) stage work, *Carmina burana* (1937). In formulating his ideas he sought inspiration in two earlier traditions in particular, those of classical Greek tragedy and Italian Baroque stage music. The latter interest no doubt accounted for his attraction in his twenties to Monteverdi's works for the stage. He arranged the music of the three early ones, of 1607–8 – the lament from *Arianna* and the *Ballo delle ingrate* as well as *Orfeo* – in 1923–5. Given the dance element in the two larger works, this activity was presumably connected too with his educational work, for it was in 1924 that he helped found the Günther-schule in Munich for gymnastics, music and dance; his colleague in this enterprise, Dorothee Günther, prepared the German texts of the three Monteverdi works. It may well be significant that, with one minor exception (also using the music of an early composer), these are his only productions from before 1930 that he did not withdraw, for they can perhaps be seen as preparations for, or at least antecedents of, the long series of original stage works from his later career. He soon began work on *Il ritorno d'Ulisse* and *L'incoronazione di Poppea* too but abandoned it, possibly because their very different nature compared with the early works – for example, the long stretches of recitative and the virtual absence of dances – was less germane to his own aspirations as a composer for the stage and made them less susceptible to conversion into the kind of conception that he strove for. Yet he continued to be gripped by the other three works and produced revised versions of them in 1939–40. They were eventually published as a triptych in 1957 under the title *Lamenti* and given as such under Ferdinand Leitner at the 1958 Schwetzingen Festival.

The first version of *Orpheus* (as it was called) dates from 1923, and it was first performed at the National-Theater, Mannheim, on 25 March 1925. It was sung in Dorothee Günther's German adaptation, and, interestingly enough, Orff scored the music for as many of the original instruments as possible, an experiment that aroused a good deal of interest but that he largely abandoned later on. A second version dates from 1929 and the third, definitive version from 1939. This was first given under Karl Böhm at the Staatsoper, Dresden, on 4 October 1940 in a double bill with *Carmina burana*; the vocal score appeared in the same year. The scoring was for modern orchestra, though a somewhat idiosyncratic one, still including theorbos and using two basset-horns and a bass clarinet together to evoke the sound of the *organi di legno*, and without horns or any other clarinets. In the programme book for the 1940 production Orff explained that such an orchestra would give the style of the work an immediacy that a 'historical orchestra' could not, making it not a 'copy . . . of an opera of the early 17th century' but enhancing it as 'a masterpiece of a past age' speaking to us today 'in our language'.[32]

A modern orchestra is indeed more appropriate to Orff's approach to Monteverdi. It is surprising, however, to find so distinguished a musicologist as Curt Sachs defending Orff's methods at the time of the 1925 performances in the following terms:

To present Monteverdi's work in its original form to a modern audience in the theatre of to-day would be a greater injustice to the spirit of the work and of Monteverdi than a tactful revision with a due sense of artistic and historical responsibility.[33]

In any case 'tactful revision' is scarcely an adequate description of Orff's treatment of the work, even in the first version. In its 1939 form it is compressed into three acts, lasting altogether about an hour and performed without a break. As a prologue in place of La

Musica a narrator declaims the Old High German Orpheus story (*c.* 1000) by the monk Notker Labeo, after Boethius. Throughout, the work is extensively cut and reordered and generally more fully scored than the original. The result seems less an edition of Monteverdi than a work by Orff after Monteverdi. In the present context, then, there seems little point in cataloguing the changes.[34] A brief description of Orff's treatment of the Act II chorus, 'Ahi, caso acerbo', in the course of a much recast passage, will, however, give some idea of his conception: it is turned into an elemental, doomladen outburst, in the wrong metre, inflated by loud dynamics, liberally accented, and accompanied mainly by wind instruments (at one point the lower voices are reinforced by the quasi-organ sound mentioned above). To hear *Orpheus* is bound to be a totally different experience from attending a performance of what can conventionally be accepted as an edition, however unfaithful, of Monteverdi's original. There is perhaps a case for judging it by different criteria, as a deeply felt, not untypical product of the German theatre of the 1920s.

In Italy in the 1930s, performances of early Italian music were encouraged by the Fascist regime: the first modern Italian stage performance of *Orfeo* at Perugia on 19 September 1934 was only one such production subsidised by the state. Two new restructurings of the work, in their freedom and 'impurity' superficially analogous to Orff's, and no doubt encouraged by those responsible for the productions, can be seen as elaborate manifestations of self-conscious nationalism: a version by Giacomo Benvenuti (1885–1943) performed under Tullio Serafin at the Teatro Reale dell'Opera, Rome, on 27 December 1934, the libretto being adapted by Arturo Rossato;[35] and one by Ottorino Respighi (1879–1936) given under Gino Marinuzzi at the Teatro alla Scala, Milan, on 16 March 1935, with the libretto adapted by Claudio Guastalla, the librettist of all of Respighi's own later operas. The appearance of Respighi's version so soon after Benvenuti's led to one of those public feuds that infect Italian cultural life from time to time; it was fostered by those who saw the powerful Respighi as upstaging the more retiring and less known Benvenuti, protected though he was by no less a figure than Toscanini. Guastalla's journal gives an account of the conflict from the point of view of a not disinterested observer.[36] As far as Monteverdi is concerned, the trend of which the two versions of *Orfeo* form a part appears to have reached a climax in 1943 with the display of jingoistic nationalism informing the commemoration of the tercentenary of his death. Benvenuti initiated two national series of early music, *Istituzioni e monumenti dell'arte musicale italiana*, followed by *I classici musicali italiani*, in which he published a second, drastically purified edition of *Orfeo* in 1942.

Among the many altered features of Benvenuti's first, 1934 version – described as 'rhythmic transcription, realisation and instrumentation' – the most extraordinary is the way in which Monteverdi's score is filled out with other music, mainly by Monteverdi himself. In Act I scene 2 (Monteverdi's Act II), after Eurydice's death has been reported her body is borne away to the sounds of the Lament of the Nymph, *Amor*, from Monteverdi's eighth book of madrigals (1638), a late ground-bass piece whose style is decidedly at odds with that of the Monteverdi of 1607. Benvenuti's second act runs from the start of Monteverdi's third act as far as his fourth-act chorus 'Pietade, oggi', into which is inserted a fifteen-part canzona from Giovanni Gabrieli's *Sacrae symphoniae* (1597). Until it eventually picks up where his second act left off, Act III scene 1 in Benvenuti amounts to a masque-like, pastoral divertissement celebrating Orpheus's triumph and consisting entirely of imported music: the *moresca* from the end of the opera (it is heard there too), a reprise of the chorus 'Lasciate i monti' from (Benvenuti's) Act I scene 1, then a sequence of three pieces from later madrigal books by Monteverdi of varying degrees of stylistic incongruity – the duets *Bel pastor* (Book 9, 1651) and *Chioma* [*sic*] *d'oro* (Book 7, 1619), the latter with a particularly fussy accompaniment, and the five-part Petrarch setting *Zefiro torna e 'l bel tempo rimena* (Book 6, 1614), transposed up a fourth – the whole rounded off with reprises of pieces from earlier in the opera: Orpheus's song 'Ecco pur ch'a voi ritorno' from the beginning of Act I scene 2 and part of the chorus 'Ecco Orfeo' from the end of Act I scene 1, the latter interrupted by the Gabrieli canzona. The stage direction for the action accompanying *Zefiro torna* gives some idea of the approach: *Chiome d'oro* has just been sung and danced, whereupon 'shepherds, shepherdesses and nymphs regroup here and there under the trees around the little temple and in the middle of the meadow. They all raise up a flowering branch, which they wave and thus gently invoke the spring.' The whole conception must have seemed superficially plausible, but it is dramatically otiose and musically indefensible; and one cannot help suspecting that Monteverdi himself is being celebrated nationalistically as a glory of the Italian past. Numerous other 'impurities' in Benvenuti's score – transpositions, added accents and dynamics and further unidiomatic realisations – reinforce the impression of a lack of confidence in the Striggio–Monteverdi original.[37] But to some extent Benvenuti – now freed from the demands of an ostentatious theatrical production – made amends with his 1942 version, which is comparatively restrained and scholarly, and the published vocal score is accompanied by a serious sixteen-page essay by him about the opera and its background and his edition. The work is presented complete, and the keyboard part, though often unstylish, rarely becomes conspicuously bizarre; but here too there are superfluous accents and dynamics and added tempo directions, some of them of a romantic cast, which have no place in a would-be scholarly text.

Respighi's 'orchestral realisation' is no less impure than Benvenuti's first version but was perhaps less overtly nationalistic in conception: in an interview at the time he spoke fervently of his response to the beauty of Monteverdi's work and of his desire to recover 'an immortal masterpiece'; but he did add that he wished to present it in 'a free interpretation . . . above all in the spirit of our time'.[38] The excesses of his version, apparently matching the production to which the work was subjected in the theatre, can perhaps be seen as a late flowering of that fondness for the sensual, gaudy and decorative earlier expressed at its best through the 'hedonistic pictorialism'[39] of symphonic poems such as *Fountains of Rome* but less apparent in his best-known arrangements of early music such as *The Birds* and in those of his own works in which he adopted a deliberately archaising manner. In his cavalier treatment of *Orfeo*, the last three acts are telescoped into one, individual pieces are transposed, and *Chiome d'oro* appears again, this time in a version for chorus and orchestra tacked on to the end of Act I; voice parts are reallocated, small ensembles inflated into choruses, harmony distorted and the orchestra filled out and made to play not just too continuously but what too often amount to jarringly modern or sentimental conceptions. A prime example of the latter is the use of horns and harp with tremolando strings to play the sinfonia during which Charon falls asleep in Act III. The last statement of the ritornello in the prologue, moreover, is hummed, unaccompanied, by an off-stage chorus (prompted, perhaps, by the famous scene in Act II of Puccini's *Madama Butterfly*), whereupon Act I steals in as a romanticised aubade to the sound of a hushed orchestral prelude, newly composed, based on the duet (in this version, chorus) 'E dopo l'aspro gel' from near the end of the act whose figuration persists 'symphonically' against the opening recitative; there is more off-stage humming during most of 'Possente spirto' and elsewhere besides – surely one of the most incongruous of all the distortions of Monteverdi's music over the years. On the whole, Respighi's version strikes one as an opulent vulgarisation of Monteverdi's original that is perhaps as characteristic of a prominent strain in Italian theatre in the 1930s as Orff's version is of a dominant tendency in German theatre of the 1920s. Some critics of the time certainly saw how alien and 'impure' it was: 'The Monteverdi–Respighi *Orfeo*', said one, 'is a very beautiful thing, but Monteverdi's *Orfeo* is something else altogether.' It is more surprising to find the elderly Mascagni apparently speaking up for musicological rectitude and dismissing such reworkings as 'truly unseemly'.[40]

Of the five remaining composers who prepared versions of *Orfeo*, three did so for prominent public occasions. It is perhaps not surprising, therefore, that, in varying degrees, they too felt that the work had to be doctored in order to appeal to audiences presumably unfamiliar with early-seventeenth-century opera. The version by Vito Frazzi (1888–1975) was timed to coincide with the 1943 commemoration. It was revived at Florence and Vicenza in 1949, and again at the Florence Festival of 1957 in a performance which was described by Reginald Smith Brindle, writing in the *Musical Times* (1957, p. 448):

The performance of Monteverdi's *Orfeo* in Boboli Gardens has aroused storms of criticism. First, because it was never meant for open-air performance. Second, because Vito Frazzi's scoring for modern orchestra offended tradition, and lastly because of the 'modern' producing techniques which permitted the use of even loudspeakers and tape-recorders. These three acts of vandalism have been placed in increasing degrees of criminality. The first is pardonable, even justifiable. An open-air performance in this lovely setting has something to give, and *Orfeo* has been presented in a new, fascinating light. True, the opera has become almost a ballet, but this has been done with exquisite taste. The second is a thorny problem. Monteverdi's score lacks sufficient indications of instrumentation, but what there are indicates his love of a constant play of colour and the use of timbres not always in homophonic blocks, but in horizontal lines. Of the thirty-six instruments indicated, few remain in their original form, but all have fairly faithful modern equivalents. Vito Frazzi's scoring of anachronistic instruments – oboes, bassoons, clarinets, tubas, Hammond organs, grand pianos, etc. – is quite unjustifiable. But his score has an even worse aspect – the romantic figuration, which is disastrous.

As for the criminality of various modern 'techniques', I can only assume somebody has gone mad, running over the Boboli hillside, scattering wires, loudspeakers and tape-recorders in his wake. The effect was hideous.

Valentino Bucchi (1916–76), a pupil of Frazzi, published a guide to the opera when it was staged in Frazzi's version in the 1949 Maggio Musicale and himself prepared an edition of the work for a broadcast on Italian radio from Milan in 1967 (it was televised in January 1968 and was also issued on gramophone records). It is no doubt significant that, with the growth of scholarly interest in Monteverdi during the post-war years, reflected in the critical tone of Smith Brindle's review, there was a twenty-four-year gap – much the longest encountered in this narrative since d'Indy's edition – between the versions of Frazzi and Bucchi, and that both seem to have been stimulated primarily by anniversary celebrations. Bucchi's version was one of a number emanating from Italy and Britain during, or shortly before, the quatercentenary year. As a composer Bucchi showed a certain interest in early music: in 1952 he turned to medieval sources for two of his stage works, an opera and a vocal ballet. In three press articles prompted by the performances of his version of *Orfeo* he set out his view of the work and the nature of his version, which he called a 'rilettura' (literally, 'rereading').[41] He respected the melodic lines and the rhythms of the original and claimed to have provided a faithful continuo part. He did, however, tamper with the structure – a 'necessary liberty', which he did not attempt to justify; the Pluto–Proserpine scene, for one, disappeared yet again, just as at the hands of Eitner and d'Indy long ago. As for the instrumentation, Bucchi still echoed the choices posed by Frank Howes (see below, p. 100) and others years before. With far less justification at this late date, he firmly rejected the use of original instruments or copies – such an instrument is 'not a real living thing but a museum piece' – in favour of a largely modern orchestra yet one that he deployed in five groups in a manner that he saw as recalling Baroque practice: strings (two obbligato violins, eight violins, four cellos and four double basses); wind and brass (eighteen, including four horns); first harp and two guitars; second harp and harpsichord; organ and percussion. The impression one derives is of a score midway between a scholarly edition and a free transcription.

Bruno Maderna (1920–73), as composer, conductor and teacher, was a highly influential figure in progressive musical circles, not only in Italy but in northern Europe too, from the early 1950s onwards. He made a surprisingly large number of arrangements of early music, from Josquin Desprez to Vivaldi; his reinterpretation of *Orfeo*, commissioned for the Holland Festival of 1967 (the year in which he joined the staff of the Rotterdam Conservatory), is the biggest of them. Because it appeared at a time when the ethos of the scholar–performer was in the ascendant it seems all the more incongruous, as though an extinct exotic species were being disinterred. Procedures characteristic of the species reappear: there are wholesale transpositions; Orpheus is converted into a light baritone, and tenor shepherds become either basses or soprano nymphs; obbligato parts are added; vocal lines are rendered inflexible by the intrusive ministrations of orchestral textures redolent of nineteenth-century German opera – the orchestra is of full symphony size, including thirty-eight strings (with a pronounced bias towards the lower instruments). All these features combine, with a vengeance, to destroy Monteverdi's conception utterly.

Until 1984 it seemed likely that Maderna's would be the last example of the elaborate transformation of *Orfeo* into an alien guise such as we have seen produced by Respighi, among others. For the 1984 Florence Maggio Musicale, however, the Italian composer Luciano Berio (b. 1925), director of the festival, conceived a version of the opera in which Monteverdi's opera would be used as the basis of a 'happening', with a committee of five young Italian composers each 'realising' a section of the score. The resulting version was, according to Hugh Canning (*The Observer*, 8 July 1984), staged by Pier Luigi Pizzi as an open-air 'popular pageant' in the courtyard of the Pitti Palace. Canning continues:

Thus Orfeo himself, Britain's Peter Knapp, sang against the historically pure backing of a period ensemble, a rock group, the lugubrious chorale of a wind band, and the extra-terrestrial soundscape of an electronic tape . . . Pizzi's shock tactics proved no less riveting: as Act Four moved towards its climax – Orfeo's forbidden glance at his wife's shade – the huge studded front doors of the palace flew open and in roared three skull-faced motorbikers, Angels of Hell come to transport Euridice back to Hades . . . Had it 'happened' in a conventional theatre, it would probably have provoked a scandal . . . but Berio, who organised an unusual, stimulating and polemical festival, had already pre-empted such a reaction by inviting Roger Norrington and Kay Lawrence's Early Opera Project, with Belgian tenor Guy de Mey and a young British ensemble, to reconstruct what he called a 'historical' version of Monteverdi's opera in the Vasari-decorated Salone del Cinquecento.

The Norrington–Lawrence version of *Orfeo* is discussed in the next part of this survey.

Scholarly versions and 'authentic' performances

A more 'faithful' approach to the editing of the opera was initiated in the 1920s by two of the leading figures in the revival of interest in Monteverdi: one was a composer, Gian Francesco Malipiero (1882–1973), and one, J. A. Westrup (1904–75), a scholar. Many Italian composers from Malipiero's generation onwards – Casella, Dallapiccola and Petrassi, for example – felt stifled by the oppressive nineteenth-century Italian operatic tradition and turned to earlier Italian music, both vocal and (especially) instrumental, as a stimulus for their own music. Malipiero reacted likewise;[42] moreover, his involvement with such music seems to have been decisive in helping him recover from a personal crisis in his career as a composer. Though he consulted one of the manuscripts of *L'incoronazione di Poppea* as early as 1902, it was Orefice's version of *Orfeo* – both the obvious fascination of the music and the equally obvious inadequacy of its presentation – that fired his enthusiasm for Monteverdi and prompted him to send for a copy of the 1609 edition. This in turn impelled him to prepare the first complete edition of the works of Monteverdi – an undertaking that, as he said later, displayed not so much courage as, rather, ignorance of how many works there were.[43] He longed to see Monteverdi's operas regularly staged on a similar basis to Mozart's at Salzburg and Wagner's at Bayreuth, and he later revealed something of the spirit that moved him in his editorial work: 'why cannot we research into the art of our past with the sole aim of satisfying that legitimate curiosity that reflects a spiritual aspiration, without thereby becoming shackled by the fetters of musicology?'[44] In some of his essays he writes not simply as a composer but as a nationalistic one, to some extent reflecting the aspirations of the Italy of Mussolini (who became prime minister in 1922 and established a one-party dictatorship in 1926). Indeed the Monteverdi complete edition was 'protected' by the overtly nationalistic D'Annunzio, by now an erstwhile associate of Mussolini given to displays of patriotism and bravado – 'poet, hero and cad', in E. M. Forster's words – who yet played a major role in fostering both the new Italian music and the revival of interest in music of the Italian past.[45] But it is clear too how keenly Malipiero empathised with Monteverdi across the centuries, and he never allowed the trappings of ostentatious nationalism to invade his work.

Orfeo appeared in Malipiero's complete edition in 1930, in a literal transcription of the original. His editing, here and elsewhere in the edition, has not always been kindly received, and his work needs to be superseded now. Confining discussion to the *Orfeo* volume, it is true that there are omissions, misprints and misunderstandings (for example of the metre of the Act II chorus 'Ahi, caso acerbo'), that instrumental parts are inadequately assigned to specific instruments, that the continuo realisation is sketchy, indeed that none at all is provided in instrumental pieces and most choruses; nor is there a critical commentary. The work could not be performed simply by following what Malipiero offered, but at least he provided a reasonable basis for the editions of others; the publication in 1927 of a facsimile edition of the 1609 edition[46] also made it possible now to consult the original more conveniently.

Malipiero had worked on *Orfeo* some ten years before it came out in his complete edition: he published a vocal score in London in 1923 – 'naturally with a foreign publisher', to quote Guglielmo Barblan's wry comment on then-current attitudes of Italian publishers;[47] the preface is dated 1920. This score is less satisfactory than the 1930 one: for instance, halving of note values in many of the instrumental pieces gives a misleading impression, and when applied to 'Possente spirto' it produces a riot of extremely short note values; the values even of some of the more recitative-like passages are halved too. But at least the music is complete, and the keyboard accompaniment is clearly identifiable as editorial by being printed in smaller notes, a standard modern practice by no means universal then. It is naturally somewhat different from the realisation in the 1930 edition. It is, however, generally simple, though it is disfigured, as the later one of course is not, by cumbersome literal reductions of the choral parts. In 1928 Malipiero prepared a chamber orchestral score which was used when the opera was given at Leningrad in December of that year.

A Malipiero edition (presumably one of these earlier ones) was used for the first stage performance of *Orfeo* in the United States, at Smith College, Northampton, Mass., on 11 May 1929, when it was played in a double bill with Handel's cantata *Apollo e Dafne*. The performance was given by the Music Department of the college, which in previous years had also given Monteverdi's *Combattimento di Tancredi et Clorinda* and *L'incoronazione di Poppea*. The performance was directed by the German-born composer and conductor Werner Josten, then a professor at Smith College. Richard Aldrich's review (*New York Times*, 12 May 1929) tells us little about the performance itself, except that Acts I and V were omitted (just as in d'Indy's performance of 1904) and that the work was staged

in a setting typical of the Renaissance theatre, with an architectural effect intended to suggest the classical ideals of that period . . . The scenic effects and the lighting within the baroque framework of the Mantuan Hall were ingeniously and effectively contrived.

Like many of the critics of early-twentieth-century productions, Aldrich felt it necessary to don the scholar's hat and explain the early history of opera to his readers; he was, though, clearly puzzled by *Orfeo* itself and was reduced to plagiarising the comments on the music, quoted above (pp. 88–9), made by the reviewer of the 1912 New York performance.

Orfeo was first heard in Britain in a concert performance with piano in London on 8 March 1924; this took place at the Institut Français, which probably accounted for the choice of d'Indy's twenty-year-old version rather than the one by Malipiero published only a year earlier. It stimulated an interested response, including an article by Frank Howes,[48] who was about to embark upon his long career as a music critic – and arbiter of taste – on *The Times*. The following year the newly formed Oxford University Operatic Society (soon to be Opera Club), dissatisfied with Malipiero's 1923 edition, asked the undergraduate J. A. Westrup to prepare a new edition, which was performed on the stage at Oxford on 7–9 December 1925 – 'the origin . . . of his reputation as a musical scholar'.[49] Howes clearly understood that performances of *Orfeo* with piano would no longer do, and at a time when the use of authentic copies of all the instruments was still impracticable he set out, albeit too starkly, the choices facing those wishing to prepare the work for performance:[50]

We could either hand the whole score over to Sir Edward Elgar and get him to give us a modern version complete with tubas and triangles – this would be the course that Monteverde himself would have wished to see adopted – or, unable to divest ourselves entirely of our antiquarian scruples, we might prefer to keep as near the original as possible, and merely make a few substitutions for the impossibly obsolete instruments.

Now that the desirability of presenting a complete score was beginning to be accepted, the divergences of opinion among editors and conductors tended to centre instead on the realisation of the orchestral and continuo parts and went on doing so over the next forty years or so: they perpetuate, on more restricted ground, the differences of opinion between composer and scholar highlighted above (see pp. 87–8) by Cesari's reaction to Orefice's edition of *Orfeo*. As Howes's words show, the issue could only too easily become clouded with tendentious remarks about 'antiquarian scruples' and gratuitous assumptions about Monteverdi's wishes.

In an authoritative article the following year in the same columns as Howes,[51] Westrup judiciously reviewed, and dismissed, previous editions of *Orfeo*, including Malipiero's 1923 one, and justified the adoption, in his edition, of the second of Howes's alternatives quoted above. He used oboes and clarinets in unison instead of cornetts and made other reasonable adjustments and compromises, of which the least satisfactory must have been the allocation of the keyboard continuo to piano and harmonium and the decision to sing 'Possente spirto' in the plain rather than the elaborated version. The work was given complete (except for part of the Act V lament), in English,[52] and the continuo part was realised discreetly, by William Harris. It is not too much to say that this edition by a twenty-one-year-old Oxford undergraduate, complemented by the most balanced article on Monteverdi that had yet appeared in English, was the biggest single advance – and may even be said to have remained so – in the rediscovery of the real *Orfeo* and of understanding of Monteverdi as a musical dramatist. It is a great pity that, except for a single aria,[53] the edition remained unpublished, for it was consequently less influential than it deserved to be: the subsequent elaborate versions of *Orfeo* discussed above show to what extent Westrup's view of Monteverdi needed to be disseminated.

The Oxford performances, with Sumner Austin in the title role, and the parts of Music and the Messenger played by Denne Parker, were directed by a professional producer, W. Nugent Monck. They were played against the simplest of settings (see Fig. 5), though with a carefully considered colour scheme for the costumes, in which 'dark blue and pale green [made] a setting of low tones for the sad emotions, while the white of Orpheus's robe and the colours of the chorus [expressed] the happier moments in the story' (*The Times*, 8 December 1925).

Westrup's decision to play the opera virtually complete and in a manner as near as possible to the original was certainly vindicated by the critical reaction. Frank Howes, writing in the *Musical Times* (1926, p. 61), was forced to admit that 'Mr. Westrup's orchestration ... worked out well; it was both economical and dramatically effec-

Fig. 5. A scene from the Oxford University Opera Club production, 1925 (*The Times*, 8 December 1925)

tive'; and, together with other critics, he was convinced that the opera really could work in performance. Ernest Newman (*The Sunday Times*, 13 December 1925) commented:

And what of the work itself? We have all read it for ourselves, but how does it bear the ordeal of stage presentation after three hundred and eighteen years, before an audience that has a totally different conception of opera? For my own part I found it astonishingly alive. It goes off in interest towards the end, but that is the fault of the librettist and of the period; the necessity for a happy ending to a tragic mythological story crippled both the operatic poet and the operatic composer for a good century and a half after Monteverdi's time . . . I doubt whether finer recitative than Monteverdi's at its best can be found again in opera until we come to Wagner.

H. C. Colles, chief music critic of *The Times*, took a different view of the quality of the libretto, at least with respect to the messenger scene of Act II:

Mr. Westrup, in a note printed with the English version, speaks of the libretto of the *Orfeo*, probably [*sic*] by Alessandro Striggio, as possessing no outstanding merit. No doubt he is right from the literary point of view, but from the stage point of view it is masterly. Orpheus's questions and interjections, which just delay the delivery of the message long enough to make the full effect of its import felt, show the writer's experience not only of the stage itself but of musical necessities.

(*The Times*, 12 December 1925)

He concluded:

There was no conscious archaism. Monteverde was heard as on equal terms with the great musical dramatists from Purcell to Wagner and was proved to be of their company.

Westrup's edition was revived at the Royal College of Music in London in 1926, at Liverpool in 1927, and, from 30 December 1929, in three stage performances at the Scala Theatre, Charlotte Street, London, during the first week of the London Opera Festival. This ambitious project, directed by Robert Stuart, the translator of Westrup's edition, spanned three weeks, and also included performances of Purcell's *Dido and Aeneas*, Handel's *Giulio Cesare*, Mozart's *La finta giardiniera*, and Weber's *Der Freischütz* conducted by Sir Thomas Beecham. Monteverdi's *Orfeo*, with a professional cast headed by Dennis Noble as Orpheus, opened the festival. The performance was conducted by Westrup and produced by Robert Stuart, with Boris Ord as continuo-player (a harpsichord had been found for this revival). The production retained the simplicity of setting devised for Oxford:

. . . mere dark draperies, a flight of shallow steps on either hand, and a neutral background, brightly lit, before which moved the Grecian flowing-clad figures. Everything depended on the judicious employment of multi-coloured lighting: and its employment certainly was judicious.

(*The Sunday Times*, 5 January 1930)

The first night of the production, representing the first complete performance of *Orfeo* in the present century, was attended by the Italian ambassador and the critics and, apparently, by very few others. An unsigned article in *The Times* for 4 January 1930, ostensibly covering the conference of the Incorporated Society of Musicians at Chester, contained undisguised criticism of a musical Establishment which could bemoan the musician's lot but fail to support such an enterprising venture:

[The] New Scala productions are the application of the results of amateur productions in the universities to a company of professional singers and players in London. For them, if for no one else, the occasion is properly a festival; it celebrates the consolidation of a piece of careful research and artistic reconstruction on which they deserve the warmest congratulation. Alas, that the congratulations of the first nights should have been offered only by a few personal friends, a few of the more enterprising members of the Imperial League of Opera, including its founder [Beecham], and a few professional critics who tried to look as though they had paid for their seats and who actually in some cases did pay for their programmes!

Apart from these one looked in vain through the scattered audience for the faces of well-known musicians, the people who, for example, one counts on seeing at concerts of the Royal Philharmonic Society and on not seeing on Puccini nights at Covent Garden. That is the type of musician to whom the first complete performance of Monteverde's *Orfeo* after 300 years might be expected to appeal. A few of the more eminent of them were necessarily withdrawn to Chester for the I.S.M. conference, and it may have been as unfortunate that the opening of the Festival clashed with the conference as that it clashed with Christmas. Perhaps next week the New Scala Theatre will be crowded with musicians who conduct or otherwise take part in an annual performance of *Messiah* and who will be treading on each other's heels with eagerness to discover what an opera by Handel, *Julius Caesar*, a work in its day as famous as the greatest of his oratorios, is really like when it is put on the stage.

In the event, the festival, though an artistic success, was a financial disaster. It was thirty-five years before another professional pro-duction of *Orfeo* was mounted in Britain.

A decade after the first performance of Westrup's edition another was prepared, likewise early in his career and never published, by another prominent Monteverdi scholar, Hans F. Redlich (1903–68). It was given in concert form at Zurich on 10 February 1936. An article Redlich published at the time[54] gives some idea of its nature and indicates his thoughtful approach to his task. He scored the work mainly for modern instruments, though he included bass viols in his string section; he replaced the two cornetts by four oboes.

The next edition to be considered here was by the one composer whose work remains to be discussed. Of all the composers who have worked on *Orfeo*, Paul Hindemith (1895–1963) was, I think, the only one who really believed in the power of the work to communicate in a performance approximating as closely as possible to those of Monteverdi's day. Yet it is important to note the circumstances in which his version originated, in 1943 (possibly prompted by the tercentenary of Monteverdi's death). He was living in an academic environment, at Yale University, and he may have conceived it for performance by the school of music there, not for a typical opera or festival audience, though – contrary to what has been stated in print – no performance in fact took place. But it is no coincidence that this was the most faithful performing edition since Westrup's, the last one prepared within a university. Hindemith had made many editions of Baroque music in Germany from the 1920s and often played it on the viola d'amore, and his interest in early music was now intensified by his new surroundings. He directed many performances of early music at Yale which were to some extent intended to illustrate his lectures on the history of music, a situation similar to d'Indy's at the Schola Cantorum forty years earlier. As far as possible, he scored for authentic instruments in *Orfeo*, an approach consistent with his long-standing enthusiasm for the viola d'amore. Its academic origins notwithstanding, the edition appeared successfully on the public stage at the 1954 Vienna Festival, conducted by Hindemith and with Gino Sinimberghi in the title role. The instruments used for the performance were, in the main, borrowed from museums and private collections, though the recorders were modern copies by Dolmetsch. A further attempt at period reconstruction was made in the choice of sets (see Fig. 6), which were modelled by Leopold Lindtberg on designs used for Cesti's grandiose court opera *Il pomo d'oro* at Vienna in 1668. Hindemith's performance was very well received. One reviewer called it 'a masterpiece of scholarship and integrity', and Nikolaus Harnoncourt has spoken of the tremendous impact it had on him ('the effect of a lightning flash'). A vocal score was issued privately in 1953.[55]

By the 1950s there was a developing tendency for scholar–

Fig. 6. Stage set for the Vienna Festival production, 1954

performers to prepare versions of *Orfeo* for purely local performance, perhaps basing their work on an existing plain edition such as
Malipiero's of 1930 and with no thought of publication: examples
are Thurston Dart's edition, given in the gardens of Girton College,
Cambridge, on 8 June 1950, and Alceo Toni's edition, using only
strings and organ for accompaniment, which was given by the
Piccola Scala Company, Milan, on 1 April 1957 (see Fig. 7); and of
course available performing editions were still being used for other
performances. One important new published edition did, however,
appear, from the Swiss cellist and bass-viol-player August
Wenzinger (b. 1905). It was first given at the Sommerliche Musik-
tage, Hitzacker, Lower Saxony, in 1955, when a score was published; a performance was soon issued on gramophone records (see
Discography, 1955), through which the edition, and indeed the
work itself, became widely known and admired. The issue of
Wenzinger's score and recording marked a crucial stage in the post-
war rediscovery of *Orfeo*, for potential audiences as well as a new
generation of performers and critics now had available not only two
reasonable editions of the opera (Malipiero's and Wenzinger's) but
also an easily accessible performance using the original instrumentation. Moreover, the decade immediately following the end of the
war had also seen the publication of several studies of Monteverdi
– by Domenico De' Paoli, Hans Redlich and Leo Schrade[56] – and
books on opera – by Anna Amalie Abert, Donald Jay Grout and
Joseph Kerman[57] – which accepted *Orfeo* as a viable work of music
theatre. The foundations were laid, then, for a rediscovery of the
opera that was more firmly and broadly based than hitherto.

Wenzinger's edition remained in use until the early 1970s, with
performances at Hanover (1966), Munich (1968) and Lyons (1973).
In 1960 it formed the basis of a performance by the New York City
Opera which marked the American operatic début of the French
baritone Gérard Souzay, who took the title role. (Souzay, incidentally, studied with Claire Croiza, who had played the Messenger in
the French stage performances of 1911 and 1913.) Since the original
instrumentation was used (with the exception of modern strings), it
is surprising to find that the performance was directed by Leopold
Stokowski, whose lush arrangements represent his more usual
attitude towards early music.

The performance was treated to a long, enthusiastic and perceptive preview by Harold C. Schonberg, writing in the *New York
Times* (25 September 1960), who pointed out, among other things,

Fig. 7. A scene from Act I of the version edited by Alceo Toni for the Piccola Scala, Milan, 1957

the importance of the introduction of the LP record in 1948 to the post-war revival of interest in Renaissance and Baroque music. Schonberg's enthusiasm, however, was dealt a severe blow at the performance on 29 September, at which *Orfeo* was used as a companion piece to Dallapiccola's *Il prigioniero*:

It is customary for a conductor to take certain cuts in most operas. But what Leopold Stokowski gave us last night represented in effect a digest version: the heart of 'Orfeo', so to speak. At a rough guess, a third of the score was omitted. The choruses especially were cut, and so were the orchestral ritornellos. Even the biggest aria in the opera, 'Possente spirto', had a good-sized slash in the middle. Thus it can scarcely be said that last night we saw 'Orfeo' plain. In its original form 'Orfeo' is in five acts [Stokowski gave it as a single, continuous action] and runs almost two hours. It need not share the program with another work; it is long enough and important enough, not to mention beautiful enough, to have been the entire evening's opera.

And the cause for regret is compounded by the fact that the settings and general presentation were quite lovely. It was a highly stylized performance in good taste.

Winthrop Sargeant, writing in the *New Yorker* (8 October 1960), gives details of the production:

The production was nothing short of enchanting. Christopher West, who staged it, and Donald Oenslager, who designed the scenery and costumes, chose to present the old work not in an antique Greek setting but in the style of Monteverdi's own day, making use of all the lavish accoutrements that one associates with the seventeenth-century masque. Orpheus was splendidly dressed as a late-Renaissance pseudo-Roman warrior, complete with plumed helmet; Charon, riding in his Stygian boat, looked something like one of those American Indians in seventeenth-century prints; the gates of Hades were depicted as the open maw of a gigantic animal; in the last act, Apollo descended from Heaven in a cloud-borne chariot; and there were no end of other scenic wonders (including appropriate ballet sequences, choreographed by Robert Joffrey) that both charmed the eye and startled the mind of anyone aware of the City Opera's limited budget.

Of the editions of the mid-1960s yet to be mentioned, four – by Cesare Brero, Raymond Leppard, Herbert Handt and Harold Badger – have, like Bucchi's, remained unpublished and thus comparatively little known; a fifth edition, prepared by Edward H. Tarr (b. 1936) for a recording of the opera issued in 1967 (see Discography), was published, and was also used for a performance at Antwerp in 1977. The edition prepared by Raymond Leppard (b. 1927) for Sadler's Wells (later the English National) Opera in 1965 was less free and empirical than his controversial interpretations of *Poppea* and of operas by Cavalli. It was scored, as far as possible, for original instruments (though clarinets were substituted for cornetts) and given in a production by Frank Hauser, with rich scene and costume designs by Yolanda Sonnabend. John Wakefield in the title role, Patricia Kern as the Messenger, Stafford Dean as Pluto and Noel Mangin as Charon were singled out for praise by the critics, but the critic of *The Times* opined that 'the rest of the cast, and the chorus, should be sent home to learn that hit-or-miss intonation and wobbly vibrato may pass in *Cavalleria* but in Monteverdi simply sound incompetent' (*The Times*, 6 October 1965). The most controversial aspect of the performance at the time seems to have been that it was sung in Italian.

The remaining edition from this period, that of Denis Stevens (b. 1922), published in 1967, has been perhaps the most widely studied, though not the most widely performed, of all editions of *Orfeo*. It quickly joined Wenzinger's as one of the two most influential editions in fostering the necessity and desire for scholarly presentations of the work. (Stevens also introduced the publication, in 1972, of a facsimile of the 1615 edition.)

Stevens's edition was given, under Gianfranco Rivoli (who also conducted Brero's edition at Aix-en-Provence in 1964), at the Sao Carlo Opera House, Lisbon, on 18 May 1967 and subsequently revived in the same year at Madrid and on 1 February 1979 at the Juilliard American Opera Center in a performance under Peter Herman Adler. The Sao Carlo performance featured a by no means whole-hearted re-creation of the original instrumentation but did attempt 'gestures and groupings preserved in illustrations from the period', and 'ornate costumes and head-dresses were matched by *trompe l'oeil* scenery of distant prospects between palace pillars' (*The Times*, 25 May 1967). The revival at the Juilliard, 'New York's first full staging of "Orfeo"', as Andrew Porter pointed out in a thoughtful and wide-ranging review (*The New Yorker*, 19 February 1979), played to packed houses but was not a critical success. Porter's comments reveal his understanding that productions of early-seventeenth-century opera should exploit an intimate relationship between the singer–actors and their accompanists, without the overt intervention of a conductor:

The edition used was that of Denis Stevens, which is a scholarly and practical score devised to make 'Orfeo' accessible to companies or music schools that lag behind the times in not being able to muster a full complement of original instruments . . . Be that as it may, Stevens is not to be held responsible for what happened at the Juilliard, where the recitatives and ariosi were actually *conducted*. (It would make as little sense to have a conductor onstage at a lieder recital, indicating tempo and accents to the singer and accompanist.)

By the late 1960s *Orfeo* could assuredly be said to have been 'rediscovered' by a wide public and in reasonably faithful editions, and the decade was crowned by the issue, in 1969, of the fine recording of the opera by Nikolaus Harnoncourt (b. 1929). It was to be another six years, however, before Harnoncourt's version reached the stage. When it did, at the Zurich Opera on 20 December 1975 (see Fig. 8), it was given as the first of a trilogy of the three surviving Monteverdi operas and in a production which was subsequently filmed for television (Unitel Films, Munich), taken in 1978 and 1979 to Germany, Austria, Britain and Italy (where it was given at La Scala, Milan), and issued on record (see Discography, 1981). In these performances the title role was taken by the baritone Philippe Huttenlocher. Harnoncourt directed a further performance with the Netherlands Opera in 1976 with the tenor Nigel Rogers in the title role.

Fig. 8. Philippe Huttenlocher as Orpheus, seen against the setting for Acts I and II of the Zurich Opera production, 1975

Criticism of the Zurich Opera *Orfeo* focused on two aspects of the performance: the style of singing cultivated – 'emasculated chant', as Peter Heyworth put it (*The Observer*, 3 September 1978) – and the work of the producer, Jean-Pierre Ponnelle. The excellence of the instrumentalists, performing on authentic instruments, was generally acclaimed, and the rhythmic freedom and apparent spontaneity of Harnoncourt's musical direction ('more dramatic than on his recordings') was noted by more than one critic. Ponnelle was responsible for both the set design and the production of the opera, which was given as a 'play within a play' and in an authentic continuous performance. The single set represented a courtyard in the ducal palace at Mantua:

> The chorus represented the members of the court, who formed the stage audience. The orchestra was also part of the scene; the players were in costume, and performed on a platform raised above the pit. A circular surround behind the three main entrances acted as a movable horizon, and defined the different settings of the opera: the fields of Thrace, the Underworld and, in the last scene, the realm of Apollo.
>
> (Heinz Kern, in *Opera*, p. 566)

The production began with the entrance of the Duke of Mantua, who then took the role of Apollo, and the Duchess, who doubled as Music and Hope; they welcomed Pluto and Proserpine on to the stage as visiting nobility. One effect of this device was to reinforce one of the possible interpretations of *Orfeo*: that the Gonzagas were intended to see in its heroic characters a reflection of themselves. In this interpretation, Orpheus represents Francesco Gonzaga, the young, impetuous son who is rescued from his despair by Apollo (his father, Vincenzo Gonzaga). The main drawback of Ponnelle's conception seems to have been that the 'Mantuan' framework distanced the real audience from the full emotional force of the drama. Further criticism was levelled at the acrobatic antics of the courtiers/ chorus during the first act and the early part of the second, Ponnelle's solution to the 'problem' of enlivening the apparently static nature of this section of the drama; for, though this production adopted the principle of continuous performance, there was no exit to the temple in Act I: during the final chorus of the act Orpheus and Eurydice remained on stage, gazing into each other's eyes. Act III, on the other hand, was accomplished more successfully, with Charon a monstrous figure who dominated the scene and gave easy passage to a number of 'the faceless dead' while barring Orpheus's path.

Ponnelle's production, though controversial, presented a solution to the problem of creating an intimacy of scale appropriate to *Orfeo* when working in a large theatre. A quite different solution to the same problem was offered in the production first given by the English National Opera in 1981 and revived in 1983. Here the musical aspects of the performance, given in a fine edition by John Eliot Gardiner (b. 1943), were universally acclaimed, as was the singing of the tenor Anthony Rolfe Johnson, the 1981 Orpheus. As well as re-creating Monteverdi's original orchestra (with the exception of modern strings), Gardiner adopted the approach of making *Orfeo* a small 'company' opera as it had been in 1607: that is, the work was performed by a small ensemble of soloists with as few extraneous chorus members as possible. The producer, David Freeman (who in Chapter 9 below writes about his approach to the opera), then welded the ensemble into a responsive company of actors through the use of preparatory theatrical exercises and games. The production was played, as though in a timeless peasant community, against a simple backdrop of hanging draperies (see Fig. 9). The performance was not continuous, but the taking of intervals between Acts II and III and between Acts IV and V seemed a reasonable compromise. The combination of Gardiner's edition, the excellence and involvement of the singers and Freeman's committed production resulted in a compelling piece of music theatre which provoked extremes of praise and anger from the critics. Their comments ranged from Max Loppert's 'an evening of mind-boggling fatuity' (*Financial Times*, 22 August 1981) to Peter Heyworth's 'a blend of dramatic intelligence, musical understanding and a phenomenal grasp of stage detail' (*The Observer*, 23 August 1981). At both ends of the critical spectrum, however, the reaction was very different from the *succès d'estime* so often accorded to *Orfeo* earlier in the century.

Two British productions which preceded the English National Opera's *Orfeo* were less controversial, though no less powerful. The first was performed at Oxford on 18 February 1975 to celebrate the fiftieth anniversary of the founding of the University Opera Club and its important inaugural performance of *Orfeo*. The editor and the translator of the 1925 edition, Sir Jack Westrup and Robert L. Stuart, were present in the audience when the opera was given in a new edition by Jane Glover (b. 1949) and in a new English translation by Anne Ridler, which has subsequently been used by both Kent Opera (1976) and the English National Opera (1981). This was

Fig. 9. Anthony Rolfe Johnson as Orpheus and Patricia O'Neill as Eurydice, in Act I of the English National Opera production, 1981

the first British production to attempt a fully authentic reconstruction of Monteverdi's orchestra and continuo groupings (Jane Glover writes in Chapter 8 about the problems involved in doing this). The results prompted Stanley Sadie to remark 'There have been good editions before but none I have heard makes such good musical and dramatic sense' (*The Times*, 20 February 1975), and he particularly admired in the performance a 'readiness to let the music move really quickly'. The title role was sung by a baritone, Ian Caddy. The costumes for the production, whether by accident or not, employed the same emblematic use of colour that had characterised Westrup's 1925 performance – green for the shepherds, buff for Orpheus, red for Pluto, gold for Apollo. Unlike the other British productions discussed here, which employed a pedestrian Apollo, the Oxford performance included his descent in a machine.

In the year following the Oxford performance, the small, flexible professional company Kent Opera staged performances in an edition by Roger Norrington (b. 1934). This, too, employed authentic instrumentation (only twenty instrumentalists), and it prefigured the English National Opera production by presenting the work as an 'ensemble' opera for fifteen singers in an imaginative, stylised production designed for small theatres by Jonathan Miller. As at Oxford, the role of Orpheus was sung by a baritone, Peter Knapp. The sets for the production, based on paintings by Daniel Lang after Poussin (see Fig. 10), were mounted on panels which could be revolved to effect rapid changes of scene, a technique similar to the device of *periaktoi* used in the Renaissance theatre.[58] After its initial performances at the Theatre Royal, Bath, the Kent Opera production was taken on tour before being given at the Collegiate Theatre, London, on 21 March 1977 and at the Everyman Theatre, Cheltenham, on 14 July 1978; it was also filmed for television. Following the London performance, Winton Dean wrote in the *Musical Times* (1977, p. 496): 'This production, with the same company's *Poppea*, should be a model for any future approach to Italian opera of the 17th century.'

Though the Kent Opera production has not itself been revived, Roger Norrington subsequently prepared another edition which was first given in the Salone del Cinquecento of the Palazzo Vecchio, Florence, on 19 June 1984 as part of the Maggio Musicale (see Fig. 11) and revived at the Teatro Olimpico, Rome, on 4 October 1984. This production, in which Norrington collaborated with the dance and movement specialist Kay Lawrence, was in

Fig. 10. Peter Knapp as Orpheus, seen against the setting for Acts I and II of the Kent Opera production, 1976

Fig. 11. Guy de Mey as Orpheus and Emma Kirkby as Eurydice, in Act IV of the Early Opera Project production in Florence, 1984

many respects the most refined and thorough re-creation yet attempted of the opera's original performance manner: a small, versatile group of instrumentalists placed on either side of the stage, with no conductor; a small company of singers led by a tenor Orpheus (Guy de Mey) and in late-Renaissance costumes; a seventeenth-century style of acting and of stage lighting (though candles were ruled out by fire regulations); a continuous perform- ance (though Eurydice made her exit at the end of Act I rather than in mid-act). According to Nicholas Kenyon, writing in *The Times* (28 June 1984):

The overall impression is of a successful – indeed an historic – attempt to bring the drama of Monteverdi's time alive for us, which strikes home to a remarkable extent. If it is not seen in Britain we will put ourselves lament- ably behind the times in one of the most interesting musical and dramatic developments of our age.

All of these recent versions of *Orfeo*, then, have aimed at authen- ticity in varying degrees, and disputes about the editing of the music tend now to be concerned with specific matters. The type of con- troversy about basic approaches to editing prompted for so long by the treatment of *Orfeo* now focuses, as far as Monteverdi's operas are concerned, on his late, Venetian works and also on those of his successor, Cavalli, where the quantity of recitative and the exiguous original instrumental forces have continued to tempt adapters and arrangers, as they did earlier in this century, to excesses that have offended scholarly editors and critics scarcely less than the freest of those discussed in the previous section of this chapter. Of *Orfeo*, however, it can be asserted with some confidence that audiences who have experienced the compelling power of Monteverdi's con- ception through recent 'authentic' editions will never again tolerate its impairment by gratuitous cuts and recomposition and inapposite rescoring.[59] Yet it could be argued that – as with arrangements of other early masterpieces – even the most extreme of the free adap- tations may have been instrumental in winning acceptance for what Monteverdi wrote and for more faithful representations of it. And, notwithstanding the present single-minded concern for authentic- ity, the time may well be approaching when, together with such things as the orchestral transcriptions of Bach by Respighi, Stokowski and Henry Wood, the adaptations of *Orfeo* are revived as documents of the art of arrangement and of the history of musical taste in the twentieth century.

6 A review of Vincent d'Indy's performance (Paris, 1904)

ROMAIN ROLLAND
Translated by Wendy Perkins

The outstanding musical event of this month (I do not mean the one that has most struck the public, but if we were to concern ourselves with the opinion of the public! . . .), the most significant event has been the performance of Monteverdi's *Orfeo* at the *Schola*. For all the musicians who heard it this performance was a revelation. In *Orfeo* we have not merely an historical curiosity, but a masterpiece that is virtually the only example of a vanished art. Vanished? Who knows? For, strange to say, this art seems on the point of being reborn in our midst, and this *favola in musica* from the beginning of the seventeenth century may offer precious ideas, even models, for those among our young composers who are, at this moment, trying to create a more supple, more realistic style of lyrical declamation, and one that is free from Germanic influences.

Perhaps I might recall the historical circumstances in which *Orfeo* came into being.

Some ten years had passed since opera was created at Florence. I choose the term 'opera' and not 'musical theatre' for, as I have shown in a recent article,[1] theatrical representations which were sung throughout had been given in Florence since the fifteenth century; and it was only at the beginning of the sixteenth century that it was decided to remove song from such performances, a decision which at the time seemed a novel departure. It is a peculiar irony (such ironies are frequent in history) that dramatic innovation consisted at the beginning of the sixteenth century in removing music from drama, and at the end of the same century in putting music back into drama. Such is the perpetual see-saw of artistic progress.

In the operas created between 1590 and 1600, therefore, it was not a question of inventing the form of dramatic song, but rather of finding a way of *speaking in music* ('quasi in armonia favellare', as Caccini puts it); and it is this that is generally forgotten, for, as we

119

shall see, opera took a quite different route almost immediately after Monteverdi's *Orfeo*.

A simple list of the founders of opera is revealing. In it we find society figures, dilettantes or scholars: Count Bardi, Jacopo Corsi, Vincenzo Galilei (the great Galileo's father); here, too, we find the director of spectacles and festivals in Florence, Emilio de' Cavalieri; a poet, Rinuccini; a poetess, Laura Guidiccioni; two singers, Peri and Caccini. No group is missing from the list . . . except musicians; and by that I mean genuine composers. And this already tells us much about the reform which the founders of opera wished to achieve. It was, in effect, a dramatic and not a musical reform. It must be seen as the final stage of the natural evolution of Italian theatre and the logical transformation of Tasso's pastoral comedy. Tasso himself, very much a musician, greatly preoccupied with musical questions, contributed not a little to this transformation. The reformers were seeking not to enrich music and to open up for it a new field – namely drama – but to enrich poetry and to increase its expressive resources a hundredfold by adding music to it; and that is something quite different. They wished to create a kind of tragedy recited in music. The reformers did not hesitate to proscribe without compunction all the learned polyphony of their time, together with orchestration, which, though youthful and as yet unsure of itself, was already so brilliant and so evocative. These they condemned as hindering full understanding of the declamation, for they intended to keep only the line of the song, which was, in a sense, speech clothed in music, with a rudimentary accompaniment.

Truth to tell, there was never, I think, more than one single example of this new art, this declaimed music or musical declamation: Peri's *Euridice*. For even in the music of Peri's rival, Caccini, the singer's virtuosity leads to pure vocalisation and an artificial style of song, neither of which accords with the rigorous logic of the system. Peri, endowed with great intelligence and, if I may say so, with a certain paucity of musical ideas (in other words with much the same qualities and deficiencies as those of Gluck), was just the composer to accomplish perfectly the reform envisaged in Florence, and he is almost the only composer who can give us a finished model of the melo-dramatic ideal of this school. He himself says that he had sought 'a form of song which, nobler than ordinary speech, and less regular in pattern than sung melody, was halfway between the two' ('un'armonia, che avanzanda quella del parlare ordinario, scendesse tanto dalla melodia del cantare, che pigliasse forma di cosa mezzana'). He made a close study of those inflections which, in ordinary conversation amid the scarcely detectable variations and nuances of the spoken word, might serve as a basis for the new language of recitative. At the same time he studied the intonations used in joy, in grief, and for the expression of the passions. This was a daunting task of notation and transposition from the spoken to the musical language. The first occasion on which Peri ventured before the public with a piece written entirely in this style (with his *Dafne* of 1597 [1598], performed in the presence of the Grand Duke and his court) produced an emotional response impossible to describe. The audience that had come to hear it with a great deal of apprehension was moved to tears, and everyone felt that it was the beginning of a new art-form. *Euridice*, in 1600, finally established this art-form and spread its renown throughout the world. But its beautiful musical declamation had no definable existence outside dramatic representation. Its interest lay essentially in the precise, lively accuracy of its accentuation and even, perhaps, in the diction and performance of the actor, who, as it happens, was the composer himself. For it was Peri who played the role of Orpheus in his *Euridice*; and this great singer, 'whose beautiful voice', so it was said, 'modulated with inexpressible sweetness, especially in haunting melancholy songs', was in fact the very soul of his work. Seven years after the first performance of *Euridice*, Marco da Gagliano was already observing 'that one could not fully understand the grace, force and nature of Peri's airs if one had not heard him sing them himself; for with his artistry in song and his dramatic rendition he was able at will to move his audience to tears or laughter'. This was, therefore, an art-form which, in spite of its perfection, was doomed to disappear because it was not sufficiently independent of particular conditions and particular actors, because it was simply not sufficiently musical; and even in its hour of glory it seems not to have succeeded in reaching beyond a very refined circle, the most aristocratic élite of Florence no doubt, but a mere handful of people nonetheless.

Here it was that the genius of Claudio Monteverdi of Cremona intervened. He was forty years old when he wrote *Orfeo* in 1607, and it was his first dramatic work. Until then he had scarcely composed anything but madrigals for several voices; and afterwards he continued to write madrigals, exploiting both the old polyphonic music and the new Florentine music, even taking up again certain of his most celebrated pieces, such as the *lamento* from *Arianna*, to arrange them for five voices. In this way he showed that he was, above all, a musician, and that he did not intend to destroy the old art for the sake of the new, but to have them live side by side in perfect sympathy and to effect a union between them. Moreover, by birth and temperament he was an Italian of the North, a colourist in the Venetian manner, a master of the orchestra; and he was not a man to be content with the pure and noble line of Florentine recitative. For him this had to be brought to life with the changing play of light and shade, of reflections, of varying nuances, of modulations, of varying timbres. Nevertheless, at the time of *Orfeo* he, like all his contemporaries, was fascinated by the attempts being made in Florence to 'speak in music'; but he brought to his researches a soul of quite exceptional vitality and musical resources of immense richness. It is this free spirit, so full of passion and music, disciplining itself to the exact observation of nature and to the faithful notation of musical speech, which gives *Orfeo* its peerless charm. Musicians of his stamp are almost always compelled by their genius to dismiss anything which attempts to impose restrictions on music. Monteverdi himself would soon follow this path and become preoccupied with writing beautiful melodies rather than genuine airs which capture the emotions of the poetry. All the more reason, then, to linger over this rare work, in which the balance between poetry and music is maintained and in which they are so intimately united that they seem to be at one in expressing a life which is harmonious and free.

Freedom: that is the most striking aspect of this art. Constantly changing impressions, a delicate sensitivity to the truth, curious rhythms and sonorities, a movement, a variety which, in his time, scandalised the representatives of academic art.[2] On every page there are evocative instrumental ritornellos, refined and brilliant in colouring, joyous poetic dances, serene pastoral airs, choruses so solid in design; but above all, recitatives of translucent fluidity. The melody seems to flow like a stream; a purity of soul shines through it. The most ephemeral emotions, the most fleeting nuances are reflected in it with a measured, supple precision. All this music resembles an atmosphere so limpid that a scarcely perceptible shift of expression, a shadow passing in the soul, can be clearly discerned there; and this surface, this soul, possess a tenderness, a melancholy, an indescribable sweetness. Oh! Gluck's Orpheus appears a mere operatic virtuoso beside this graceful, high-strung young creature from Umbria [*sic*]! And how heavy, impoverished and artificial all declamation seems, not only in Gluck, but in every opera since Monteverdi, from Cavalli to our own day, beside this music of the heart ('e 'l cantar che nell'anima si sente', as Petrarch puts it)! Four or five pages seem to me divine: Orpheus's air at the beginning of the second act, when he greets the fields and the woods with joyful tenderness – 'Ecco pur ch'a voi ritorno, care selve e piaggie amate'; his lamentations in the Underworld – 'Orfeo son'io' (Act III), containing those passages of vocalisation without words, strange and inspired, close to sobbing; the proud, youthful exuberance of the fourth act, when he emerges from the Underworld, leading Eurydice – 'Qual honor di te fia degno, mia cetra onnipotente'; and, above all, in the second act, the recitative of the Messenger who announces the death of Eurydice to Orpheus. This is, to my mind, truly the highest point which musical declamation has ever reached. The artistry is so great that it is forgotten; heart speaks to heart, and one is penetrated by grief both profound and chaste, of sublime innocence.

Our new school of composers might look for models and arguments here to support them in their conviction that there exists, that there must exist, a musical art superior to that which has been imposed on us for two centuries by a degenerate Italy and her pupil Germany: an art less solemn, less constrained, less subservient to the formalism of classical rhetoric, to the tyranny of the bar-line, to the conventions of a theatre of declaiming puppets; in their conviction, too, that the emancipation of music envisaged and desired by the impetuous nature of a Beethoven, or by the inspired ignorance of a Berlioz, is far from being accomplished, and that this dream of a freer, more human art is not a chimera; for, many centuries ago, the young and audacious genius of the Renaissance had, for a moment, achieved it. A moment so fleeting! Monteverdi himself does not seem afterwards to have sought to press this revolution further. Just as we see him abandoning the large orchestra of *Orfeo* (thirty-six instruments) and limiting himself in the *Ballo delle ingrate* of 1608 to a quartet of viols, clavicembalo and chitarrone, and in the *Combattimento di Tancredi e Clorinda* of 1624 to a string quartet, clavicembalo and contrabasso da gamba, thus aiming at homogeneity, rather than richness of style, so, in his last opera, *L'incoronazione di Poppea* of 1642, he sacrifices freedom and musical truth to beauty of line. Here we no longer have the impalpable texture of musical poetry that we admire in *Orfeo*. Here already we have the conventional grand structure of the classical

Italo-German opera. Here we have beautiful arias, beautiful duos, fixed forms to which life must adapt whether it wishes to or not. All the genius in the world will try in vain to make these forms more flexible. From now on, the idea is adapted to the form, and not the form to the idea as the creators of Florentine opera had dreamed it should be.

Why was this dream not fulfilled? Those respectful of the *fait accompli*, and keen to discover in the events of history a kind of inevitability and justice, will naturally be quick to say that it was because Peri's and Monteverdi's type of opera was not viable, and that the opera of Cavalli and Lully was superior. But for those (of whom I am one) who do not believe that the best necessarily triumphs, for those who see in the success or failure, the victory or defeat of men or ideas evidence not of their merits or demerits, but of a blind force and, even, of chance, such simple optimism (such optimism *à la* Candide) is inappropriate. I believe that the liberating reform of Monteverdi came to nothing, like so many other inspired ideas of the Italian Renaissance, because the Italian Renaissance was itself slowly dying at that moment, crushed by all kinds of political and religious despotisms, which it is not my purpose to discuss here. The free spirit of Italy longs for subjection; music, in common with the other arts, tends towards domestication. It is clear that, in this order of things, the France of Louis XIV and the Germany of the Prussian Sergeant-Major [Friedrich Wilhelm I] ought to have the prize. Now that our minds are struggling for emancipation once again, they are rediscovering the way for themselves and trying to take up the unfinished task of the world's most liberated age.

I am a long way from the concert at the *Schola*. I return to it and beg forgiveness for such a long digression. The two performances of *Orfeo*, on 25 February and 2 March, were a delight. M. Bourgeois sang the part of Orpheus – which is so difficult – with a great deal of feeling and remarkable intelligence. This young artist seems to me among those whose future is totally assured. Mlle Marthe Legrand was an enormous success in the wonderful role of the Messenger, which she delivered with the skill, simplicity and artistry which we have come to expect. Mlle Pironnet was applauded for her singing of the role of Music, who introduces the tragedy. The orchestra was most intriguing.[3] Above all, though, we must give thanks to M. Vincent d'Indy, for this beautiful concert really owed most to him. Not only was it he who directed the performance and communicated to everyone the spirit and vitality of *Orfeo*; he also brought it to life again and returned it to the beauty it once had, freeing it from the clumsy restorations which have disfigured it.[4] We owe our pleasure to him; but I am quite sure that no one experienced deeper pleasure than he did in rendering this act of homage to one of the greatest and most neglected of musical geniuses.

7 Orpheus: the neoclassic vision*

JOSEPH KERMAN

Io la Musica son, ch'ai dolci accenti
so far tranquillo ogni turbato core,
ed or di nobil' ira ed or d'amore
poss' infiammar le più gelate menti.

THE PROLOGUE, MUSIC, IN MONTEVERDI'S ORFEO

First there was the neoclassic vision of a drama reanimated by the co-operation of music. Doubts grew up only later.

The vision itself came as a climax to the whole tendency of Renaissance musical speculation and practice. In the sixteenth century, for the first time, the problems of musical expressivity became central for many theorists and composers; here as elsewhere, the Renaissance contributes the essential modern point of view. Long before the first classicizing librettos of the Florentines, humanists had insisted that if music in ancient times had imitated and stirred the emotions with matchless power, it could and should again. Musicians, accordingly, had devoted their attention to the means of emotional expression, experimenting sometimes with great psychological understanding, and over the years with developing ingenuity and effectiveness. The dominant musical form was the madrigal, a short vocal piece bound intimately to its poem – at best, and most characteristically, to a Petrarchan sonnet, an isolated stanza from Ariosto, or a lyric by Tasso. Images, moods and 'affects' were translated into musical terms. The rich tradition of the Italian madrigal, from Cipriano de Rore to Luca Marenzio and Claudio Monteverdi, determined the expressive course of music during the last half of the *cinquecento*.

The ultimate step, perhaps an inevitable one, was from the lyric to the dramatic: music was to step on to the stage, as Monteverdi's Prologue does, in order to inflame variously even *le più gelate menti*, the most frigid of minds. To attain its most far-reaching influence, music had to aspire to the high form of drama. This remained an

---

* Slightly revised by the author, and reprinted here without the complementary discussion of Gluck's *Orfeo ed Euridice*.

aspiration, no doubt, except for a few works; in any case it was less a deliberate goal than the natural outcome of *fin de siècle* essays in exaggerated expressivity. Many currents led in to the famous musical 'revolution' of 1600, from which we date a little too crudely the beginning of modern music, the invention of the *basso continuo* or thoroughbass, the triumph of melody over counterpoint, and the first opera. This revolution is best seen as a violent, baroque extension of tendencies of the prior century. In many ways Monteverdi cuts off sharply from Cipriano de Rore and Palestrina, but the continuity is also clear; the first great opera composer was also the last great madrigalist. Musical drama was the last and most extreme product of the sixteenth century's faith in the moving power of music.

To the humanists and those who shared their enthusiasms at second hand, evidence for the great power of music was everywhere convincing. They knew that the Greek lyrics had been sung, and likewise the tragedies themselves – certainly in part, if not entirely. In 1585 a version of *Œdipus tyrannus* was performed with the choruses confidently set to music by one of the most important madrigalists, Andrea Gabrieli. But an even deeper inspiration was to be found in the musical stories revered by classic authors – by Plato himself, who would have banished certain modes of music as too powerful, too dangerous for the well-being of the state. Great musical exploits are told of Amphion and Eunomus, Terpander and Timotheus, Pan and Apollo. The legend of the Thracian singer Orpheus is especially well developed, problematic, and rich, and is remarkable for the simple beauty of its action. Already in its classic sources the myth is halfway to the dramatic form in which Politian and Rinuccini, Lope de Vega, Monteverdi and Gluck, Cocteau, Milhaud, and Stravinsky were subsequently tempted to shape it.

The lasting myths contain in them the lasting problems of man. The myth of Orpheus, furthermore, deals with man specifically as artist, and one is drawn inevitably to see in it, mirrored with a kind of proleptic vision, the peculiar problems of the opera composer. Initially Orpheus is the supreme lyric artist. In the classic view he is the ideal of the prize-winning *kitharista* – or, in Christian allegory, the evangelical psalmist who charmed the melancholy Saul. To the fourteenth century, he is the minstrel who exacts his boon from the Fairy King; to the sixteenth, perhaps, the madrigalist; to the nineteenth, proud Walther who persuades the German pedants. The eighteenth century painted him, tremulously, as the amiable singer of Metastasio's faint verses who entranced the King of Spain. But for Orpheus the lyric singer, the crisis of life becomes the crisis of his lyric art: art must now move into action, onto the tragic stage of life. It is a sublime attempt. Can its symbolic boldness have escaped the musicians of 1600, seeking new power in the stronger forms of drama? Orpheus' new triumph is to fashion the lament that harrows hell out of his own great sorrowing emotion – this too they must have specially marked, wrestling as they were with new emotional means, harrowing, dangerous to manage. The fundamental conflict of the myth transcends that time and this medium, and extends to every artist. It is the problem of emotion and its control, the summoning of feeling to an intensity and communicability and form which the action of life heeds and death provisionally respects. All this Orpheus as artist achieves. But as man he cannot shape his emotions to Pluto's shrewd decree; face to face with the situation, he looks back, and fails. Life and art are not necessarily one.

The quality of Orpheus's failure here is obscure in the myth, but for the dramatist it is the crux of the matter. Around it, Monteverdi and – in a later age – Gluck attempted to crystallize the very different dramatic ideas that guide their versions of the legend. To be sure, this 'problem of control' is an abstraction; few artists, and certainly not Monteverdi or Gluck, have drawn so clean and scientific an issue. Nor did Orpheus, in the simple, unelaborated myth. It is the dramatist's task to clarify the issue for Orpheus. The critic's is to clarify the parallel issue, the artist's problem of control; not for the dramatist, but for an audience which needs to grasp the dramatist's methods in order to share his vision.

The first two operas that have been preserved are settings by Jacopo Peri and Giulio Caccini of the *Euridice*, by the Florentine humanist poet Ottavio Rinuccini, in 1600. The first great opera is Monteverdi's *La favola d'Orfeo*, written at Mantua in 1607; and *Orfeo* is the first opera to reveal the characteristic composer's struggle with the libretto. The composer is the dramatist, and his particular powers will determine the integrity of the drama. From his point of view, then, those elements in the libretto which suit his powers can be realized; other elements are either triumphantly distorted, or do not matter, or defeat him. In the end, the libretto is the limitation. But from another point of view, it is usually true that the composer's powers have hardly been shown beforehand, and come out only in the musical setting of the libretto. In the beginning, the libretto is the inspiration.

So it was with Monteverdi. He was not a master of recitative who went to Alessandro Striggio for a libretto to incorporate this special strength. Striggio, let us say, brought him the book; and, in setting it, Monteverdi discovered recitative – he did not invent it, but in the deepest sense he certainly discovered it. From then on recitative was his greatest achievement. It forms the basis for *Orfeo*, and completely dominates and determines his masterpiece of thirty-five years later, *L'incoronazione di Poppea*.

Recitative is one of the fundamental, constant elements of operatic dramaturgy. But actually it already began to decay into convention with Monteverdi's pupils, and in spite of impressive renewals in later centuries, it has never been used again with Monteverdi's confidence, imagination, and conviction. As a result, it is hard for us today to think of recitative as anything but second best, a necessary link between arias. In 1600, however, there was as yet no concept of the considered emotional experience that later composers were to elaborate in purely musical forms – Bach in the fugue, Beethoven in the symphony, Handel and Verdi in the aria. It remained for Gluck to bring this modern concept of musical coherence to the Orpheus legend; Monteverdi understood nothing of it; in the tradition that he knew, musical expressivity was directed only to the painting of moods and images in madrigals. Now there was a more specifically neoclassic ideal: music instead should imitate the accents of passionate speech as best represented by the grand, exaggerated rhetoric of a great actor. Music should follow the cadence and thus the moving implication of the individual word, with little heed to the phrase, the sentence, or even the total feeling. The result was recitative, tumbling emotion, a continuing heart-cry, undistanced, 'the naked human voice' behind the measured voice of the poet. Its magnificence and immediacy stem exactly from its impulsive nature, from its lack of forming control.

Monteverdi met this ideal with a perfect genius for declamation; words formed themselves musically for him. And to whip the recitative line into passion, he harrowed every available musical means for tension. Declamation guided him to sudden halts and spurting cascades in rhythm, and to precipitous, intense rises and falls in melodic line. Though he sometimes juxtaposes chords in radical ways, his basic harmonies are generally simple; harmonic tension is implemented by dissonance between the voice and the chords below. Occasionally he even emphasizes violent dissonance above a harmony without any suggestion of relief (in technical terms resolution, passage into calmer consonance). Or when, more usually, he does resolve dissonance, the effect may be partial and bitter, or else compromised with new subsidiary tensions introduced in passing by searing extra-harmonic notes. The great advantage of the modern monodic style of the 1600's, the 'new music', was that the voice could range unencumbered above the *basso continuo*, which all alone provided a simple harmonic support. Rhythm, line, and dissonance were actually freed for the most expressive contortions. In the essential simplicity of the total texture, they could not destroy the clear, quiet authority of the bass.

Monteverdi's use of syncopation is particularly striking. Syncopation is rhythmic tension, just as dissonance is harmonic tension; traditionally the two had been carefully used together, mainly for the purpose of strengthening a coming cadence. But Monteverdi made syncopation of the recitative line into a positive mannerism, producing a curious sense of ready displacement, a latitude that allows the singer to drag or rush irrespective of the sober metrical beat. In the musical example below, the lower lines show Monteverdi's syncopated recitative line and its bass; above I have tried to reconstruct the conventional, non-syncopated version of that line which the bass would normally imply. Six times the voice seems to come in too late for its accompaniment – and usually its lateness has caused a sharp, scarcely resolved dissonance. At the end the voice twice stumbles in ahead of time, with an even more excruciating effect. This has just the expressive force of *rubato*:

- po - se tut - te le gra-zie sue___ cor -te - se_il Cie - lo

No doubt Monteverdi wanted the dissonances for their own sake, but he was also interested in an impression of unbridled ebb and flow, and in the immediacy of response which this creates. It is as though the singer were in such transports that he can no longer restrain himself to the artifice of the steadily marching bass. The example, moreover, is simple in that Monteverdi here has regular movement in the bass, for a special reason; usually the bass is also erratic, giving a remarkable sense of flexibility, torsion, and expressivity to the whole complex. The musician tries to capture the metrical fluidity of poetry, poetry as spoken on the stage. The result is a declamatory style of unexampled raw emotionality.

This art of recitative is what Monteverdi brought to the story of Orpheus, an artist who could move hell by his grief, a lover who could not dominate his passions. Striggio's libretto does everything to refine a view of Orpheus as an unreflective creature of impulse, acting strongly and with the greatest instinctive bravery. In the first act we hear him only briefly, breaking into the Arcadian atmosphere with an enthusiastic hymn to the Sun, rejoicing in his success at finally winning Eurydice. But in Act II the pastoral tone is shattered by a most explosive Messenger, Silvia, '*ninfa gentile*', who suddenly and for the first time reveals the full force of Monteverdi's recitative. Her superb, rapid lament acts as a kind of trigger for Orpheus' emotion; his part in this act is also small, an abrupt, intense, half-unconscious decision to seek Eurydice in Hades. In Act III he is on the bank of Styx with Hope, who must leave him, to his very articulate distress. Hopeless, he nonetheless sings a huge formal lament to Charon; the lament breaks off into an informal plea which is even more impassioned, and which does at last gain him admission. Rather ambiguously, though: Charon, evidently a half-comic character, is still adamant, but falls asleep (like Cerberus in mythology). In Act IV, when Eurydice is released, the drama quickens as it reveals Orpheus' rather terrible insufficiency. His reaction is neither gratitude nor real affection, but a hymn of praise to himself and to his lyre. Fearing that Eurydice may be snatched back, he turns fitfully to see her, as much out of over-confidence as for love. When she fades away from him, he utters another piercing cry, such as Monteverdi alone could handle in recitative. How inadequate Gluck is at this place, in the heat of the moment! Monteverdi's Orpheus is agonized, and the Infernal Chorus mercifully cuts him off.

This chorus observes that success comes only to those who can moderate their feelings, a moral which indeed is spoken by everybody: by a Spirit who warns of *giovenil desio* as he fetches Eurydice, by Eurydice herself in her dying words '*Così per troppo amor . . .* ', and in the next act by Apollo *ex machina*, who echoes her speech and further rebukes his son: '*Non è consiglio / di generoso petto / servir al proprio affetto*'. But Orpheus learns nothing. In Act V, before Apollo comes to him, he is lamenting again in Thrace, with more intensity than ever, but with scarcely any higher awareness. And his subsequent ascent to heaven is more or less meaningless, the most disappointing thing in the opera.

To distinguish between the attitudes of the librettist and those of the composer is often hard. Striggio was experimenting, just as Monteverdi was. While the first act of the libretto is purely lyric in quality, like the *Euridice* of Rinuccini, the later acts show striking dramatic tendencies, especially by contrast with Rinuccini. But Striggio did nothing to bridge the gap between Orpheus' heroic achievements in song or action and the callow impulse (to consider it coldly) which is his only response to them. In a libretto, poetry can do nothing for Orpheus; even if Striggio had the poetic art, he lacked the time and the form. But through Monteverdi's recitative, impulse becomes passion; it is impossible to consider Orpheus coldly. What seems in the book to be instinct or caprice becomes under the pressure of the music an absolutely compelling emotion, so that we are no more in doubt of Orpheus' integrity than are the wild beasts of Thrace and the creatures of Hades, whom he likewise sways. A libretto provides a framework, but the essential dramatic articulation is provided by the music. By means of Monteverdi's recitative, Striggio's blank or contradictory character attains tragic reality.

Monteverdi also grasped the need for elements to bind and weight the primary texture of recitative, to control it from the outside, since it knew no inner restraint. He used short songs, brief orchestral sections called *ritornelli* or *sinfonie*, and choruses ranging

in style from serious madrigals to light fa-la's. None is very expressive in itself, indeed many can be said to be awkward, neutral, and
antiquated; but they make a perfect ballast for the form. In the task
of dramatic construction, Monteverdi was helped by having a poem
shaped along bold, simple lines. Striggio appears to have worked
from a sort of ideal scheme for an act, a scheme which forms itself
during Acts I and II, reaches full articulation in Acts III and IV, and
decays in Act V. His tendency was to start each act with a static situation, follow it by a single important action, show Orpheus' reaction
to it, and then sum up in a choral conclusion. Especially the great
Infernal Chorus, flanked by the trombones and *cornetti* which alone
survive in Monteverdi's hell, beautifully reflects the success of
Orpheus in Act III, and then his failure in Act IV. The solemn
Venetian madrigal polyphony, stiffly controlled as though
sculptured, answers and deepens the impassioned voice. *Orfeo*
shows a wonderful sense of clear dramatic movement; Striggio had
not studied and translated Greek plays for nothing. And Monteverdi, past master of the highly developed choral art of the sixteenth
century, was able to give the chorus, in particular, a dramatic
importance second only to that of the recitative.

As I have said, one virtue of the libretto is that it gives Orpheus
many occasions to react violently in moments of crisis: the news of
Eurydice's death, the departure of Hope, the rejection by Charon,
the return of Eurydice, and her second death. These moments are
precisely suited to Monteverdi's power, and mark indelibly the
character of the drama. But at two crucial points in the play,
Orpheus is confronted with the necessity of dealing with considered
feeling after the moment of pain has passed; he is to summon up all
his art, his control, to comprehend pain in a purer consciousness.
For a later composer, these would have been natural 'aria
situations'.

The first of them is the formal lament to Charon; and Monteverdi, who could not write a true aria, triumphantly distorted the
libretto. Striggio wrote six tercets of *terza rima* – knowing that
Monteverdi was usually very respectful of poetic form. Monteverdi
set the first four tercets as an increasingly brilliant musical display,
with fabulous coloratura for the singer, broken by ornate instrumental interludes. But as this does not impress Charon, Orpheus
forgets himself abruptly and delivers the fifth tercet as a free and (in
context) doubly piercing recitative. Then, by a wonderful inspiration, the final tercet is completely calm, without coloratura or
passion; Orpheus and the instruments come together for the only

time in the opera, in a style vaguely ecclesiastical, part-music to which Orpheus kneels with the viols, exposing most purely the quiet bass pattern which had united the earlier stanzas. Charon is indeed stony-hearted. With intolerable passion, the recitative plea is resumed, culminating in the famous refrain '*Rendetemi il mio ben, Tartarei Numi*'. As Orpheus enters Charon's boat, the Infernal Chorus speaks its sober sentence:

> Nulla impresa per uom si tenta invano
> Nè contr'a lui più sa Natura armarse . . .
>
> No undertaking of man is tried in vain,
> Nor can Nature arm against him further . . .

The other 'aria situation' is of course the scene in Act V, which begins with a fifty-line lament for the despairing Orpheus. Striggio built the passage metrically to a pulsing climax; apparently the idea was to carry Orpheus forward from mere depression and bantering with his echo to a state of ecstasy in which he could sing a hymn (at last) to Eurydice. It is worth emphasizing that previously Orpheus has sung only in praise of his success in winning her, and then again in praise of his lyre. But Striggio's long lament turned out to be one of those elements in a libretto which defeat a composer. Monteverdi's recitative is perhaps never so impassioned and powerful as here, but he had no way to present the more serene vision that Orpheus may be expected to attain as he looks back on events from the Thracian fields. Monteverdi must have been dimly conscious of a 'problem of control' in recitative. He attempted to organize it by means of refrains, sequences, rhythmic and melodic goals, even sometimes by a sort of tonal plan, and most strikingly by loose repetitive structure in the bass. That is, the free flow of the declamation is unified by the repetition in the bass of a fairly extensive pattern. Even this device, however, does not produce the cohesion of musical substance that gives consistency to emotional effect. Recitative is still too bound to the words; the technique of the aria was not yet developed. Having learned nothing, Orpheus is still reacting on impulse.

And when the force of instant passion fails for Orpheus, Monteverdi was at a loss for a further action or a final comment. I see no reason to doubt that Monteverdi saw into the delicate balance between character and action implicit in a drama. He was able to develop Orpheus' character in music so that his actions have dignity and sense; Orpheus' failure in Act IV begins to touch us tragically.

But in the implied tragic end of an Orpheus play, there is another necessary balance: between the consciousness that grows in the hero and the tragic fate for which this prepares him, and which it lets him then transcend. Orpheus must somehow rise to meet, or deserve, or require the tragic fate. This progress Monteverdi could not show. So the conclusion of the drama presented a serious problem.

Monteverdi solved the problem by conducting Orpheus to heaven, with the prospect of meditating upon Eurydice fixed among the stars. It must be said that this Platonic apotheosis is musically and intellectually blank. But at least it is an act, and ends the piece efficiently; that is more than Striggio would have done; he meant originally to bring in the Bacchantes, but unlike Politian did not venture to offend the court by having them tear Orpheus. Monteverdi, we may well imagine, could only have deplored this undramatic prevarication. Even if Orpheus could not be shown to progress in Act V, dramatic form demanded some full action, some solid realization in terms of plot. Custom would not have deterred Monteverdi from carrying through Striggio's hint of tragedy if he had wished. Perhaps he refused to do so on account of an instinct of his own limitation.

Apotheosizing Apollo has no personality at all. But earlier, there have been beautifully pure little pictures of minor characters. The first is the passionate Messenger of Act II, who, after Orpheus has sung and left, continues her tremendous lament, self-centered as the hero himself, even infecting the Nymphs and Shepherds with her recitative refrain. In the next act, an even smaller role, parallel in function to that of the Messenger, is Charon; grotesque, scabrous, bitter with memories of violation and deceit. After Orpheus' song, Charon grumbles over the same bass pattern that had accompanied his original outburst; he is touched but determined not to budge. The vivid consistency of characterization and the opportunity provided for Orpheus to intensify his plea more than make up for Charon's unlikely drowsiness. He is a genuine test both of Orpheus' bravery and of the power of song.

Finally, there is the earnest figure of Music, who sings a simple strophic song as Prologue. She carries on her shoulders the artistic anxiety of the time. As, at the end, her song changes from gay to sad and she charges the birds and waves and winds to silence themselves, we wonder – will they yield in Mantua, as once they did in Thrace? Twice during the course of the drama Music is heard to return, as though to enquire and encourage, dumbly through the viols of her original *ritornello*. Can passion move into action? In the Vienna of Gluck, Calzabigi, and Durazzo, a century and a half later, the issue was again to be in doubt, in a new atmosphere of experimentation with the means of musical expression. The matter was still not to be settled unequivocally.

*
*　*

Heroic opera, the quintessential art-form of the baroque, had its beginning when Monteverdi showed suddenly what the form was worth. The great tradition came to an end when Gluck transformed it, and transformed it in his own terms. Orpheus begins and ends an era. The era embraces many neoclassicisms: the late humanism of the Florentine and Mantuan courts; the *grand siècle* order of Lully and Quinault; the delightful, preposterous fantasy of the Arcadian Academy, with Crescimbeni, Farinelli, and Metastasio; the serene Roman ideal of Goethe, Winckelmann, and Gluck. At every point someone had a vague vision of a modern analogy to the Greek drama; and musical drama somehow came into being. Between the time of Monteverdi and that of Gluck, recitative erupted and decayed, while the aria developed, over-developed, and finally realized itself. It was the time of the true classical tradition of opera.

The lyre of Orpheus extends its charm even farther back, to Peri and Caccini in 1600, and even farther forward, almost to 1800: an *Orpheus* written for London by Joseph Haydn (but never performed) was among the very last of the *opere serie*, decrepit and long past its time. Orpheus' dramatic conflict falls easily into the favorite baroque formulation of instinct and duty, emotion and reason, 'love and honor'. But a special fascination for the opera composer lay in the almost explicit parallel between Orpheus' action and Orpheus' art. The task for the artist is to assert a purifying control over the emotional source of art, to form and focus it until he can move hell – and also move the audience in the theater. For the man, the trial demands heroism beyond that of daring hell: it is to control his own flood of passion when finally Eurydice returns – and also to convince the audience of the integrity of his actions. With Monteverdi, for whom raw passion was the main reality, the conflict was never solved. With Gluck, whose reality was the sublimation of feeling, the conflict was less solved than passed over; sublimation brought him practically to the sublime, to Elysium.

Gluck had reached a point of artistic sophistication at which the problem of emotional discipline was only too simply met. The danger was in losing the very roots of passion. Both dramatists failed in the ultimate task of articulation, lowering their expressive sights and frankly deflecting the conclusion.

Perhaps it was just as well; at least they assumed no more than they knew. This negative virtue stands out in contrast with the next curious operatic metamorphosis of the Orpheus idea, another hundred years later, at another period of expressive experimentation and 'reform'. In *Die Meistersinger*, Richard Wagner attacked the problem of control head on, specifically, and with his usual relentless enthusiasm. The singer who will not brook laws of art or of orderly bourgeois society is gently taught self-control and musical form, both together, by a higher being who rescues him as arbitrarily as Cupid or Apollo, but who insists on rationalizing the rescue. The complacent tale ends with an unearned hymn to German Art, as the fantastic dramatic machinery purrs to its calculated close. All questions are answered, but no serious ones have been asked; it is not hell that has to be appeased, but the pedants of Nuremberg and the journalists of Vienna. And blind, proud, instinctive Walther has none of Monteverdi's burning passion or of Gluck's heroic self-awareness. The dramatic life in *Die Meistersinger* lies in something that began as a counterpoint to the central idea and then gradually displaced it: the drama of Sachs. It is there, and in other operas, that Wagner asked his important questions.

'*Die heil'ge deutsche Kunst*' – 'Frau Musica' makes a substantial substitute for Monteverdi's shadowy Prologue. But the latter nonetheless remains to haunt our imagination. We imagine her, perhaps, restless on the bank of Styx with Orpheus as he pleads, vainly now, for another opportunity. Like Orpheus, she has her partial success, which is more meaningful than the full victory of others. Like Orpheus, she will continue to confront the dramatist with her elusive, animating challenge:

> I am Music, who with dulcet accents
> Know how to soothe each troubled heart,
> And now with passion, now with noble rage,
> My power can inflame the coldest mind.

RECREATING 'ORFEO' FOR THE MODERN STAGE

8 *Solving the musical problems*

JANE GLOVER

It is almost inevitable that the first products of a brand-new art-form should be attended by problems. The earliest operas are no exception; and modern editors of seventeenth-century opera scores almost invariably encounter all manner of difficulties and conundrums which have to be solved before such works can go into the rehearsal room. Compared with the enormous number of manuscript scores from the latter part of the seventeenth century, the printed scores of Monteverdi's *Orfeo*, like those of the two *Euridice* settings by Peri and Caccini which preceded it, are remarkably clear in content and intention. But there are confusions. These can arise from an original slip of the pen, or from a printing error, or from plain omission. Most commonly they arise from the composer's simply taking for granted the conventions of contemporary performance practice, and bequeathing his work to posterity in a shorthand which was comprehensible at the time. In any event the editor has to employ detective methods, based largely upon knowledge of the seventeenth-century context, but partly also upon straightforward common sense.

After the opening of the Teatro San Cassiano at Venice in 1637, operas were conceived for, performed on and subsequently discarded by the ferocious treadmill of operatic showbusiness. The purpose they served was an immediate one, and their prominence therefore short-lived. As a result, it was never deemed necessary to preserve them for posterity by printing them, and the remarkable number of manuscripts that survive from this period do so by the most fortuitous of accidents. But *Orfeo* preceded this great wave of commercial activity, and did reach the safe haven of the printing presses. The score survives in two printed editions, both published in the composer's lifetime by the celebrated Venetian publishing house of Amadino. The first edition appeared in 1609, two years after the opera's premiere. The second followed in 1615, by which time Monteverdi had left the Mantuan court, where he had experienced the extremes of fulfilment and disappointment, and was contentedly esconced in his brilliant new post of *maestro di cappella* at St Mark's, Venice. The first edition is available in Sandberger's facsimile reprint (Augsburg, 1927). More accessibly, it has been transcribed by Monteverdi's tireless champion Gian Francesco Malipiero in Volume XI of his collected edition of the composer's works. If we check this against the facsimile it is clear that Malipiero made some minor mistranscriptions, and there is one major omission. But it is otherwise relatively accurate and therefore perfectly usable. So, for convenience, all page references in the following discussion of the opera are to the Malipiero edition.

The published score of *Orfeo* is certainly complete, in that no note is missing. Furthermore, Monteverdi printed two lists at the beginning of the score, one of the *dramatis personae* and one of the instruments involved in performing the work. There is thus a very clear idea of what forces are needed. But two basic problems arise with regard to these lists: first, that they are both confusing and inaccurate; and secondly, that within the score itself instructions as to how and where the forces should be deployed are incomplete.

These, then, are the problems which the editor–conductor must solve before *Orfeo* can be translated into the vital and passionate stage work that it is. His solutions will fall into four main categories: deployment of instruments (this is the most extensive category), deployment of vocal forces, minor editorial adjustments, and, finally, the work he does in the rehearsal room which actually makes the music live. The following discussions thus approach the musical problems in that order. It must be added that the ensuing judgments are based on experience, that of preparing an edition for a series of performances.[1] I cannot in any way claim that my solutions are definitive; and indeed subsequent editor–conductors have made their own editions,[2] which inevitably differ from mine to a greater or lesser degree. But, in all humility, it must be said that my edition, neither more nor less than those of my colleagues, worked.

Deployment of instruments

The following is the list of instruments printed by Monteverdi at the front of his score:

Duoi Gravicembani
Duoi Contrabassi de Viola

Dieci Viole da brazzo
Un Arpa doppia
Duoi Violini piccoli alla Francese
Duoi Chitaroni [but elsewhere three are specified]
Duoi Organi di legno
Tre bassi da gamba
Quattro Tromboni [elsewhere five]
Un Regale
Duoi Cornetti
Un Flautino alla Vigesima seconda [elsewhere two]
Un Clarino con tre trombe sordine

This list is in itself confusing. The order is arbitrary, and the quantitative errors misleading. In fact, the instruments divide into three groups: strings, brass and continuo. The 'Dieci Viole da brazzo' are ten members of the violin family: that is, they form a five-part string ensemble (two ensembles if we observe the instruction on p. 48 that an ensemble of strings should also be located on the stage) of first and second violins, first and second violas, and violoncello. They are supported by 'Duoi Contrabassi de Viola' (double basses), which double the fifth line. In addition there are the 'Duoi Violini piccoli alla Francese', small violins for specific soloistic moments (the ritornellos to 'Ecco pur ch'a voi ritorno' in Act II, p. 41; to 'Possente spirto' in Act III, p. 84; and to 'Qual honor' in Act IV, p. 121). These two solo violins need not, however, require extra players, as they never play in conjunction with the full string ensemble.

Among the brass instruments there are five trombones and two cornetts, which together play the 'infernal' sinfonias in Acts III and IV. The 'Clarino con tre trombe sordine' contribute only to the toccata which opens the work, and will be considered separately.

The remainder of the instruments constitute an imposing array of continuo forces: two harpsichords, a double harp, three chitarroni, two organs, three gambas and a regal. The fact that there are three gambas implies three separate continuo groups. Two of these have each a harpsichord, an organ, a chitarrone and a gamba (one also has the regal), and the third consists of the harp, a chitarrone and a gamba. Again, both the first two groups require only one keyboard-player each, with two or three instruments at his disposal. The division into these three groups need not be too rigorously observed: it may be desirable, for example, to use two or three of the chitarroni together, with one gamba. Thus, there is an enormous variety of potential continuo combinations. And Monteverdi gives some indication of how the instruments should be placed. Among his all-too-exiguous instructions, he does ask that at the beginning of Act V (p. 138) two organs and two chitarroni should accompany Orfeo's song, with one group on the left of the stage area and the other on the right.[3]

There remains a handful of miscellaneous instruments: the two recorders ('flautini'), which occasionally support and colour the strings, and the 'Clarino con tre trombe sordine', which play the toccata only. The fact that this D major toccata is virtually identical to the opening of Monteverdi's Vespers (1610) suggests that it was a familiar Mantuan toccata, regularly used to open any large ceremonial occasion. Here, as Monteverdi instructs, the toccata is played three times to announce the imminent start of the performance (rather like interval bells).[4] It will be observed that the two lowest lines of the toccata are pedals only, so a total of only three trumpets (the clarino and two others) is needed, supported by two of the trombones. And, finally, Monteverdi mentions the use of 'ceteroni'. He does not include them in the list of instruments at the beginning of the score, but refers to them in an instruction at the end of Act IV:

Tacciono li Cornetti, Tromboni & Regali, & entrano a sonare il presente Ritornello, le viole da Braccio, Organi, Clavicembani, contrabasso, & Arpe, & Chitaroni, & Ceteroni, et si muta la Sena.

Literally, these 'ceteroni' are 'large citterns' (see Chapter 4, note 14). As they are listed only on this occasion, it is just possible to ignore them; but if a meticulous editor is in genuine doubt about authenticity he can add them to the group of continuo instruments and so find even greater flexibility.

Having clarified the nature and number of instruments, the next step is to determine the manner in which they are to be used. Scattered throughout the score are a few of Monteverdi's own instructions as to which instruments should be playing (a complete list of these instructions is printed in Appendix 3). While these are by no means comprehensive, they are certainly sufficiently numerous to give a precise idea of the instrumental colours Monteverdi had in mind.

Two crucial directions appear between Acts II and III and between Acts IV and V. The first of these is the one Malipiero omitted from his transcription; it should read:

Qui entrano li Tromb[oni] Corn[etti] & Regali, & taciono le Viole da bracio, & Organi di legno, Clavacem[bali], & si muta la Sena.

while, conversely, the second reads:

Tacciono li Cornetti, Tromboni & Regali, & entrano a sonare il presente Ritornello, le viole da braccio, Organi, Clavicembani, contrabasso, & Arpe, & Chitaroni, & Ceteroni, & si muta la Sena.

From these instructions, it is quite clear that there are two completely separate instrumental colours, each inextricably bound to one of the two locations of the opera. The first consists of strings, organs, harpsichords, plucked continuo instruments, and also recorders, and is associated with those scenes which take place in the fields of Thrace (Acts I, II and V). As if to emphasise that this particular instrumental colour represents these pastoral scenes, the haunting D minor ritornello first heard in the prologue (p. 2ff) is repeated at the end of the second act (p. 74), and again at the beginning of Act V (p. 137). This means that however the transition from the Thracian fields to Hades (and vice versa) is accomplished in visual terms, the audience is left in no doubt aurally as to where the next scene takes place. (Incidentally, the use of this aural topographical pointer also offers the attractive notion that time has stood still during Orfeo's descent to the Underworld.) Monteverdi's rubric at the beginning of the first-act chorus 'Lasciate i monti' (p. 14) reinforces this practice:

Questo Balletto fu cantato al suono di cinque Viole da braccio, tre Chittaroni, duoi Clavicembani. un Arpa doppia, un contrabasso de Viola, & un Flautino alla vigesima seconda.

The rubric at the head of the preceding chorus, 'Vieni Imeneo' (p. 11) – 'Questo Canto fu concertato al suono de tutti gli stromenti' – should, however, be interpreted in the context of the pastoral colours and not in the context of the complete instrumental quorum.

In addition to the main body of pastoral instruments, there are the two 'violini piccoli' for the beginning of Act II (p. 41), distinguished from the rest of the violins by reference to 'violini ordinari' for the ensuing ritornello (p. 43). There are also the two 'flautini', one listed for 'Lasciate i monti' on p. 14, and two for the ritornellos to 'Qui le Napee vezzose' on pp. 45–6. It might be inferred that these 'flautini' can be used occasionally for additional colour elsewhere in the opera. Finally in this instrumental grouping there are the basic continuo instruments of harpsichords, organs, harp and chitarroni: that is, everything but the regal.

As Monteverdi's clear instructions show, the other main instrumental colour consists of cornetts, trombones and regal, and is associated entirely with the scenes in Hades (Acts III and IV). Thus, the sinfonias '*a 7*' (in fact in eight parts) on pp. 75, 105, 112, 128 and 135 are played by two cornetts, five trombones and the regal on the continuo line, while the five-part sinfonia on p. 83 is played by trombones alone.[5] They also accompany the choruses on pp. 107, 120 and 130, with the addition of regal, organ and bass stringed instruments on the continuo line, as dictated in Monteverdi's instruction on p. 107.

Within this clear pattern, of string-based sound for pastoral scenes and brass-based sound for infernal scenes, there are exceptions. Strings do appear in Hades, in the following circumstances. Two solo violins are used in the first and fourth stanzas of 'Possente spirto' in Act III (pp. 84 and 96); but here, like the two cornetts and double harp which share the ritornellos, they are employed entirely to emphasise the virtuoso nature of this, the central musical and dramatic focus of the opera.[6] They also play the ritornellos to 'Qual honor' in Act IV (p. 121); but their appearance in this context may be accounted for by the fact that in this joyous little aria Orfeo is happily (and prematurely, as it happens) anticipating his return to the Thracian fields with Euridice.

The full string ensemble also occurs on two occasions in the Hades scenes. The first is the string accompaniment to 'Sol tu, nobile Dio' at the end of 'Possente spirto' (p. 99). After so much virtuoso entreaty comes this simplest of heartfelt pleas. Monteverdi dictates that the strings should play this 'Pian piano', thus contrasting in every way with the brass sounds which preceded this crucial juncture of the opera. Throughout this centrepiece, exceptional devices have been used in every way, vocal and instrumental. The second occasion where strings appear in Hades is the sinfonia on p. 103, during which Caronte falls asleep, giving Orfeo the opportunity to slip unnoticed across the Styx. This is an echo of the sinfonia on p. 83 which introduced 'Possente spirto'; and it is interesting that this very sinfonia reappears in Act V (p. 144), as a devastating reminder of what Orfeo endured in Hades, just before Apollo descends with comfort and a solution. For this sinfonia, then, Monteverdi again specifies the use of strings, and a 'Pian piano' dynamic to mark the echo, the closing of the prayer, and Caronte's falling asleep.

The only remaining problem in sorting out the deployment of instruments in the closed numbers is in the scoring of the opening toccata. As has already been seen, the toccata is separate from the opera as such (which opens with the D minor ritornello), and is the only part of the score to employ the 'Clarino con tre trombe sordine' listed on the frontispiece. Monteverdi's instruction (apart from making it clear that muting the trumpets raises their pitch so that the printed C major sounds as D major) merely states that the toccata is played before the rise of the curtain 'tre volte con tutti li stromenti'. Since it is to be played three times, one possible method of scoring it is to build up the instrumentation on each repetition. Thus, the first statement might be for brass alone, with the regal; the second would add the strings, and the third would add everything else (the recorders to the top line, and the remaining continuo instruments).

The next problem is how to allocate the continuo instruments to unmeasured recitatives and to arias with no other instrumental accompaniment. In the whole score there are only twelve indications from Monteverdi of what to use for this sort of music. But, again, even these few pointers are crucial to an understanding of his concept of exploiting continuo to achieve contrast and effect.

The two most dramatic moments in the opera (which, incidentally, are fundamental to the symmetrical structure of the work) are the entry of the Messenger in Act II, and Orfeo's turning to look at Euridice, against the orders of Plutone, in Act IV. In each case Monteverdi tells us exactly what to do, both at the precise moment and in the context of what precedes it.

The whole wedding-party atmosphere of the beginning of the second act, with its jovial choruses, duets and arias, has in musical terms been entirely built on string sounds with harpsichords and chitarroni. For the shepherds' duet 'In questo prato adorno' (p. 44) Monteverdi specifies an accompaniment of 'un clavicembano & un chitarrone'; for the succeeding ritornello (p. 45) 'duoi Chitaroni [&] un clavicembano' (Malipiero mistranscribed this rubric) with the recorders; and for the ritornellos to Orfeo's jolly 'Vi ricorda o bosch'ombrosi' (p. 48) 'duoi Clavicembani & tre chitarroni' with the strings. But at the devastating entry of the Messenger (p. 56), cutting into the festive C major music and thrusting it into A minor, Monteverdi decrees 'un organo di legno & un Chit[arrone]'. After her first desolate cries of 'Ahi caso acerbo, ahi fat'empio e crudele,

/ ahi stelle ingiuriose, ahi ciel avaro' (structurally central to the ensuing pages, in both text and music), the shepherd's interruption 'Qual suon dolente il lieto dì pertuba?' is accompanied by 'un Clavic[embalo], Chitar[rone] & Viola da bracio'. Thus, the contrast of sound, matching the contrast of mood, is specifically bespoken by Monteverdi. And from these two instructions it follows that the ensuing narrative of the Messenger is accompanied entirely by the organ and chitarrone, and the interjections of the various shepherds by harpsichord, chitarrone and viola da braccio. It is interesting to note also that the organ colour is then transferred to Orfeo when he finally utters after his long silence ('Tu se' morta', p. 62).

Monteverdi took similar care at the corresponding moment in Act IV. In the build-up to it, Plutone agrees to let Orfeo have his Euridice (on certain conditions); the spirits rejoice for Orfeo, who sings his little triumph aria (with those violins). Then comes the beginning of his doubt, straight out of his aria. He talks himself into mistrusting Plutone ('Ma che temi mio core? / Ciò che vieta Pluton comanda Amore') when there is a dreadful noise offstage ('Qui si fa strepito dietro la tela', p. 125). He begins to panic ('Ma che odo?'); but Monteverdi tells us still to use the harpsichord and chitarrone sound ('Clavicembano, Viola da braccio, & Chittarone'). As a result of his panic, Orfeo turns to look at Euridice, and accompanied by one organ ('al suono del Organo di legno') he begins to sing to her. But she vanishes ('Ma qual Eclissi, ohimè, v'oscura?'), and the more abrasive harpsichord–chitarrone sounds return. So his one, abbreviated line of passion and tenderness was accompanied by three chords on the organ. Again, Monteverdi supplied the perfect contrasts for the pivotal moment.

It follows, then, that the task of the editor in deploying his vast continuo forces is to follow Monteverdi's lead and to use them in such a way as to give maximum variety and, therefore, dramatic impetus to the text. Each 'speech' should be in contrast to its predecessor and its successor. This applies also in strophic arias, such as the proclamations of La Musica in the prologue. Often, using colours from the text as indications of the sounds to be added (for example a harp for La Musica's third stanza, 'Io su Cetera d'or', p. 5), there is ample scope in the range of continuo instruments to give each stanza a colour and a texture of its own.

The most difficult and challenging section of the opera, for purposes of allocating continuo instruments, is Orfeo's long soliloquy from the opening of Act V to the entry of Apollo. (After this, the dialogue effect makes the task more straightforward.) In fact Orfeo's speech falls into five clear sections.[7] The first (p. 138) states his return to the 'campi di Tracia', which shared his grief before he left. The second, beginning 'Voi vi doleste o monti' (p. 139), is an echo section, in which the pastoral surroundings echo his lamenting. The third and fourth sections, respectively beginning 'Ma tu, anima mia' (p. 142) and 'Tu bella fusti' (p. 142), are contrasted passages (the latter more measured than the former) addressed to Euridice's shade. In the final section, beginning 'Hor l'altre donne son superbe e perfide' (p. 143), Orfeo vows never to look at another woman. With such defined and contrasted subject-matter, it is perfectly possible to treat the sections as strophes, rather like those of La Musica's prologue or of Orfeo's own strophic aria 'Vi ricorda o bosch'ombrosi', and to allocate contrasting continuo groups accordingly. (The echoes in the second section provide an agreeable opportunity for delicate editorial manipulation.)

Vocal scoring

Monteverdi's list of *Personaggi*, printed with that of the *Stromenti* at the beginning of the score, is as follows:

> La Musica Prologo
> Orfeo
> Euridice
> Choro di Ninfe, e Pastori
> Speranza
> Caronte
> Choro di Spiriti infernali
> Proserpina
> Plutone
> Apollo
> Choro de Pastori che fecero la moresca nel fine.

Leaving aside for the moment the matter of the choruses (and the perhaps confusing indication that there are three of them), there seem to be eight principal singers. Of these, the most important, clearly, are Orfeo himself, a high baritone or low tenor (Signor Francesco Rasi, the original Orfeo, was a singer of exceptional range and extraordinarily deft coloratura: see above, pp. 5–6); Euridice, a gentle soprano; and Caronte, a deep bass. The remaining named principals, La Musica, Speranza, Proserpina, Plutone, and Apollo, can only be considered in the context of the other solo parts which are not listed, but whose music is often substantial and vitally important. The most obvious of these is the Messenger in Act II, and in addition to her there are various nymphs and shepherds in Acts I and II, and spirits in Act IV. The main editorial problem with regard to vocal scoring, then, lies in the logical yet economical distribution of these various unlisted roles.

One solution is to view the whole opera as an ensemble work, in which all the singers apart from Orfeo and Euridice come from the chorus.[8] If this is to be done, then clearly the members of the chorus must be hand-picked, and each one a potential soloist. This may present its own problems, either of impracticability in an established company where the chorus is fixed, or in the difficulty of blending these hand-picked soloists into a homogeneous ensemble for the choruses themselves. Once these problems are overcome or avoided, the solution works well. It may, however, be noted that in the preface to his opera *Dafne* (1608) Gagliano stated first that the chorus should be 'formed of not fewer than sixteen or eighteen people', and later that 'in the following scene, as in all the others, the soloists must not be confused with members of the chorus'.[9] An alternative solution, therefore, is to divide the many minor roles, named and unnamed, among a small number of principal singers.

The first obvious doubling is that of La Musica in the prologue with Speranza in Act III. Their dramatic function is similar in each case. Then the nymph in Act I, who sings a solo on p. 12 and in a trio on p. 34, can also play the Messenger in Act II.[10] This is highly logical, as the Messenger Silvia is reported by one of the shepherds to be the 'dolcissima compagna della bell'Euridice' (p. 57). This same singer can then with ease go on to play Proserpina in Act IV. From all the music labelled simply for shepherds, there seem to emerge two important roles, one tenor and one baritone, and one slightly less important, an alto. The tenor and baritone shepherds, who carry much of the first and second acts, can easily double Apollo (Act V) and Plutone (Act IV) respectively. This leaves four small parts: the third (alto) shepherd in Acts I and II, and the three spirits (two tenors and bass) in Act IV. These last four roles can be taken by members of the chorus.

So, labelling the two solo shepherds Pastore I (tenor) and Pastore II (baritone), and the chorus shepherd (alto) Pastore III, the logical breakdown and distribution of all the unlisted roles in Acts I and II of *Orfeo* is as follows:

Act I	p. 9	'In questo lieto e fortunato giorno'	Pastore II
	p. 12	'Muse honor di Parnasso'	Nymph (Silvia)

	p. 19	'Ma tu gentil cantor'	Pastore III
	p. 30	'Ma s'il nostro gioir'	Pastore I
	p. 32[11]	'Alcun non sia'	Pastori I and II
	p. 34	'Che poi che nembo'	Silvia, Pastori III and II
	p. 37	'E dopo l'aspro gel'	Pastori III and I
Act II	p. 42	'Mira ch'a se n'alletta'	Pastore I
	p. 44	'In questo prato adorno'	Pastori I and II
	p. 46	'Qui le Napee vezzose'	Pastori I and II
	p. 56	'Mira, deh mira Orfeo'	Pastore I
	p. 57	'Qual suon dolente'	Pastore I
	p. 57	'Questa e Silvia'	Pastore III
	p. 61	'Ahi caso acerbo'	Pastore I
	p. 62	'A l'amara novella'	Pastore II
	p. 68	'Chi ne consola ahi lassi?'	Pastori I and II
	p. 71	'Ma dove, ah dove?'	Pastori I and II.

Finally, in considering problems of vocal scoring, there is the chorus. Monteverdi lists three separate choruses in his list of *Personaggi*: 'Choro di Ninfe, e Pastori', 'Choro di Spiriti infernali', and 'Choro de Pastori che fecero la moresca nel fine'. The same people are clearly involved in all three, and Monteverdi's distinction among them merely indicates the different dramatic roles they play at different stages of the opera, and therefore the different functions they serve. The 'Choro di Spiriti infernali' is, however, scored differently from the 'Choro di Ninfe, e Pastori'. The nymphs and shepherds in Acts I, II and V are straightforwardly scored for two sopranos (the second of whom explores a lower register), alto, tenor and bass, while the infernal spirits in Acts III and IV are for three tenors, baritone and bass. Remembering that Gagliano, in his preface to *Dafne*, said that he would prefer a chorus of at least sixteen to eighteen people, a total of four voices per part in the pastoral choruses works well. This leaves a certain flexibility for vocal distribution in the infernal choruses. The altos should all sing the top line (and even some plucky sopranos in our experience), all the tenors should sing the second line, and the remaining lines can be divided evenly between the baritones and basses. This gives, as Monteverdi intended, a rich, sonorous texture, matching the trombone accompaniment and the general darkness of the setting.

Minor editorial adjustments

In addition to carrying out the above editorial practices, many of which simply involve following Monteverdi's example, some further adjustments are needed to clarify the score in performance. First, it is occasionally necessary to stiffen the bass line by the addition of a double bass, at 16-foot pitch, when the music moves in definitely measured sections. An example of this is Orfeo's very first speech in Act I, 'Rosa del ciel' (p. 20). It begins on a long opening pedal; but as he describes his own exquisite joy at his marriage to Euridice, the bass line moves. And the addition here of a double bass emphasises the transition into measured music and eases the flow. Another poignant example is in the heart-rending refrain 'Rendetemi il mio ben' in Act III (pp. 102 and 105). As it is a refrain, a stronger bass line supports its aural recognition.

Secondly, there is the question of re-barring. The original barring, based on the limited conventions of the time (C, 3/2 etc.), does occasionally produce misleading results which it is the duty of the editor to clarify. The inflections and metrical stresses of the text constantly supply the true rhythmic proportions. A protracted section at the beginning of Act II is a good illustration. Orfeo's 'Ecco pur' (p. 41), barred in 4/2, is actually in 3/2 and begins on the upbeat: Ex. 1. Thus its preceding sinfonia (p. 39) is similarly in 3/2 beginning on the upbeat, and the ritornello and solo for Pastore I which follow are in 4/2 beginning on the upbeat: Ex. 2. Then the ritornello, p. 43, is in 6/4, beginning on the upbeat; and the music returns to 4/2 at the ritornello following the shepherds' duet (p. 45). With the use of such editorial practice, the whole flow of the music now looks as smooth and logical as it in fact sounds, and any initial confusion is removed.[12] There are, in addition, a number of less dramatic places where it is simpler to divide 4/2 bars into 4/4 for greater control. The aria 'Qual honor' in Act IV (p. 121) is an obvious example of this, as are the ritornello and chorus 'Vanne Orfeo' in Act V (p. 150).

The third minor adjustment that an editor might make is the occasional reorganisation of the bass line to interpret the text. By

Ex. 1

old barring   new barring

Ex. 2

the removing of ties and the reiteration of chords, a line may be given greater point, even in the least measured music. The opening of Orfeo's 'Rosa del ciel' (p. 20), for example, consists of six 4/2 bars on a pedal G. The occasional repetition of the chord under certain crucial words aerates the passage in a delicate, unobtrusive manner: Ex. 3. When the opera is being performed in translation, of course, the chord reiteration would be slightly different: Ex. 4.[13]

Finally, there is the question of the adjustment of accidentals. Occasionally these have been omitted in one or other of the seventeenth-century printed versions. Checking one against the other does yield some clarifications. A case in point is the ritornello following the Act I chorus 'Lasciate i monti' (p. 17). In the second bar there is an F on the fifth crotchet, which corresponds to that in the ninth bar of the same ritornello. The 1615 edition prints the F in bar 9 as F sharp, which implies that the F in the second bar should likewise be sharpened. Otherwise it is safe to apply the usual procedures: sharps in rising passages, naturals in falling passages. Thus the final *moresca*, for example (p. 153), should include the following adjustments: bar 3 (violin 2) F sharp; bar 11 (violin 2) F sharp, G sharp; bar 15 (violin 2) B natural, C sharp; bar 15 (bass line) C natural, B flat.

Ex. 3

Ex. 4

Rehearsal-room procedures

The remaining problems in editing *Orfeo* for performance are all solved in the second stage of preparation, that is in the rehearsal room. For it is only here, where there is a working relationship among the performers, that the final subtleties can be achieved. Thus the 'realisation' of the continuo parts and their relationship to the singers, questions of dynamics, ornamentation, tempo and tempo-relationships are all matters on which agreement is reached on a collective basis.

One of the most substantial questions is the extent of the freedom in apparently unmeasured music. Like all Italian composers of this period, Monteverdi simply gave common-time signatures at the beginning of a passage, and the interpreter must follow the inflections of the speech rhythms to liberate the stresses of the text. In general, then, the music is fairly free but always observant of an inherent measured tactus ('pulse' rather than 'beat' in this context).[14] With composers of the generation after Monteverdi, such as Cavalli or Cesti, much of the recitative is very free indeed; and to perform this it is often necessary to ignore the note values completely. A singer should simply learn the text as an actor does, and then 'recite' it within the melodic and harmonic framework supplied by the composers. But with Monteverdi it is essential that the inherent tactus should prevail, for he was so skilful a word-setter that to deviate from his inner rhythmic impulse is often to dismantle the metrical values of the text. Furthermore, a basic adherence to the measured tactus exploits the full effect of the most extraordinary chromatic moments. Passages such as Euridice's 'Ahi vista troppo dolce' in Act IV (p. 126), or Orfeo's ensuing 'Dove t'en vai?' (p. 127) can sound merely wayward if taken too freely. When sung in tempo, the heart-rending harmonies are all the more poignant.

But there are some occasions where, always for dramatic reasons, the fracture of this fundamental rhythm is implicit. The most striking example is in the exchange between Orfeo and the Messenger in Act II (pp. 58–9). Orfeo's agitated series of questions – 'D'onde vieni? ove vai? Ninfa che porti?' – contains an in-built *accelerando* which must be observed. The tempo is re-established as the Messenger continues; is broken again as Orfeo breaks in with 'Ohimè, che odo?' (the devastating harmonic shift emphasising the rhythmic interruption); and gradually unwinds as she spells out his loss ('La tua diletta sposa è morta'), and he accepts it ('Ohimè').

After a very significant semibreve rest, the Messenger continues with her desolate narrative.

With regard to tempos and their relationships in measured music, it is reasonable to conclude that most tempos do flow easily into each other, even when the time-signature implies a new beginning. A handful of examples will illustrate this, of which the first is the very opening of the opera. The whole of the prologue and its enfolding D minor ritornello leads smoothly into Pastore II's 'In questo lieto e fortunato giorno' (p. 9) and then into the chorus 'Vieni Imeneo'. This does not sound monotonous, merely logical. At the next chorus, 'Lasciate i monti' (p. 14), the balletto-type mood implies a quicker tempo, but again the various sections of the chorus and its ritornello are related. Thus the relationship is old ♩ = new ♪ where the 4/2 section goes into the 6/4 section, and ♩ = ♩ where the ritornello begins. In Act II, the relationship between Pastore I's little strophic aria 'Mira ch'a se n'alletta' (p. 42) and the ritornello which follows (p. 43, before the duet) is ♩ = ♩. ; and, conversely, the relationship is ♩. = ♩ from the duet into the recorder ritornello (p. 45). Thus with the re-barring referred to above, Ex. 5 becomes Ex. 6.

Another crucial passage where the tempos are related is in the general festive music of Act II before the entry of the Messenger. The last strophe of Orfeo's aria 'Vi ricorda' must be related to Pastore I's 'Mira, deh mira Orfeo' which follows it (pp. 55–6) in order to maintain the musico-dramatic impetus which the Messenger destroys: old ♩ = new ♪ makes this connection successfully.

Finally, there are the questions of vocal ornamentation and continuo realisation, considered here together in that both must always sound spontaneous and immediate, however much careful discussion and deliberation has gone into them. In general, vocal lines should not be greatly embellished, partly because nothing must detract from the deliberately virtuoso nature of the central aria 'Possente spirto' in Act III, and partly because they simply do not require it. But countless cadential closes do call for some decoration, such as the two identical 'nostri concenti' cadences in the very opening of Act I (pp. 9 and 10). When seeking for a guide to cadential ornamentation, of course, an editor and his singers need only turn to 'Possente spirto'. It is a remarkable compendium of contemporary techniques and virtuoso displays, and the presence of its unornamented version (lest a potential performer be deterred by the heavy demands of the fuller version) makes it additionally a

Ex. 5

Ex. 6

virtual demonstration-case of how to ornament particular progressions and cadences. Until a singer is well versed in the general style, it is perhaps advisable for him to learn a number of separate formulae, which can be applied at will to cadences as they occur. But the spirit of spontaneity must remain. Once an ornament has become too firmly glued to its cadence, it not only sounds ponderous and studied, but also serves only to obscure the very façade that it seeks to embellish.

As to the realisation of continuo parts, no editor should ever impose rigid, immalleable ideas on his players. Various basic principles may be stated and encouraged, such as the necessity for continuo instruments to be supportive but unobtrusive, and to achieve this by variety of rhythm and texture rather than by melodic invention. Beyond that, any editorial dictation is an affront to the players, and a damper on the spontaneous flow of the music.

Orfeo is undoubtedly a masterpiece. This is astonishing, coming as early as it does in the history of opera. Musical masterpieces are difficult to ruin, but they can be transformed into something other than their composers intended, by the application of inappropriate interpretative methods. But by following the performance practices implicit in Monteverdi's own instructions, *Orfeo* can be re-created in a manner close to that of its original performance, and so delight modern audiences as it did those of the early seventeenth century.

9 Telling the story

DAVID FREEMAN

There are two great Western traditions of religious drama, the Greek and the medieval. The works that belong to these traditions are religious not only because religious/mythological themes are discussed, but also because the social context of their original presentation depended for its significance upon a series of beliefs shared by performers and audience. A largely homogeneous audience was common to both these traditions, which lent to even the much more sophisticated Greek works a certain quality of folk theatre or festival, so that the social significance of their presentation was essentially different from that of being entertained in the theatre: it was a type of mystery or initiation.

Monteverdi and Striggio, it seems to me, penetrated to something of this quality of mystery, of religious festival drama, in *Orfeo*; but it is very hard to say just why that should be so. Perhaps it was because they were both in a sense amateurs: the genre 'opera' had not yet been invented and they were both experimenting in their 'favola in musica' against a background of only ten years of precedents. Perhaps it was also because the attempts of the humanists to recreate Greek tragedy was born of an idealism and enthusiasm for Greek mythology, philosophy and forms which, for a brief period in history, created a climate in which religious drama could be written. Certainly, although *Orfeo* was written for the Mantuan court, it is not its origins as a Renaissance courtly entertainment that give the work its stamp, but rather the rigour, economy and lack of sentimentality of the humanists' view of the Greek world. For a brief moment Greek values and figures live again with the directness of their fifth-century models. One need only compare *Orfeo* with Monteverdi's other surviving treatment of a Greek theme, *Il ritorno d'Ulisse in patria*, for that to be apparent. A comparison with the other great treatment of the Orpheus myth in operatic literature, Gluck's *Orfeo*, makes the difference even

156

clearer, for here we have a neoclassical work discussing religious/ mythological themes in a secular theatrical context.

One of the major problems in presenting a religious drama, and especially a Greek tragedy, is to find a social context for it which can have some validity today. The brilliance of Pasolini's *Edipo Re*, for instance, seems to me to lie in the transference of the Oedipus myth from its urbane fifth-century context to a much more primitive and superstitious society in which blood feuds and oracles seem natural. The classical Greek context, by virtue of the fact that it has meant classical style ever since the Renaissance, has ceased to be a genuine social context for anything. The figures we associate with classical Greece – the figures on the vases – are not people, but idealisations; useful, perhaps, for a neoclassical, idealised view of Greek tragedy, but not for a religious drama requiring a social context which allows for human weakness, not just heroic flaws. The great classical tragedies and their themes are frequently discussed, but rarely performed, a fact which points to the difficulty of finding a valid context for their presentation today.

Having rejected the Mantuan and classical Greek contexts, the association I finally attempted to make in my own production of *Orfeo* was with Oberammergau. The performers were to be members of a close-knit peasant society which, by its nature, is comparatively unchanging and therefore timeless. They wore clothes that were a mixture of ethnic and Western elements (see Fig. 9), the sort of clothes that one might conceivably see worn by peasants somewhere between Turkey and Afghanistan: a man wearing a Western suit coat with a traditional shirt and a turban, perhaps. Clothes, not costumes: all consisted of elements which could be found in London today, so that the distancing, calming effect of stage costumes would be lost to the audience.

This near naivety of presentation was also emphasised in the setting: the theatre. Any attempt to pretend that we were not in a theatre, to build up the illusion of a peasant village in more detail, would also have had a distancing, lulling effect. There was to be no realism, but the tangibility of realism; no peasant village to escape into, merely some elements of peasant life brought into a theatre. A theatre remains doggedly a theatre, no matter what the window-dressing: very real, but also capable of being anything. The real situation consisted of an audience coming to see a performance of *Orfeo*, a religious drama which they would have to accept as taking place in the theatre before them, not a magical mystery tour into another world. The audience would have to decide whether or not they would partake of this other kind of mystery, but they could not do anything else with it; only acceptance or rejection should be possible.

In creating this mythical village, all the performers developed characters within the context of the village, functions which they would fulfil when not playing the story of Orpheus: widow, tavern-keeper, shepherd. Not only did this give consequence to their actions in the acts on earth, it also emphasised the ritual quality of the piece. They were not really Orpheus and Eurydice, they were peasants enacting the myth of Orpheus and Eurydice. But, as happens in Kazantzakis's *Christ recrucified*, the peasants identify increasingly with their roles until they are taken over by them. A ritual has inevitability; something happening for the first time is unpredictable. The peasant playing Orpheus has prepared himself for the task; he has been chosen to do so. At the beginning, the others sympathise with the ordeal he will have to go through, to put himself through. He elects to play Orpheus, rather like Christ submitting to his father's will in going to Calvary.

To emphasise this ritual quality, the whole story was acted out in miniature during the ritornellos of the prologue. It was all there: the wedding, the messenger's tale, crossing the Styx, the second loss of Eurydice in Hades, the ascent to heaven with Apollo. It was like the argument of a seventeenth-century poem. It was also a way of telling the story, just as the opera itself is a way of telling the story, a story that has been told many times before, and will be again. And because it was a ritual and not a reality, or, rather, because it had the reality of a ritual and not the reality of everyday life, it was possible at the end for all to reassume the role of the peasants who put on the story and to dance the celebratory *moresca*. Even Orpheus and Apollo, who have gone to heaven, join in because it was all theatre. And because it was all theatre, a ritual, the question of why a peasant society should put on the story of Orpheus is irrelevant. Why should a Greek hero sing seventeenth-century Italian music? More important, why should we still be listening?

Ultimately, when we get beyond all the intellectual explanations and fabrications, the discussions about greatness and significance, we are still listening because the piece still seems to have something to say to us; it still moves us. But even this invests the whole idea with a type of bogus objectivity. We listen because we want to; not a very impressive intellectual construct, but all the intellectual constructs remain descriptions of that fact.

So far, I have described some of the problems involved in staging *Orfeo*. I have not offered an interpretation of the 'meaning' of the piece. Trying to suggest what a great work of art means seems to me as elusive and pointless a task as trying to decide what it is that makes the work so great. Not only do I not know what *Orfeo* means, I do not even know what my staging of it means. Nor do I wish to know. My staging of the piece was not an interpretation; it was an attempt to tell the story in as allusive, tangible, ambivalent and unsentimental a way as possible. The version that I produced in 1981 found certain solutions (and failed to find some). When I restaged the work in 1983 I found in some cases quite different solutions. In 1981, all the performers worked very closely with the designers choosing clothes suitable for their characters. In 1983 the clothes, though in the same style, were different because many of the performers were different. Every article of clothing a person wore had been individually considered and chosen by him, and that process formed an integral part of character development for the performers. In 1981 there was one singer per role; in 1983 certain doublings were made. I mention all this in order to emphasise the very practical nature of staging a work and the uniqueness of any live performance situation, which is dependent as much on performer and audience as on the script. And I use the word 'script' deliberately, because although it is quite possible to consider *Orfeo* as music or literature, if one is to have any but an obsequious relationship to it in a theatrical context, the piece must remain at some level a script. So, having robbed myself of the possibility of offering an interpretation of the meaning of *Orfeo*, but not wishing merely to give you a description of my staging (which is better seen), let me offer a few more problems and, in some cases, hesitant solutions.

There are two main characters in *Orfeo*: Orpheus and the Chorus. With a chorus there are two basic alternatives: to generalise or to individualise. The first is most useful for the chorus as commentator, the second for the chorus as participant. In *Orfeo* the chorus participates on earth, and comments at the end of the Hades scenes in a moralising way. A generalised chorus requires not only unity of musical and dramatic statement, but also unity of gesture and movement, in order to create a sense of collective choric identity. This was achieved at the ends of Acts III and IV by their simply dropping their roles in the drama and addressing the audience in a line, without moving. In the acts on earth, individualisation of the chorus was based upon the depiction of the peasant village. This had the advantage of creating much longer dramatic movements than are at first apparent, especially in Acts I and II. As the piece is written many characters appear only once; but the creation of the peasant characters could be followed from beginning to end.

Orpheus himself presents a different problem. He is the greatest of singers, yet this is something of a paradox in a work in which everyone sings. In the classical accounts, Orpheus appears closer to the concept of the poet–singer, the seer who spoke for his times, rather than the opera singer. It was not the prettiness of his voice, but the extent of his suffering and his ability to express the knowledge that suffering lent him which made him the singer. He was one of the Argonauts, and the quest for the Golden Fleece took place before he met Eurydice. He was no callow youth, but a seasoned hero, albeit untypical since his strength lay in music rather than muscle. He wrote his own songs: more Mick Jagger than Montserrat Caballé. In a peasant village he need not, perhaps should not, be glamorous.

The basic structural units of Acts I and II are very short – madrigalian choruses and ensembles, ritornellos, brief solos – though Monteverdi and Striggio use repetition to create larger structures. One way of unifying these two acts in 1981 was by use of character; another was through the use of dance. All the dances were simple folk dances: folk dances, that is, in the sense that each told a simple story. For example, in the ritornello after 'Ma se 'l nostro gioir dal ciel deriva' Orpheus acted out his first search for Eurydice, for, fascinatingly, despite his great skill as a singer she was at first not interested in him. The ritornello is played three times. During the first playing Orpheus reached out for Eurydice, but could not make contact and retired in confusion. The second time, two of the peasants played the male/female roles in the dance, and they successfully reached out to touch each other. This was a dance of coming together, a way of seeing what leads up to the marriage. The two peasants who showed Orpheus and Eurydice how to come together were later to take the roles of Proserpine, who pleads for Orpheus and Eurydice to come together again, and Pluto, who ultimately expels Orpheus from the Underworld. During the third playing of the ritornello, Orpheus and Eurydice, and the future

Pluto and Proserpine, danced in parallel. Proserpine sympathises with Eurydice's fate: it is not unlike her own. The duets and trio which come between these dances are also about the initial rejection and ultimate acceptance of Orpheus by Eurydice. The message, as at the ends of Acts III and IV, concerns steadfastness. It is said three times, using three examples: the personal despair of Orpheus which, as we know, gave way to eventual happiness and resolution in marriage; the terror of a storm which gives way to sunshine; the frost of winter which gives way to the flowers of spring.

A further way of creating longer dramatic movements was achieved by dividing the first two acts up into four large dramatic actions, the first three those of predictable ritual, wedding and prayer, and celebration, the fourth the unexpected catastrophe. The timing of the catastrophe, which interrupts the contentment and optimism of 'Mira, deh mira Orfeo' rather than the more obvious climax of Orpheus's 'Vi ricorda o bosch'ombrosi', points to the human scale of events. Monteverdi and Striggio are not just interested in an emotional bloodbath. It is, finally, much more complex for the Sword of Damocles to fall when we are enjoying life than when we are exulting in it. There is more room for human weakness. The scene can have an almost comical quality which leads to a far greater poignancy and emotional complexity.

After declaring that he will go to the Underworld, Orpheus collapsed and was carried upstage, beyond the acting area, covered with clothes, waiting, in a sense, to be buried. The society, the village, loses not only Eurydice but also Orpheus, through his decision to go to the Underworld. Perhaps Orpheus stays unconscious and dreams the journey to Hades. Perhaps the only way for him to reach the Underworld is to undergo a ritual burial. We never know, for in Act III he is already approaching the Styx, and when Act V begins he is in the same prostrate, unconscious position.

In Act V, when Orpheus awakes (or returns to earth), he appeals to nature to lament the loss of Eurydice with him. He has no regrets about his conduct in the Underworld. There is no self-blame for turning around. He has been involved in a ritualised quest and the result was pre-determined. He has no awareness that he might have altered the course of events. The echo is Nature's response: the inanimate being so moved by Orpheus's suffering that it cannot remain silent. He cannot be consoled, though there is something faintly ludicrous when he berates the echo for giving him back only the second half of each sentence. Orpheus's capacity for self-irony and his complete lack of self-recrimination about events in the Underworld again point to the human scale of the tragedy. There is no heroic moralising or bombast. Indeed, it is the very human scale of events before and after the death of Eurydice which lends an heroic quality to Orpheus's attempts to win her back from the Underworld. A hero behaving heroically is merely behaving according to pattern; but for a human to overcome his fear and insecurity is far more complex and moving. This suggests another most important advantage in playing the work in the context of some sort of society – the possibility of humour in a basically tragic work. If all is tragic, then the tragic becomes commonplace.

After the echo lament Orpheus lapses into a reverie about Eurydice. In a sense he is now thinking about the past, since Eurydice is dead. One interpretation of Orpheus's turning around to see Eurydice in Hades is that it represents a corruption, a crude dramatic version of the idea that he must not let the past that she represents come between himself and the future. If he succeeds in getting out of Hades, he must love a new Eurydice, not the old one who is dead, just as in any relationship the person one knew yester-day is in a sense dead, and one can only effectively relate to the per-son one now sees. It is not the act of turning around, not a childish condition imposed by a spiteful Pluto, which leads to Orpheus's downfall; and Orpheus's weakness is not just a question of curiosity or lack of steadfastness, as with Elsa in *Lohengrin*. It is a question of man's place in time.

By dreaming of the past in Act V, then, Orpheus is making the same mistake a second time, and it leads him to reject all other women. At this point the classical sources give various elaborations of the end of the myth: that the women rejected by Orpheus became so incensed that they tore him limb from limb like Pentheus; that his head floated down a river singing and landed on an island where it became an oracle which rivalled Apollo's own Delphic Oracle, causing Apollo finally to silence his own son's song. There is even some suggestion that Orpheus may have taken up with boys. Orpheus began his lament in a desert. So eloquent was his com-plaint that animals and even trees and rocks came to listen, trans-forming the desert into a paradise. The text of the opera implies some of this, and even where it does not the Mantuan audience would have understood the background, since most educated people knew, often by heart, the accounts in Virgil and Ovid.

The ending which appears in Monteverdi's score circumvents the tragedy. The dangers are there to be perceived, both philosophical, in Orpheus's dwelling in the past, and actual, by his rejection of women and the possibility of their revenge if the ritual were to be played out in the usual way. One may speculate why the tragic ending is averted; one may refer to contemporary conventions. But it does not really matter. The question is how to avert the feeling that the end of the opera is not an adequate response to the vitality of the opening, the tragedy of the Messenger scene, or the epic solemnity of the Underworld acts. For this, it seems to me necessary, first, that the events of the first half of Act V concerning Orpheus's lamenting should have some sort of reality, so that one is not just confronted by a static if beautiful lyric about how sad and plaintive it is to be Orpheus without Eurydice. We need to suggest, rather, that the action is continuing, that Orpheus's song in sorrow is just as dynamic as in any other situation, that the situation is indeed becoming increasingly dangerous for Orpheus, so that Apollo's intervention is not merely dénouement, but necessity. The second dramaturgical necessity is that Apollo should not be a sudden apparition whom we see for the first time in Act V. This would reduce him to the status of an invented god, a conventional trick to resolve the piece. This could never be anything but unsatisfying artistically, emotionally and formally. My solution was to have Apollo appear in the first act during 'Rosa del Ciel', so that his intervention in the final act could have something of the effect of a successful *da capo* – inevitable, spontaneous and surprising at the same time. Not an artificial ending, but a coming full circle. This solution also satisfies one of the aspects of the myth which Monteverdi and Striggio did not elucidate, but also did not contradict – Apollo's relationship to his son Orpheus. Apollo gave the gift of music to Orpheus and finally silences him, or, in this case, removes him to another sphere.

I have left Acts III and IV until last because it seems to me that the problems they pose in terms of staging require radically different solutions from those of the acts on earth, though I am not sure about this and may well seek other solutions when restaging the work. Certainly the danger of finding a very different theatrical context for the Underworld scenes is that the work will split into two; but on the other hand the music is very different, the structures tend to be longer (especially in Act III), and the nature of the action is different too.

Orpheus needs opposition. If there is no significant opposition, the significance of his heroic attempt is diminished. The only real opposition that he meets in Striggio's text is from Charon, and even the nature of that confrontation is undercut in a deliberately ironic way. Orpheus sings his most extended aria, 'Possente spirto', in order that Charon will acquiesce and let him pass; but the song is a failure, and only after rejecting Orpheus's plea does Charon fall asleep.

Fortunately, the Greeks had very specific views on what Hades was like and it is this very tangible place that we tried to create on stage, using particularly the descriptions of Virgil and Dante. For though Dante's is a Christian hell, it is obviously modelled on that of Virgil, and it was impossible for Striggio and Monteverdi, as Italians writing in 1607, to do so without a knowledge of the *Inferno*. There is, indeed, even the direct quotation by Speranza in Act III: 'Lasciate ogni speranza voi ch'entrate'.

So, in order to make Orpheus's task difficult enough, and also to continue the idea of a mystery play in which the village took part communally, the chorus remained on stage during these two acts. In Act III they played souls who had not been buried properly, and therefore had to wait a hundred years on the banks of the Styx before they could be taken across by Charon, and Orpheus had to fight his way through them. In Act IV they played souls in torment, based upon some of the specific information we have about how such figures as Tantalus and Sisyphus were punished. Each soul had to perform some insoluble task, repeatedly, into eternity: the task itself based upon the crime he had committed.

Orpheus physically calmed each spirit, rather like a laying on of hands, in Act IV, before the chorus 'Pietade oggi', which consequently became a chorus of participation rather than of comment. This helped solve another problem. We never hear the song with which Orpheus persuades Proserpine to intercede for him and gain Pluto's permission for Eurydice's release; it is only during 'Possente spirto' in Act III that Orpheus moves the Underworld, when he is (strictly speaking) not even in Hades. This makes it very important to link the two acts as closely as possible so that, in a sense, the emotional effect of 'Possente spirto' can carry over into Act IV; but the 'laying on of hands' also added to the struggle that Orpheus had in winning back Eurydice. The victory must be earned.

In such a classical view of the Underworld, just what the naked spirits should wear presents a problem. It seemed to me that if the villagers stayed in their village costumes a necessary abstraction and freedom or beauty of movement would not be possible. But I am not sure that the idea of their wearing the rags of clothes they might once have worn on earth was the best solution. It certainly allowed for a type of sensuality, which is very important, for however terrible the Underworld of Dante or Virgil may be, it is a terrible beauty. But it did lead to a break with unity which disturbed some people. In another way, too, it was a risky option. At its best it led to a genuine confrontation between Orpheus and the Underworld and it was a way of allowing terror to happen on stage. I say 'allow' because terror is usually an involuntary reaction, not something one can act as a performer. It is something one can only set up and allow to happen. But of course in less successful performances that is exactly what happened: there was an acted torment. Of course, one could accept the idea that acting in opera should be merely representational: music with illustrations, rather like a book with illustrations. Then one is left with a pantomime along the lines of what often happens in the last scene of Verdi's *Falstaff*, in the 'Pizzica, pizzica' section. But clearly we were seeking something else, something very difficult to achieve, so that there was a considerable difference from one performance to another. We were seeking an understanding of violence and death from which many of us, especially in more polite circles, are protected today, but which was part of everyday life in 1607. Striggio himself died during an epidemic of plague which claimed one in four of the population of Venice in 1630. But what would the atmosphere of London be like today if one in four of its population was dying of an incurable disease?

I mention all this, which may appear to be a long way from an interpretation of *Orfeo*, because in practice I find it is not. The whole process of putting on an opera, and of writing one for that matter, is a series of solutions at a particular time and place, under particular circumstances, which makes one come to question the whole idea of a universal work of art in any sphere. When we call a work of art 'universal', we mean that we still appreciate it today; how needlessly grandiose! In that sense, *Orfeo* was not nearly as universal in 1607 as it is today, and a hundred years ago it had no universality whatever.

I do not wish at all to denigrate Monteverdi's and Striggio's creation. In a romantic frame of mind I am as likely to call the work 'universal' as anyone else. The work is important, but it is not more important than the people who perform and watch it. It is actually a tool through which they can communicate with each other at a level, and about issues, with which the normal run of conversation, body language and social ritual cannot cope. If it becomes an object of worship, it quickly and easily becomes a form of cultural escapism. The transience inherent in any work of art is even more marked in a particular production of a work performed in the vernacular. Hence the impossibility of my giving you an interpretation of what *Orfeo* means.

One last example. In 1981 Hope (La Speranza) was played by a singer who otherwise performed as chorus, as did everyone else. In 1983, for a variety of reasons, there were a number of doublings of roles. Hope was played by the singer who performed Eurydice as well as a choral role. When Orpheus is advised that he must abandon hope, what does that mean? Surely his hope is to recover Eurydice. He must put himself in the hands of fate and accept what comes; to hope to recover her would be presumptuous. He may plead for her, but not hope. He abandons his old vision of Eurydice. When he turns to see her he is clinging to that vision again: he hopes again too soon. Can such an idea be right or wrong? I think it can only work or not work. It is a way of telling the story.

Correspondence relating to the early Mantuan performances

IAIN FENLON

The letters that follow (including those previously cited by other authors) are newly transcribed from originals in the Archivio di Stato, Florence (Archivio Mediceo) – ASF (AM) – and the Archivio di Stato, Mantua (Archivio Gonzaga) – ASM (AG). Original spelling, punctuation and use of accents are retained; abbreviations are realised except in forms of address.

I am grateful to the staffs of the two archives for their assistance. Steven Botterill of Queens' College, Cambridge, has provided the English translations of the letters.

1. ASM (AG) 2162. Letter of Francesco Gonzaga, Mantua 5 January 1607, to Ferdinando Gonzaga in Pisa

. . . Io ho determinato di far recitare una favola in Musica questo Carnevale, ma perche quì habbiamo pochi soprani, e poco buoni, vorrei che V.E. mi favorisse di farmi sapere se son costi certi castrati ch'Io sentii già quando fui in Toscana che servono il Gran Duca, i quali mi piacquero all'hora assai, che d'un di loro cioè di quello che V.E. giudicasse migliore havrei pensiero di valermi ogni volta ch'ella credesse, ch'il Gran Duca non fusse per negar di prestarlo per quindici di solamente quand'ella gliel dimandasse, mi avisi però V.E. di tutto questo ch'Io se mi risolverò di valermene lo scriverò a lei, perche mi favorisca presso il Gran Duca . . .

> . . . I have decided to have a play in music performed at Carnival this year, but as we have very few sopranos here, and those few not good, I should be grateful if Your Excellency would be kind enough to tell me if those castrati I heard when I was in Tuscany are still there. I mean the ones in the Grand Duke's service, whom I so much enjoyed hearing during my visit. My intention is to borrow one of them (whichever Your Excellency thinks the best), as long as you agree that the Grand Duke will not refuse to lend him, if you yourself do the asking, for a fortnight at most. Please will Your Excellency let me know about this, so that if I do decide to use one of these singers I can write to you asking for your support in my approach to the Grand Duke . . .

2. ASM (AG) 2162. Letter of Ferdinando Gonzaga, Pisa 14 January 1607, to Francesco Gonzaga in Mantua.

. . . Io conforme al commandamento di V.A. ho ritrovato un soprano castrato quale veramente non è di quelli che V.A. senti ma ha recitato due o tre volte cantando in comedie ottimammente questo e allievo di Giulio Romano [Giulio Caccini] e salariato del G. Duca . . .

167

. . . In accordance with Your Highness's orders I have engaged a castrato, who is, in fact, not one of those whom Your Highness heard; but he has performed with great success in musical plays on two or three occasions. He is a pupil of Giulio Romano [Giulio Caccini] and receives a stipend from the Grand Duke . . .

3. ASM (AG) 2162. letter of Francesco Gonzaga, Mantua 17 January 1607, to Ferdinando Gonzaga in Pisa.

. . . la qui congiunta lettera per il Gran Duca, nella quale Io lo prego a favorirmi di prestarmi uno de' suoi Castrati per questo Carnevale da valermene nella recitazione cantata d'una favola s'apparecchia nella nostra accademia, come altre volte le ho scritto. E perchè spero che S.A. per sua bontà non me 'l sia per negare affinche non si perda tempo con aspettar da lei la risposta, le mando la parte per il detto Castrato, acciochè la possa studiare e metterla ben à memoria in caso ch'il Gran Duca me 'l conceda, et al principio del mese, che viene potrà porsi in viaggio per questa volta pregando V.E. a volerlo proveder di danar per il bisogno del viaggio, che gliele farò buoni quì in qualche cosa di suo servizio . . .

> . . . Enclosed with this you will find a letter for the Grand Duke, in which I ask him to be so kind as to lend me one of his castrati for the coming Carnival, so that I can use him in the performance of a musical play which is currently being composed in our Academy. I have already written to you about this. Because I hope that His Highness will be good enough not to refuse my request, and in order not to waste time waiting for your reply, I am sending you the said castrato's part, so that he can study it and learn it thoroughly, should the Grand Duke lend him to me. He should be able to set out at the beginning of next month; on this occasion I must ask Your Excellency to give him some money to cover the expenses of his journey, which I will repay by being of service to you here in any way that I can . . .

4. ASM (AG) 2162. Letter of Francesco Gonzaga, Mantua 2 February 1607, to Ferdinando Gonzaga in Pisa.

. . . quando V.E. riceverà questa mia, il castrato, ch'Io desidero sarà giunto quà, ò almeno sarà in viaggio, . . . senza questo soprano non si potrebbe in modo veruno rappresentare [la favola].

> . . . By the time Your Excellency receives this, my much-needed castrato will have arrived here, or will at least be on his way . . . without this soprano it would be quite impossible to stage [the play] at all . . .

5. ASM (AG) 2162. Letter of Ferdinando Gonzaga, Pisa
5 February 1607, to Francesco Gonzaga in Mantua.

. . . L'essibitor di questa è Giovanni Gualberto giovine castrato ch'io mando à V.A.S. per servirsene nella rappresentatione della sua comedia. Lui stesso dirà à bocca la difficoltà che hà nell'imparar la parte che se glie data nella quale ne hà alla mente à quest'hora il Prologo, ma il restante non già perche ricerca troppo voci . . .

> . . . This is to introduce Giovanni Gualberto, a young castrato whom I am sending to your Highness to take part in the performance of your play. You will hear from his own lips of the difficulty he has had in learning the part which was given him; so far he has managed to commit only the prologue to memory, the rest proving impossible because it contains too many notes . . . [on the phrase 'troppo voci', see Chapter 1, note 26]

6. ASM (AG) 2162. Letter of Francesco Gonzaga, Mantua
9 February 1607, to Ferdinando Gonzaga in Pisa.

. . . Io mi credeva che a quest'hora dovesse esser qui il castrato, e veramente sarebbe necessario, che quanto prima venisse, poiche non solo haverà da dir la parte già mandatagli, ma gli bisognerà imparar quella di Proserpina per mancamento di chi l'haveva da rappresentare. Pero lo sto di giorno in giorno aspettando con gran desiderio che senza lui la favola andrebbe in nulla. V.E. intanto mi favorisca di ringraziar il Gran Duca della cortesia usatami, si come farò ancor Io con mia lettera al ritorno del Castrato costà . . .

> . . . I had expected that the castrato would have arrived by now, and indeed it is essential that he should be here as soon as possible. He will now have not only to play the part that was sent to him, but also to learn that of Proserpine, as the singer who was to take the role can no longer do so. So I am awaiting him from day to day with great eagerness, as without him the play would be a complete failure. Meanwhile, I must ask Your Excellency to thank the Grand Duke for the kindness he has shown me; I will thank him myself by letter when the castrato returns to you . . .

7. ASM (AG) 2162. Letter of Francesco Gonzaga, Mantua
16 February 1607, to Ferdinando Gonzaga in Pisa.

. . . Giunse hieri il Castrato . . . [lui] non sappia altro ch'il Prologo, poiche non dubitando che non haverà tempo d'imparar l'altra parte per questo Carnevale, nel qual caso mi bisognerebbe differir la rappresentazione della favola sine à questa Pasqua, questa mattina però hà incominciato a studiare, non solo la musica, ma le parole ancora, e pure se havesse imparata la parte con tutto che ricercasse troppo voci come dice V.E. saprebbe almeno l'aria, e la musica si sarebbe accomodata à suo dosso, et

hora non si spenderebbe tanto tempo in far ch'l havesse à imparar à
mente . . .

> . . . the castrato arrived yesterday . . . he knows only the prologue,
> and seems to think that he will not have time to learn the other
> part before the Carnival; in which case I shall have no choice but
> to postpone the performance of the play until Easter. This morn-
> ing, however, he began to study not only the music, but the words
> as well; and if he were able to learn the part (although it does con-
> tain too many notes [see Chapter 1, note 26], as Your Excellency
> says), he would at least know the melody, the music could be
> altered to suit his needs, and we would not waste so much time
> ensuring that he knows it all by heart . . .

**8. ASM (AG) 2709. Letter of Carlo Magno, Mantua
23 February 1607, to his brother Giovanni in Rome.**

. . . Hieri fu recitata la Comedia nel solito scenico Teatro et con la consueta
magnificenza et dimani sera il Ser.^{mo} Sr Prencipe ne fa recitare una,
nella sala del partimento che godeva Mad.^{ma} Ser.^{ma} di Ferrara, che
sarà singolare posciache tutti li interlocutori parleranno musicalmente
dicendosi che riuscirà benissimo onde per curiosità dubio che mi vi lasciarò
ridurre, caso che l'angustia del luogho non mi escludda . . .

> . . . The play was performed yesterday in the usual theatre and
> with all the customary splendour. Tomorrow evening the Most
> Serene Lord the Prince is to sponsor a [play] in a room in the
> apartments which the Most Serene Lady of Ferrara had the use of
> [on this interpretation of 'godeva', see Chapter 1, note 27]. It
> should be most unusual, as all the actors are to sing their parts; it
> is said on all sides that it will be a great success. No doubt I shall
> be driven to attend out of sheer curiosity, unless I am prevented
> from getting in by the lack of space . . .

**9. ASM (AG) 2162. Letter of Francesco Gonzaga, Mantua
23 February 1607, to Ferdinando Gonzaga in Pisa.**

. . . Dimani si farà la favola cantata nella nostra Accademia, poiche Gio.
Gualberto s'è portato cosi bene ch'in questo poco di tempo ch'e stato qui
non solo hà imparato bene tutta la sua parte a mente, ma la dice con molto
garbo, e con molto effetto, ond'Io ne son rimasto sodisfattissimo e perche
la favola s'è fatta stampare acciochè ciascuno degli spettatori ne possa
haver una da legere, mentre che si canterà; ne mando una copia a V.E.
siccome le manderò per quest'altro ordinario certi cartelli pubblicati per un
torneo, che si combatterà forse il di di Carnevale . . .

> . . . The musical play is to be performed in our Academy
> tomorrow, since Giovanni Gualberto has done very well in the
> short time he has been here. Not only has he thoroughly learned
> the whole of his part, he delivers it with much grace and a most
> pleasing effect; I am delighted with him. The play has been printed

so that everyone in the audience can have a copy to follow while the performance is in progress; I am sending Your Excellency a copy, and I shall let you have, by another messenger, some notices just published about a tournament which may take place on Carnival day . . .

10. ASM (AG) 2162. Letter of Francesco Gonzaga, Mantua 1 March 1607, to Ferdinando Gonzaga in Pisa.

. . . Si rappresentò la favola con tanto gusto di chiunque la senti che non contento il Sig.ʳ Duca d'esserci stato presente, ed haverla udita à provar molte volte, ha dato ordine, che di nuovo si rappresenti, e cosi si farà oggi con l'intervento di tutte le dame di questa Città, e per questa cagione si trattiene ancor quì Gio. Gualberto il quale s'è portato bene, et hà dato gran sodisfazzione col suo cantare a tutti, e particolarmente à Madama . . .

> . . . The play was performed to the great satisfaction of all who heard it. The Lord Duke, not content to have been present at this performance, or to have heard it many times in rehearsal, has ordered it to be given again; and so it will be, today, in the presence of all the ladies resident in the city. For this reason Giovanni Gualberto is to remain here at present; he has done very well, and given immense pleasure to all who have heard him sing, especially to My Lady . . .

11. ASF (AM) 2944, f. 295. Letter of Francesco Gonzaga, Mantua 8 March 1607, to the Grand Duke of Tuscany.

. . . Il ritorno del Sig.ʳ Alessandro Senesi in Toscana m'invita à rinovar in V.A. per mezo della presente la memoria dell'antico mio desiderio di servirla, baciandole affettuosamente la mano et augurandole quel colmo di tutte le felicità, ch'è dovuto ai molti meriti suoi. Mi son servito di Gio: Gualberto con molto mio gusto, et hora il rimanderei à V.A. . . . c'ha il S.ʳ Duca mio Sig.ʳᵉ di far di nuovo rappresentar la favola nella quale egli ha cantato. Onde me son presa libertà di trattenerlo ancor qui per qualche giorno confidato nella solita cortesia . . .

> . . . Signor Alessandro Senesi's return to Tuscany gives me the opportunity to remind Your Highness, in this present letter, of my long-standing desire to serve you; I kiss your hand with devotion and wish you that perfection of all happiness which is the just reward of your many merits. I have taken great pleasure in the services rendered by Giovanni Gualberto, and I should like to return him now to Your Highness . . . but My Lord the Duke wishes to have the play in which he sings performed again. I have thus taken the liberty of keeping him here for a few days more, trusting in your unfailing kindness . . .

12. ASF (AM) 2944, f. 319. Letter of Francesco Gonzaga, 30 April 1607, to the Grand Duke of Tuscany.

. . . Prego V.A. à perdonarmi, se mi son forse abusato della sua cortesia, tenendo qui tanto tempo Gio: Gualberto suo servitore poiche ha fatto cio solamente per quella confidenza che ho sempre havuta nell'indicibile sua bontà, . . . sopra il desiderio, che ho di servirla. Hora egli se ne ritorna al servizio di V.A. essendo io rimasto di lui sodisfatto, et obligato à lei infinitamente à cui rendo percio le dovute gratie . . .

> . . . I must ask Your Highness to forgive me, if I have perhaps taken advantage of your generosity by keeping your servant Giovanni Gualberto here for so long; but I did so only out of that confidence in your indescribable goodness which I have always felt, knowing it to be firmly founded on my desire to serve you. He now returns to Your Highness's service, having given me nothing but satisfaction; I am infinitely obliged to you and thank you as is right and proper . . .

13. ASM (AG) 1731. Letter of Cherubino Ferrari, Milan 22 August 1607, to Duke Vincenzo Gonzaga in Mantua.

. . . Il Monteverdi è qua in Milano, et è allogiato meco; onde ogni giorno raggioniamo di V.A., et l'uno à gara dell'altro andiamo celebrando le virtù, il valore, et di lei regie maniere. Cosi m'hà fatto vedere i versi et sentir la musica della comedia che V.A. fece fare, et certo che il Poeta et il Musico hanno si ben rappresentati gli affetti dell'animo, che nulla più. La Poesia quanto all'inventione è bella, quanto alla dispositione migliore, et quanto all'elecutione ottima; et insomma da un bell'ingegno, qual'è il Sig.ʳ Striggio, non si poteva aspettar altro. La musica altresi stando nel suo decoro serve si bene alla Poesia, che non si può sentir meglio . . .

> . . . Monteverdi is here in Milan, staying with me; and every day we talk about Your Highness and vie with one another in paying tribute to your virtues, your goodness and your royal manners. He has shown me the words and let me hear the music of the play which Your Highness had performed, and certainly both poet and musician have depicted the inclinations of the heart so skilfully that it could not have been done better. The poetry is lovely in conception, lovelier still in form, and loveliest of all in diction; and indeed no less was to be expected of a man as richly talented as Signor Striggio. The music, moreover, observing due propriety, serves the poetry so well that nothing more beautiful is to be heard anywhere . . .

Modern editions and performances

NIGEL FORTUNE and JOHN WHENHAM

A) Published editions

Of the editions of *Orfeo* currently available only two give a wholly reliable picture of the scores originally published by Monteverdi. These are the facsimiles of the 1609 and 1615 editions, published in 1927 and 1972 respectively. Malipiero's 1930 edition, despite some errors and omissions, also gives a clear impression of the original form of the score. Denis Stevens's edition, published in 1967, has the great merit for English readers of including a parallel English translation. It must, however, be read with care and in conjunction with Stevens's introduction and critical notes, since the text itself is essentially a performing edition with suggestions for ornamentation and the use of modern instruments: editorial additions and alterations are not distinguished typographically from the composer's original; Monteverdi's own instrumental specifications are presented only in an appendix; and the style of the continuo realisation does not (naturally enough) reflect more recent thinking on the subject (compare, for example, Stevens's continuo realisation with that presented on Nikolaus Harnoncourt's 1969 recording).

L'Orfeo, ed. Robert Eitner, *Publikationen älterer praktischer und theoretischer Musikwerke*, x (Leipzig, 1881).

————, ed. Vincent d'Indy (Paris, 1905).

————, ed. Giacomo Orefice (Milan, 1909).

————, [vocal score] ed. Gian Francesco Malipiero (London, 1923).

Orpheus, ed. Carl Orff [first version] [Munich, 1923, reprinted Mainz, copyright 1931].

L'Orfeo, facsimile of Monteverdi's 1609 edition, with introduction by Adolf Sandberger (Augsburg, 1927).

————, [full score] ed. Gian Francesco Malipiero, *Claudio Monteverdi: Tutte le opere*, xi ([Asolo], 1930).

————, ed. Giacomo Benvenuti [first version] (Milan, 1934).

————, ed. Ottorino Respighi (Milan, 1935).

Orpheus, ed. Carl Orff [third version] (Mainz, copyright 1939).

L'Orfeo, ed. Giacomo Benvenuti [second version], *I classici musicali italiani*, ix (Milan, 1942).

————, [vocal score] ed. Paul Hindemith (U.S.A. [n.p.], 1953).

————, ed. Michel Podolski, *Publications du Centre International des Etudes de la Musique Ancienne*, première série, i (Brussels, 1966).

173

———, ed. Bruno Maderna (Milan, 1967).
———, ed. Denis Stevens (London, 1967; corrected edn, 1968).
———, facsimile of Monteverdi's 1615 edition, with introduction by Denis Stevens (Farnborough, 1972).
———, ed. Edward H. Tarr (Paris, 1974).
———, ed. John Eliot Gardiner (London, in press)

B) Performances and unpublished editions/arrangements

In the list of performances which follows, no attempt has been made to distinguish between editions which attempt a reasonably faithful re-creation of the original and those which are free realisations and arrangements, some of which seriously misrepresent the composer's intentions. For a discussion of the latter see above, Chapter 5. For several of the performances which have been given since the Second World War no edition is cited. In a few cases this is because information on the performances was not readily available. In most cases, however, it may be assumed that the musical director of the production prepared performing materials either from the original scores or from a 'clean' edition such as that published by Malipiero in 1930. On the problems to be solved when adopting this approach see above, Chapter 8.

The list of performances before 1940 is based on that given in Loewenberg, *Annals of Opera* (3rd, rev. edn, London, 1978). When the information given here differs from that in Loewenberg's list, a short reference is given to the source of the information. For invaluable help in compiling the list of performances from 1940 onwards the editor is indebted to Mr Harold Rosenthal, who kindly allowed him to consult the relevant section of the supplement to Loewenberg's *Annals*, compiled by Mr Rosenthal, which is now in the press.

Date	Place	Comments
1904	Paris	D'Indy's edition, sung in his French translation. Concert performances under d'Indy at the Schola Cantorum on 25 February and 2 March. Repeated there 27 January, 26 February 1905.
1909	Milan	Orefice's edition. Concert performance under Amilcare Zanella (see Bussi, 'Amilcare Zanella', pp. 117–18) at the Conservatorio on 30 November. Subsequently performed at Mantua, Teatro Sociale, on 5 April 1910 and on succeeding days at Venice, Bologna, Florence, Turin and other Italian towns, and at Monte Carlo on 16 April 1910.
1910	Brussels	D'Indy's edition. Concert performance under Sylvain Dupuis at the 'Concerts

		Populaires' on 21 January (this is the date given in the review published in *The Times*, 27 January 1910).
1911	Paris	First modern stage performance. D'Indy's edition, given under Marcel Labey at the Théâtre Réjane on the afternoon of 2 May. This production was revived at the same theatre on the afternoon of 11 April 1913.
1912	New York	Orefice's edition, sung in an English translation. Concert performance under Josef Pasternack at the Metropolitan Opera House on Sunday 14 April.
1913	Chicago	Orefice's edition, sung in an English translation. Concert performance by soloists, chorus and orchestra of the Chicago Opera under Cleofonte Campanini on Sunday 5 January.
1913	Breslau	Stage performance. Hans Erdmann-Guckel's edition, sung in his own German translation. Given under Erdmann-Guckel at the Stadttheater on Sunday 8 June.
1920	Buenos Aires	Orefice's edition. 10 May.
1922	Dresden	Hans Günther's edition of Act II.
1924	London	D'Indy's edition. Concert performance, with piano accompaniment, directed by Louis Bourgeois at the Institut Français, Cromwell Gardens, on 8 March.
1925	Mannheim	Carl Orff's first version of *Orpheus*, with German text by Dorothee Günther and using some original instrumentation. Stage performance under Werner von Bülow at the National-Theater on 17 April.
1925	Oxford	First British stage performance. J. A. Westrup's edition, sung in an English translation by Robert L. Stuart. Given by the Oxford University Operatic Society under William H. Harris on 7 December. Westrup's version was revived at London, Royal College of Music (1926), and Liverpool (1927).
1928	Cologne	D'Indy's edition, sung in a German translation by H. Jalowetz. Summer.
1928	Cairo	Orefice's edition, sung in Italian at the Cairo Opera (see also Perugia, 1934).
1928	Leningrad	Malipiero's (unpublished) edition with chamber orchestra performed on

		5 December (see Nicolodi, *Gusti*, p. 124).
1929	Northampton, Mass.	First U.S. stage performance. Malipiero edition, with Acts I and V cut, given under Werner Josten at Smith College on 11 May.
1929	Munich	Orff's second (unpublished) version of *Orpheus*. Stage performance under Franz Hallasch at the Residenztheater on 10 December.
1929	London	First modern stage performance of the complete opera. J. A. Westrup's edition, sung in an English translation by Robert L. Stuart. Given at the Scala Theatre, London, on 30 December 1929 with Westrup as musical director.
1931	Vienna	Orff's second (unpublished) version of *Orpheus*. Concert performance on 14 January.
1932	Lisbon	D'Indy's edition, sung in a Portuguese translation under Ivo Cruz. Spring.
1933	Mantua	?Orefice's edition. Concert performance under Amilcare Zanella in the Sala Manto of the ducal palace on 30 April during the Settimana Mantovana (see Dioli and Nobili, *La vita*, p. 308).
1934	Perugia	First modern Italian stage performance. Orefice's edition, given at the Teatro Morlacchi on 19 September. Scenery and costumes from the 1928 Cairo production (see Nicolodi, *Gusti*, p. 131).
1934	Rome	Benvenuti's first version, with text adapted by Arturo Rossato. Stage performance under Tullio Serafin at the Teatro Reale dell'Opera on 27 December (review in *La Tribuna*, 28 December 1934). A gramophone recording of Benvenuti's version was issued in 1939 (see Discography).
1935	Milan	Respighi's edition, with text adapted by Claudio Guastalla. Stage performance under Gino Marinuzzi at the Teatro alla Scala on 16 March. Also given at Modena in May 1935.
1936	Zurich	Hans F. Redlich's edition. Concert performance on 10 February.
1936	Budapest	Respighi's edition, sung in a Hungarian translation by V. Lányi on 25 April.
1937	Buenos Aires	Benvenuti's first version. 23 July.

1940	Dresden	Orff's third version of *Orpheus*. Stage performance under Karl Böhm at the Staatsoper on 4 October. Orff's third version of *Orpheus*, a radical reworking of Monteverdi's opera (see above, pp. 90–2), has acquired a stage history of its own in German-speaking countries, with revivals at Hamburg (1942), Frankfurt-am-Main and Berlin (1943), Nuremberg (1953), Munich (1954/55 season), Mannheim (1956). Schwetzingen Festival (1958), Oldenburg (1962), Salzburg (1963), Munich (1965), Augsburg and Munich (1980). A gramophone recording of Orff's *Orpheus* was issued in 1975 (see Discography).
1941	Boston	Malipiero edition. Stage performance on 21 March.
1942	Brussels	Malipiero's 1930 edition, performed, using original instrumentation, under Paul Collaer on 2 May.
1943	Cremona	Vito Frazzi's edition. Frazzi's version was revived at the Florence Maggio Musicale (1949), at Vicenza, Teatro Olimpico (1949), and at the Florence Festival of 1957 with a performance in the Boboli Gardens.
1950	Cambridge	Thurston Dart's edition. Stage performance, under Dart, in the gardens of Girton College on 8 June.
1950	Mexico City	Stage performance under Paul Collaer at the Palace of Fine Arts. Summer.
1952	London	Broadcast performances under Walter Goehr on 6 and 9 June.
1954	Tanglewood	Stage performance of Act II at the Berkshire Festival.
1954	Italy	Malipiero edition. Broadcast performance.
1954	Vienna	Paul Hindemith's edition, using original instrumentation. Stage performance under Hindemith at the Redoutensaal, Vienna, in June during the Vienna Festival.
1955		?Erich Kraack's balletic version (see art. 'Kraack, Erich', in *MGG*). See also 1961.
1955	Hitzacker	August Wenzinger's edition, using original instrumentation. Hitzacker (Lower Saxony) Sommerliche Musik-

		tage. A gramophone recording of Wenzinger's version was issued in 1955 (see Discography).
1957	Milan	Alceo Toni's edition. Stage performance by the Piccola Scala company on 1 April. Also given at Vicenza, Teatro Olimpico (1957).
1959	Annapolis	Stage performance. Also given at the Lisner Auditorium, Washington.
1959	Drottningholm, Sweden	Stage performance by the Hanover State Opera under Albert Wolff on 31 May at the eighteenth-century opera house at Drottningholm.
1960	New York	Wenzinger's edition (abridged) with original instrumentation. Stage performance under Leopold Stokowski. Performed by the New York City Opera at the City Center on 29 September.
1960	Brussels	Performance, in a French translation by J. Paillot, under Paul Collaer on 12 November.
1961	Wuppertal	Erich Kraack's balletic version of the opera. Stage performance on 5 February. Kraack's version was revived at Duisburg (1968) and Salzburg (1971).
1961	Brussels	Performance under Edgard Doneux at La Monnaie.
1964	Versailles ·	Cesare Brero's edition. Performed by the Opera da Camera di Milano in May and June. Brero's version was also performed, under Gianfranco Rivoli, at the Aix-en-Provence Festival in 1965 using the sets from the 1964 Versailles production.
1965	Mexico City	Three performances during March, given in aid of the Morales Esteves Foundation.
1965	Cambridge	Raymond Leppard's edition, sung in Italian. Pre-London stage performance by the Sadler's Wells Company, under Leppard, at the Arts Theatre, Cambridge, on 6 July.
1965	London	Raymond Leppard's edition. Stage performance under Leppard at Sadler's Wells on 5 October. This production was revived at Sadler's Wells in subsequent years and was also given at Katonah, New York, on 28 June 1968.

1966	Hanover	Wenzinger's edition given at the Herrenhausen on 2 August.
1967		Edward Tarr's edition (see Discography).
1967	Lisbon	Denis Stevens's edition. Stage performance under Gianfranco Rivoli at the Sao Carlo Opera House. Performed 18 May during the 11th Gulbenkian Festival. Subsequently given at Madrid, Teatro della Zarzuela, in ?May/?June 1967.
1967	Milan	Valentino Bucchi's edition. Broadcast performance.
1967	Amsterdam	Bruno Maderna's edition, commissioned for the Holland Festival. Stage performance under Maderna at the Théâtre Carré on 23 June.
1967	Oxford	Concert performance under Herbert Handt at the Oxford Bach Festival.
1967	Melbourne	Concert performance under Harold Badger on 2 October at the Melba Memorial Conservatorium.
1968	Munich	Wenzinger's edition, sung in a German translation. Stage performance under Matthias Kuntzsch at the Cuvilliés-theater on 29 November.
1969	London	Semi-staged performance of Acts I and II under John Eliot Gardiner at the Henry Wood Promenade Concerts.
1969		Nikolaus Harnoncourt's edition, using original instrumentation (see Discography).
1971	Tokyo	Stage performance, sung in Japanese. Tokyo Chamber Opera. 5 October.
1972	San Francisco	Stage performance by the Spring Opera Theater under Byron Dean Ryan in February.
1973	Verona	Stage performance under Claudio Gallico. Subsequently given at Mantua, Teatro Accademico, on 9 September.
1973	Lyons	Wenzinger's edition.
1974		Jürgen Jürgens's edition, using original instrumentation (see Discography).
1975	Oxford	Stage performance, using original instrumentation, and sung in an English translation by Anne Ridler. Given by the Oxford University Opera Club under Jane Glover on 18 February.
1975	Zurich	Stage performance, using original instrumentation. Given, under Nikolaus

Harnoncourt, at the Zurich Opera on 20 December. The Zurich Opera production was subsequently given at Hamburg (26 January 1978), Vienna (May 1978), Edinburgh (29 August 1978), Berlin (October 1978), Milan (20 October 1978), and Wiesbaden (17 May 1979).

1976 Amsterdam — Stage performance, using original instrumentation. Given by the Netherlands Opera under Nikolaus Harnoncourt on 17 March.

1976 Bath — Stage performance, using original instrumentation, and sung in Anne Ridler's English translation. Given by Kent Opera under Roger Norrington on 3 June during the Bath Festival. The Kent Opera production was subsequently taken on tour before being given in London, at the Collegiate Theatre, on 21 March 1977, during the Camden Festival, and at the Everyman Theatre, Cheltenham, on 14 July 1978, during the Cheltenham Festival.

1977 Antwerp — Edward H. Tarr's edition. Given on 5 February to mark the opening of Rubens Year.

1977 Melbourne — Stage performance under Richard Divall at the Victoria State Opera on 2 July.

1977 York — Stage performance, using original instrumentation. Given under Lewis Jones at the Lyons Concert Hall, University of York, on 10 November.

1979 New York — Denis Stevens's edition. Stage performance under Peter Herman Adler at the Juilliard American Opera Center on 1 February, using sets from the 1967 Lisbon production.

1980 Berkeley — Stage performance, using original instrumentation. Given under Philip Brett in the Herz Hall of the University of California at Berkeley on 3 February.

1980 Bad Hersfeld — Stage performance attempting a reconstruction of the opera's original ending. Given, under Siegfried Heinrich, in the ruins of the eleventh-century abbey at Bad Hersfeld (near Kassel). A gramo-

		phone recording of this version was issued in 1981 (see Discography).
1981	Nottingham	Stage performance, using original instrumentation, and sung in Anne Ridler's English translation. Pre-London performance by the English National Opera under John Eliot Gardiner on 11 March.
1981	Paris	Stage performance by the Paris Opéra, under Charles Rosier, at the Palais de Chaillot on 2 April.
1981	London	Stage performance, using original instrumentation, and sung in Anne Ridler's English translation. Given by the English National Opera under John Eliot Gardiner on 20 August. Gardiner's version was revived in London by the English National Opera under Peter Robinson on 6 October 1983.
1984	Florence	Stage performance, using original instrumentation and attempting a seventeenth-century style of acting. Given, under Roger Norrington, in the Salone del Cinquecento of the Palazzo Vecchio on 19 June as part of the Maggio Musicale. Revived at Rome, Teatro Olimpico, on 4 October 1984.
1984	Florence	Version conceived by Luciano Berio. Open-air performance, as a 'popular pageant', in the courtyard of the Pitti Palace. Five young Italian composers were each commissioned to 'realise' a section of the score.
1984		Nigel Rogers's edition, using original instrumentation (see Discography).

A list of Monteverdi's instrumental specifications

JANE GLOVER

(All page references are to Claudio Monteverdi, *Tutte le opere*, ed. G. F. Malipiero, vol. xi. The orthography of the specifications is, however, that of the 1609 print.)

Toccata		'che si suona avanti il levar de la tela tre volte con tutti li stromenti, & si fa un Tuono piu alto volendo sonar le trombe con le sordine'

Act I

p. 11	Chorus: 'Vieni Imeneo'	'Questo Canto fu concertato al suono di tutti gli stromenti'
p. 14	Chorus: 'Lasciate i monti'	'Questo Balletto fu cantato al suono di cinque Viole da braccio, tre Chittaroni, duoi Clavicembani. un Arpa doppia, un contrabasso de Viola, & un Flautino alla vigesima seconda'

Act II

p. 41	Ritornello	'Questo Ritornello fu suonato di dentro da un Clavicembano, duoi Chitaroni, & duoi Violini piccioli alla Francese'
p. 43	Ritornello	'Questo Ritornello fu sonato da duoi Violini ordinarij da braccio, un Basso de Viola da braccio, un Clavicembano, & duoi Chittaroni'
p. 44	Pastori: 'In questo prato adorno'	'Un Clavicembano & un Chittarrone'
p. 45	Ritornello	'Fu sonato di dentro da duoi Chitaroni un Clavicembano, & duoi Flautini'

p. 48	Ritornello	'Fu sonato questo Ritornello di dentro da cinque Viole da braccio, un contrabasso, duoi Clavicembani & tre chitarroni'
p. 56	Messaggiera: 'Ahi, caso acerbo'	'Un organo di legno & un Chit[arrone]'
p. 57	Pastore: 'Qual suon dolente'	'Un Clavic[embalo] Chitar-[rone] & Viola da bracio'
p. 62	Orfeo: 'Tu se' morta'	'Un organo di legno & un Chitarone'
p. 68	Pastori: 'Chi ne consola'	'Duoi Pastori cantano al suono del Organo di Legno, & un Chittarone'

Between Acts II and III

| p. 76 | Printed below Sinfonia; omitted by Malipiero | 'Qui entrano li Tromb[oni] Corn[etti] & Regali, & taciono le Viole da bracio, & Organi di legno Clavacem[bali] & si muta la Sena' |

Act III

p. 81	Caronte: 'O tu ch'innanzi'	'Caronte canta al suono del Regale'
p. 84	Orfeo: 'Possente spirto'	'Orfeo al suono del Organo di legno, & un Chitarrone, canta una sola de le due parti'
p. 84		'Violino / Violino'
p. 88		'Duoi Cornetti'
p. 91		'Arpa dopia'
p. 96		'Violino / Violino / Basso da brazzo'
p. 99	Orfeo: 'Sol tu nobile Dio'	'Furno sonate le altre parti da tre Viole da braccio, & un contrabasso de Viola tocchi pian piano'
p. 103	Sinfonia	'Questa Sinfo[nia] si sonò pian piano, con Viole da bracio, un Org[ano] di leg[no] & un contrabasso de Viola da gamba'
p. 103	Orfeo: 'Ei dorma'	'Orfeo canta al suono del Organo di legno solamente'
p. 104	Orfeo: 'Mentre versan quest'occhi'	'Qui entra nella barca e passa cantando al suono del Organo di legno'
p. 107	Chorus: 'Nulla impresa'	'Coro de spirti, al suono di un Reg[ale] Org[ano] di legno,

cinque Tromb[oni] duoi Bassi da gamba, & un contrabasso de viola'

Act IV

p. 121   Orfeo: 'Qual honor'

'Violino / Violino'

p. 125   Orfeo: 'Ma che odo?'

'Qui si fa strepito dietro la tela. Segue Orfeo cantando nel Clavicembano Viola da braccio, & Chittarone'

p. 125   Orfeo: 'O dolcissimi lumi'

'Qui si volta Orfeo, & canta al suono del Organo di legno'

p. 126   Orfeo: 'Ma qual Eclissi'

'Qui canta Orfeo al suono del Clavic[embalo] Viola da braccio basso, & un chitar-[rone].

Between Acts IV and V

p. 137   Printed above Ritornello

'Tacciono li Cornetti, Tromboni & Regali, & entrano a sonare il presente Ritornello, le viole da braccio, Organi, Clavicembani, contrabasso, & Arpe, & Chitaroni, & Ceteroni, & si muta la Sena'

Act V

p. 138   Orfeo: 'Questi i campi di Tracia'

'Duoi Organi di legno, & duoi Chitaroni concertorno [sic] questo Canto sonando l'uno nel angolo sinistro de la Sena, l'altro nel destro'

Notes

Chapter 1. The Mantuan *Orfeo*

1 The Magni, sons of Paolo (a distinguished Mantuan doctor), were from an ancient local family; see ASM (D'Arco) *Famiglie mantovane*, 7 vols., v, 140–1 for further details. Giovanni served as Mantuan ambassador in Rome, France, and Spain.

2 On the surviving fragments of *Dafne* see William V. Porter, 'Peri and Corsi's "Dafne" '.

3 In, respectively, Michelangelo Buonarroti, *Descrizione delle felicissime Nozze della Cristianissima Maestà di Madama Maria Medici Regina di Francia e di Navarra* (Florence, 1600) (partly transcribed in Angelo Solerti, *Gli albori*, ii, 113), and Federico Follino, *Compendio delle sontuose feste fatte l'anno MDCVIII nella città di Mantova* (Mantua, 1608) (see Solerti, *Gli albori*, ii, 145ff).

4 Surviving copies of the 1609 and 1615 editions are located in the following libraries:

1609: Florence, Biblioteca nazionale centrale; Genoa, Biblioteca universitaria (defective copy); Modena, Biblioteca Estense; Rome, Biblioteca musicale governativa del Conservatorio di Santa Cecilia. (No copy survives in Bologna, Civico museo bibliografico musicale, despite references to such a copy in several bibliographical sources.)

1615: Brussels, Bibliothèque royale Albert 1er; London, British Library; Oxford, Christ Church Library; Wrocław (Poland), Biblioteka uniwersytecka.

Facsimile reprints of the 1609 and 1615 editions are listed in Appendix 2.

5 Some of the costume drawings and scene designs for Florentine *intermedi* are given in Nagler, *Theatre Festivals*.

6 See Nino Pirrotta, 'Teatro, scene', p. 49 (*Music and Culture*, p. 257).

7 In Eugenio Cagnani, *Raccolta d'alcune rime di scrittori mantovani* (Mantua, 1612), p. 9.

8 Transcribed in Angelo Solerti, *Musica, ballo e drammatica alla corte medicea dal 1600 al 1637* (Florence, 1905), pp. 54–7.

9 Ibid., p. 55.

10 For Bacchini's biography, see P. M. Tagmann, 'Bacchini, Girolamo M.', in *The New Grove*, i, 771.

185

11 Alessandro Striggio, *La favola d'Orfeo, rappresentata in musica il carnevale dell'anno MDCVII. Nell'accademia de gl'Invaghiti di Mantova; sotto i felici auspizij del serenissimo sig. duca begnissimo lor protettore* (Mantua, 1607). Surviving copies are held by the following libraries:

> Bologna, Biblioteca comunale dell'Archiginnasio; Genoa, Biblioteca universitaria; Wolfenbüttel, Herzog-August-Bibliothek (two copies, shelfmarks 174 Hist. and 549 Quodl.).

Another, manuscript, copy of the libretto, 'La Favola d'Orfeo canoramente recitata nell'Accademia de gl'Invaghiti di Mantoa', MS N.V.30 of the Biblioteca nazionale in Turin, was destroyed by fire in 1904 together with other manuscripts from the library of the Accademia degli Invaghiti.

12 On the Ferrarese *concerto di donne* see Anthony Newcomb, *The Madrigal at Ferrara 1579–1597* (2 vols., Princeton, 1980).

13 Vincenzo Giustiniani, 'Discorso sopra la musica de' suoi tempi' (ASL Orsucci MS 48); English translation of this passage from Iain Fenlon, *Music and Patronage*, i, 126–7.

14 Giustiniani, 'Discorso'; English translation by Carol MacClintock (n.p., 1962), pp. 70–1.

15 See Fenlon, *Music and Patronage*, i, 194.

16 On the Monteverdi–Artusi debate see Claude V. Palisca, 'The Artusi–Monteverdi controversy', in Denis Arnold and Nigel Fortune (eds.), *The New Monteverdi Companion* (London, 1985), pp. 127–58.

17 For a more extended discussion of the musical contacts and influences between Mantua, Ferrara and Florence during this period, see Fenlon, *Music and Patronage*, i, 121–62. For the best recent discussion of the *intermedio* tradition, see Pirrotta and Povoledo, *Music and Theatre*, especially Part I, Chapter 5. For the staging of *intermedi* see also Nagler, *Theatre Festivals*, and Roy Strong, *Splendour at Court*. An abbreviated description of one of the Florentine *intermedi* played in 1589 is given below, pp. 43–5.

18 It is difficult to believe that this complete series of letters was unknown to the three most important nineteenth-century historians of Mantuan music – Stefano Davari, Antonio Bertolotti and Angelo Solerti. Nevertheless, apart from the three much-quoted letters concerning the first and second performances of *Orfeo* (see Appendix 1, letters 8–10, the only passages which they excerpted concern Prince Ferdinando Gonzaga's literary and musical activities. I am grateful to Ms Susan Parisi for allowing me to consult a paper read to the American Musicological Society in November 1979 in which the importance of the complete series is briefly discussed.

19 'Relazione del Clarissimo Signor Pietro Gritti, ritornato di Ambasciator al Duca Francesco di Mantoa l'anno 1612', in A. Segarizzi (ed.), *Relazioni degli ambasciatori al senato* (4 vols., Bari, 1912–16), i, 119–20.

20 Monteverdi's *Il terzo libro della musica . . . fatta spirituale da Aquilano Coppini* (Milan, 1609) and the reprint of the *Scherzi musicali* (Venice,

1609) are dedicated to Francesco Gonzaga, as are Benedetto Pallavicino's *Il settimo libro de madrigali a cinque voci* (Venice, 1600), Floriano de' Magri's *Canzonette* (Milan, 1611) and Antonio Taroni's *Secondo libro di madrigali* (Venice, 1612).

21 Ferdinando Gonzaga, *Piae meditationes quadregisimale* (Ingolstadt, 1602).

22 Details from I. Donesmondi, *Dell'istoria ecclesiastica di Mantova*, ii (1616), pp. 370, 391. Giovanni da Mulla's 'Relazione dell'Illustrissimo Signor Gioanni da Mulla ritornato di Ambassator dal Cardinal Duca di Mantova Ferdinando 1615' is printed in A. Segarizzi (ed.), *Relazioni*, i, 140–1. For details of Ferdinando's artistic activities see the dedication to Ortensio Gentile's *Il primo libro de madrigali a cinque voci* (Venice, 1616), and P. Askew, 'Ferdinando Gonzaga's patronage of the pictorial arts: the Villa Favorita', *Art Bulletin*, lx (1978), 274–95.

23 On the Elevati and Ferdinando's connections with it see E. Strainchamps, 'New Light on the Accademia degli Elevati of Florence', *Musical Quarterly*, lxii (1976), 507ff. For Ferdinando's activities as a composer see the excerpts from the diary of Cesare di Bastiano Tinghi given in Solerti, *Musica, ballo*, pp. 37ff. (see n. 8).

24 On the Invaghiti see Fenlon, *Music and Patronage*, i, 35–7.

25 Although this letter, or at least its contents, must have been known to Bertolotti (see his *Musici alla corte dei Gonzaga in Mantova dal secolo XV al XVIII* (Milan, 1891), p. 86), the fact that it remained unpublished led some later scholars to question whether Magli was indeed a castrato, and to propose, on the basis of Florentine documentation, that he was simply a boy treble (see the letters from J. A. Westrup and Nigel Fortune to *The Music Review* – xiv (1953), 340, and xv (1954), 88 respectively – and Westrup's article 'Two first performances: Monteverdi's "Orfeo" and Mozart's "La Clemenza di Tito"', *Music and Letters*, xxxix (1958), 327–35).

26 The sense is unclear from its context here and from its use in letter 7. One possible explanation is 'too much voice' in the sense of vocal power, another might be 'too many notes'. Seventeenth-century usage suggests the latter (see the common usage in D. Bartoli, *Trattato del suono* (Rome, 1679) and throughout Giovanni Battista Doni's 'Lyra Barberina' (1632–35), published in G. B. Doni, *Lyra Barberina amphichordos: accedunt eiusdem opera*, i, ed. A. F. Gori and G. B. Passeri (Florence, 1763 / R 1975).

27 The translation of 'godeva' as 'had the use of' follows the definition given in the *Vocabolario della Accademia della Crusca* (Venice, 1623). According to the reports of the Venetian ambassadors (see Segarizzi (ed.), *Relazioni*, cited in note 19 above), the duchess did not live in the palace itself. In these circumstances it is not possible, on the basis of this passage, to identify the place where *Orfeo* was first given.

28 This conclusion agrees with that presented in Pirrotta, 'Teatro, scene', pp. 49–51 (*Music and Culture*, pp. 257–9). Against the idea that *Orfeo* was played in a small room at Mantua must be set the evidence provided by Cagnani's *Lettera cronologica* (see p. 3 and n. 7 above), in which it is stated that *Orfeo* 'was performed in the grand theatre with most noble

scenery'. It is not clear, however, to which of the Mantuan performances Cagnani might have been referring or, indeed, whether his statement should be regarded as Mantuan propaganda rather than an
objective statement of fact.

29 I am grateful to Professor Gary Tomlinson for this suggestion. On the
grounds of the quality of the verse it is difficult to believe that 'after the
successes in 1608 of the *Ballo delle ingrate* and *Arianna*, the latter of
which also concludes with the miraculous appearance of two gods,
Monteverdi turned to his librettist, Rinuccini, to provide a happy ending for the printed score of *Orfeo*', as argued by Barbara R. Hanning,
Of Poetry and Music's Power, p. 129.

30 'Io sono alla fine italiano e bisogna che fra noi c'intendiamo bene,
perché l'amicizia di questi forestieri non è procurata da loro per bene
nostro, ma solo per levarsi quanti possediamo, o per obbligarci di
servire ai loro fini, per poter tanto più facilmente assoggettarci tutti.'
Report given to the Venetian senate, 26 January 1609, by Pietro
Contarini and published in N. Barozzi and G. Berchet (eds.), *Relazioni
degli stati europei lette al senato dagli ambasciatori veneziani nel secolo
decimosettimo* (10 vols., Venice, 1856–78), series iii, vol. i, p. 102.

31 There is an operatic precedent for a *lieto fine* in Rinuccini's *Euridice*, a
piece which clearly influenced Striggio in a number of ways. For some
of them see the remarks in Gary Tomlinson, 'Madrigal, Monody', pp.
60–1 and the literature cited there in n. 1.

32 As in H. Prunières, *Monteverdi: His Life and Work* (London, 1926),
pp. 57–8, who suggests performances in Turin, Florence, and Cremona.

33 L. G. Luisi (ed.), *Discorsi e regole sopra la musica di Severo Bonini*
(Cremona, 1975), p. 110.

34 The point is discussed at length in Tomlinson, 'Madrigal, Monody', particularly pp. 80ff.

Chapter 2. The Orpheus myth and the libretto of *Orfeo*

1 The best summary of classical scholarship on the topic of Orpheus and
Orphic poetry is probably that given by Ziegler in Pauly-Wissowa's
Real-Encyclopädie der classischen Altertumswissenschaft, vol. xviii,
part 1 [1939], cols. 1200–1417. Another essay by Ziegler, 'Orpheus in
Renaissance und Neuzeit', deals more specifically with painting, poetry
and music. Further literature is cited in F. W. Sternfeld, 'The Birth of
Opera'.

2 *Seneca's Tragedies, I* (The Loeb Classical Library), trans. Frank Justus
Miller (London, 1917); lines 569–89 of *Hercules furens* refer to the
Orpheus myth.

3 *Le trasformationi* (6th edn, Venice, 1561), p. 223: 'Per Orfeo, che
racquistata Euridice, la perde per voltarsi a dietro, si dinota lo stato
dell'anima, la quale è perduta dall'huomo, qual volta egli lasciando la
ragione si volge a dietro: cioè a seguir le cose biasimevole e terrene.'

4 *Le metamorfosi di Ovidio, ridotte da Giovanni Andrea dell'Anguillara
. . . con l'annotationi di M. Gioseppe Horologgi* (7th edn, Venice, 1581),

f. 190: 'La favola di Orfeo ci mostra quanta forza, e vigore habbia
l'eloquenza, come quella ch'è figliuola di Apollo che non è altro che la
sapienza; la lira datagli da Mercurio, è l'arte del favellare
propriamente, laquale a simiglianza della lira va movendo gli affetti col
suono hora acuto, hora grave, della voce e della pronuncia, di maniera
che le selve, e i boschi si muovono per il piacere che pigliano di udire la
ben'ordinata, e pura favella dell'huomo giudicioso.'
 Such interpretation of the significance of the Orpheus myth by way of
'allegory' – that is, by perceiving a deeper spiritual meaning behind the
surface of the story – goes back to early Christianity, and a fairly consistent commentary may be constructed from perusing the remarks on
Orpheus spanning the period from Boethius's *Consolation of
Philosophy* in the sixth century to Cosimo Bartoli's *Ragionamenti* of
1567.
5 Ovid, *Metamorphoses*, II, trans. Frank Justus Miller, p. 65.
6 Virgil, *Eclogues, Georgics, Aeneid I–VI*, trans. H. Rushton Fairclough,
 p. 229. The four-fold repetition of 'te' ('of thee') in this passage demon-
 strates Virgil's use of the technique of repetition to give intensity to the
 affections, a technique frequently copied by Striggio as, for example, in
 the four 'ahi's of the Messenger's initial utterance in Act II (lines 200–1
 of the libretto) and in the three 'tu se's of Orpheus's reaction to her news
 – 'Tu se' morta' (lines 247–8 of the libretto, slightly altered in the
 musical setting). Note also Virgil's three-fold repetition of 'Eurydice' at
 the end of the passage from the *Georgics* quoted on pp. 25–6.
7 Ovid, *Metamorphoses, II*, p. 65.
8 Ibid., pp. 67–9.
9 Virgil, *Ecologues, Georgics, Aeneid I–VI*, pp. 231–3.
10 On the creation of opera and Florentine solo song see Nino Pirrotta,
 'Early Opera and Aria' in Pirrotta and Povoledo, *Music and Theatre*,
 pp. 237–80. On the membership and achievements of Count Bardi's
 'Camerata' see Claude V. Palisca, 'The "Camerata Fiorentina": a
 Reappraisal', *Studi musicali*, i (1972), 203–36. The same author's 'The
 Alterati of Florence, Pioneers in the Theory of Dramatic Music', *New
 Looks at Italian Opera*, ed. William W. Austin (Ithaca, 1968), pp. 9–38,
 gives a broader view of the Florentine intellectual and literary environment in which opera was born.
11 See Donald Jay Grout, 'The Chorus in Early Opera', p. 154.
12 Translated in Oliver Strunk, *Source Readings in Music History* (New
 York, 1950), p. 368.
13 See Ovid, *Amores*, II, 12, lines 1, 2, 5, 16 (The Loeb Classical Library),
 trans. G. Showerman (2nd edn, London, 1977).
14 Letter of 7 May 1627; see Monteverdi, *The Letters*, trans. Denis
 Stevens, p. 316.

Chapter 4. Five acts: one action

1 Federico Follino, *Compendio delle sontuose feste fatte l'anno MDCVIII
 nella città di Mantova* (Mantua, 1608), cited in Solerti, *Gli albori*, ii,
 187.

2 See Elena Povoledo, ' "Visible" *intermedi* and movable sets', in Pirrotta and Povoledo, *Music and Theatre*, p. 339. See also Pirrotta's remarks, ibid., p. 76.

3 Nino Pirrotta, 'Teatro, scene', pp. 45–64. As this book goes to press an English translation of Professor Pirrotta's article has at last appeared (in Pirrotta, *Music and Culture in Italy from the Middle Ages to the Baroque* (Cambridge, Mass., 1984), pp. 254–70).

4 Bastiano de' Rossi, *Descrizione dell'apparato e degl'Intermedi fatti per la commedia rappresentata in Firenze nelle nozze de' Serenissimi Don Ferdinano Medici e Madama Cristina di Loreno, Gran Duchi di Toscana* (Florence, 1589). The Italian text of the passage cited is given in Solerti, *Gli albori*, ii, 30–1.

5 Pirrotta, 'Teatro, scene', p. 46 (*Music and Culture*, p. 255).

6 The rubric indicating the change of scene and instrumentation between Acts II and III is printed below the first Underworld sinfonia rather than between the two instrumental movements. Malipiero omitted the rubric altogether in his 1930 edition. It is given below, in Appendix 3. The corresponding rubric between Acts IV and V is printed in the correct position, as shown in Fig. 4.

7 The techniques are described in Nicola Sabbatini, *Pratica di fabricar scene e machine ne' teatri* (Ravenna, 1638). An English version of sections of this treatise, trans. John H. McDowell, is given in Barnard Hewitt (ed)., *The Renaissance Stage* (Coral Gables, Florida: University of Miami Press, 1958); see particularly pp. 102–6 and 113–19.

8 Pirrotta ('Teatro, scene', p. 54; *Music and Culutre*, p. 261) suggests that the scene designer for *Orfeo* was probably Antonio Maria Viani, 'prefetto alle fabbriche' at Mantua.

9 Michelangelo Buonarroti, *Descrizione delle felicissime Nozze della Cristianissima Maestà di Madama Maria Medici Regina di Francia e di Navarra* (Florence, 1600); Italian text transcribed in Solerti, *Gli albori*, ii, 113.

10 A similar instrumental introduction was used (and thought of as 'usual') in the performance of Guarini's *Idropica* at Mantua in 1608: 'The torches being lit in the theatre, the usual sign of the sound of trumpets was given within the stage; and as the trumpets began to sound a third time the great curtain which masked the stage disappeared so quickly, as it were in the batting of an eyelid, that even though it rose high above, there were few who noticed how it disappeared' (Follino, *Compendio*, transcribed in Solerti, *Gli albori*, iii, 208).

11 Not Parnassus, as this has sometimes been interpreted. According to *Lemprière's Classical Dictionary*, Permessus was 'a river of Boeotia, rising in Mount Helicon, and flowing all round it. It received its name from Permessus the father of a nymph called Aganippe, who also gave her name to one of the fountains of Helicon. The river Permessus, as well as the fountain Aganippe, was sacred to the Muses.'

12 'A mountain, or rather a chain of mountains, between Thessaly, Macedonia and Epirus. It was greatly celebrated as being sacred to the Muses and to Apollo' (ibid.).

13 ' . . . a mountain of Boeotia, on the borders of Phocis. It was sacred to

the Muses, who had there a temple. The fountain Hippocrene flowed from this mountain' (ibid.).

14 In Striggio's text Music, Orpheus and the Muses are generally depicted as playing the 'cetra' (cittern, or Classical kithara) rather than the 'lira' (lyre), though 'cetra' does have 'lyre' as a secondary meaning. The cittern is a plucked string instrument with wire strings, and in the late sixteenth century a large version of this instrument, the *ceterone*, was developed for playing continuo accompaniments. *Ceteroni* appear unexpectedly in one of the instrumental specifications given at the transition from Act IV to Act V of *Orfeo* (see Appendix 3 and Fig. 4). By extension, the term 'cetra' could also embrace the *chitarrone*, an offshoot of the lute family, which was one of the standard instruments used for continuo accompaniments in the early seventeenth century. The *chitarrone* is one of the instruments which accompany Orpheus's aria 'Possente spirto' in Act III of *Orfeo* and probably represents Orpheus's 'lyre'.

  If Striggio had consistently used the term 'lira' rather than 'cetra', then a completely different situation would have obtained. During the Renaissance, 'lira' was usually interpreted as meaning a *lira da braccio*: that is, a bowed rather than a plucked string instrument. In Renaissance iconography Apollo, Orpheus, and the Muses are often depicted playing the *lira da braccio* (see Fig. 3, in which Orpheus stands before the River Styx playing what appears to be a *lira da braccio*). See Emanuel Winternitz, *Musical Instruments and their Symbolism in Western Art* (New York, 1967 / R New Haven and London, 1979), pp. 30–1, 86–98.

  Monteverdi would have been well aware of the ambiguity surrounding the depiction of the 'lyre', and so would Alessandro Striggio, whose father had played the *lira da braccio*. The accompaniment to 'Lasciate i monti' is allocated to five *viole da braccio*, three chitarroni, a double harp, a *contrabasso de viola*, and a *flautino alla vigesima seconda*. The sound of both the bowed and the plucked string instruments could, thus, be interpreted as representing the sound of the Muses playing on their 'lyres'.

15 *Istitutioni harmoniche* (rev. 3rd edn, Venice, 1573), p. 397.

16 For possible Neoplatonic overtones of the sun imagery used here, see Robert Donington, *The Rise of Opera*, pp. 155–7.

17 Malipiero edn, p. 9, bar 7; Stevens edn, p. 9, bar 13.

18 Malipiero edn, p. 38; Stevens edn, p. 36.

19 The processional nature of this instrumental movement and the idea that the temple must be located off stage were discussed as early as 1902–3 by Alfred Heuss ('Die Instrumental-Stücke des "Orfeo"', p. 192). Heuss's ideas have, however, been less widely circulated than, for example, Henry Prunières's comment 'What, we might ask, is this piece of church music, which might be the work of a Giov. Gabrieli or a Claudio Merulo, doing in this opera? The explanation is that it embodies the impression of rude strength and harsh gravity which best befits true shepherds' (*Monteverdi, his Life and Work*, trans. Marie D. Mackie, p. 71).

20 This is true of both printings of the libretto. In the absence of evidence

to the contrary, I would assume that the printed librettos represent Striggio's original text. The usual practice in the early seventeenth century was to publish the text as the poet had written it, ignoring any changes or omissions made in the musical setting.

21 Malipiero edn, pp. 48–55; Stevens edn, pp. 47–9.
22 *Istitutioni harmoniche*, p. 394.
23 Ibid., pp. 414, 399, 402.
24 The score has 'le sue chiome' (her [i.e. Eurydice's] hair). The libretto has 'le tue chiome' (your [i.e. Orpheus's] hair], a reading which makes better sense since it provides a motivation for Eurydice's otherwise irrelevant activity.
25 Malipiero edn, p. 62, bar 4; Stevens edn, p. 56, bar 296.
26 Malipiero edn, p. 66, bars 8–9; Stevens edn, pp. 61–2, bars 386–387.
27 *The Divine Comedy: Inferno*, Canto III.
28 '. . . a promontory of Laconia, the most solemn point of Europe, where Neptune had a temple. There was there a large and deep cavern, whence issued a black and unwholesome vapour, from which circumstance the poets have imagined that it was one of the entrances of hell . . . ' (*Lemprière's Classical Dictionary*).
29 Ovid, *Metamorphoses, II*, trans. Frank Justus Miller, p. 65.
30 'Erebus, a deity of hell, son of Chaos and Darkness. He married Night, by whom he had the light and the day. The poets often used the word Erebus to signify hell itself . . . ' (*Lemprière's Classical Dictionary*).
31 '. . . a river of Epirus. The word is derived from *kokuein, to weep and to lament*. Its etymology, the unwholesomeness of its water, and above all, its vicinity to the Acheron, have made the poets call it one of the rivers of hell' (ibid.).
32 Virgil, *Eclogues, Georgics, Aeneid I–VI*, trans. H. Rushton Fairclough, pp. 229–231.
33 Dante, *The Divine Comedy, 1: Inferno*, trans. John D. Sinclair, pp. 51–3.
34 The cornett, a wooden instrument with a mouthpiece like that of a brass instrument, aptly represents both classes of instrument.
35 Professor Pirrotta's suggestion (*Music and Theatre*, p. 277) that the unornamented version of the line was intended to be sung as written is not wholly convincing. At the beginning of stanza 4, for example, Monteverdi divides the syllables of the word 'Or-feo' and sets them to two notes separated by a minim rest, a nonsense in terms of Florentine-style recitative, but a clear indication to the singer improvising his own ornamentation of the points at which the syllables should fall.
36 On the use of a string ensemble with organ continuo for this sinfonia, see the letters from Michael Graubart and Sir Jack Westrup in *The Musical Times*, cxvi (1975), pp. 339 and 537 respectively. For a different opinion on the scoring of this sinfonia, see p. 143.
37 For Ovid's account of the rape of Proserpine, see *Metamorphoses*, Book V.
38 Made explicit in Ovid, *Metamorphoses*, Book X.
39 Cf. Psalm 126 (A.V. 127): 'Qui seminant in lacrimis: in exultatione metent' ('They that sow in tears shall reap in joy').

40 Possibly related to the English Morris Dance; see the article 'Moresca' by Alan Brown in *The New Grove*, xii, 572–3.
41 Monteverdi, *The Letters*, trans. Denis Stevens, p. 117.

Chapter 5. The rediscovery of *Orfeo*

1 Charles Burney, *A General History of Music* (4 vols., London, 1776–89), ed. Frank Mercer (London, 1935), ii, 517.
2 John Hawkins, *A General History of the Science and Practice of Music* (5 vols., London, 1776), 2nd repr. (London, 1875), ii, 525.
3 Mercer edn, ii, 519.
4 *Johannes Gabrieli und sein Zeitalter* (3 vols., Berlin, 1834); see especially ii, 25–6, 35–6, 44–7.
5 'Claudio Monteverdi', *Vierteljahrsschrift für Musikwissenschaft*, iii (1887), 315–450, especially 343–4.
6 *Studien zur Geschichte der italienischen Oper im 17. Jahrhundert* (2 vols., Leipzig, 1901–4).
7 *Les origines du théâtre lyrique moderne: l'histoire de l'opéra en Europe avant Lully et Scarlatti* (Paris, 1895).
8 C. Hubert H. Parry, *The Music of the Seventeenth Century*, *The Oxford History of Music*, iii (London, 1902), p. v.
9 Ibid., p. 55.
10 'The Significance of Monteverde', p. 61.
11 'Die Instrumental-Stücke'.
12 'L"Orfeo" ', p. 132.
13 See Appendix 2 for bibliographical details of modern editions and performances of *Orfeo*.
14 J. A. Westrup, 'Monteverde's "Orfeo", p. 1096: '[Eitner's] emendations are frequently unnecessary and fussy.'
15 A ponderous, almost comic, example of Eitner's rewriting is quoted in Jane Glover, 'The Metamorphoses of "Orfeo" ', p. 135. This is a useful account of some of the editions mentioned in the present survey.
16 'A propos de Pelléas et Mélisande: essai de psychologie du critique d'art', *L'occident* (Brussels, June 1902). I am most grateful to John Whenham for transcribing this and certain other passages, mainly reviews of performances, from newspapers and out-of-the-way periodicals.
17 Cesari, 'L"Orfeo" ', p. 136, note 2.
18 In *Chronique des arts et de la curiosité* (supplement to *Gazette des beaux-arts*), 4 March 1905, reprinted in Paul Dukas, *Chroniques musicales sur deux siècles, 1892–1932* (Paris, 1980), pp. 21–3. I am indebted to the late Bill Hopkins for drawing my attention to this review.
19 Dukas, *Chroniques musicales*, pp. 22–3.
20 'L'Orfeo de Monteverdi', p. 287.
21 Ibid., p. 286: 'M. Vincent d'Indy, s'aidant de la vérification du texte musical faite sur le manuscrit [*sic*] par l'érudit musicographe M. Romain Rolland, a pu écrire une réalisation aussi conscieuse que possible.'

22 See *Le Figaro* (2 May 1911).

23 In *SIM Revue musicale mensuelle*, vii (1911), 77–8.

24 From a review by 'R.L.' in *Le Figaro* (12 April 1913).

25 See Cesari, 'L' "Orfeo" ', p. 136.

26 Gabriele d'Annunzio, *Il fuoco* (Milan, 1900), pp. 160ff; Eng. trans. by Kassandra Vivaria (London, 1900), pp. 112ff. Further on this work and on D'Annunzio's involvement with music, see Domenico De' Paoli, 'Gabriele d'Annunzio, la musica e i musicisti', in *Nel centenario di Gabriele d'Annunzio* (Turin, 1963), pp. 41–125, especially 41–51. Elizabeth Roche was kind enough to draw my attention to Moore's novel.

27 'Claudio Monteverdi (1567–1643)', *Monthly Musical Record*, xl (1910), 150.

28 'L' "Orfeo" ', pp. 175–6; see also p. 168.

29 See, especially, pp. 140ff and 168ff; on pp. 138–9 Cesari presents a detailed comparative table of the cuts in the editions of Eitner, d'Indy and Orefice on which I have drawn above.

30 See Nicolodi, *Gusti*, p. 131.

31 Cf. *Monteverdis Orfeo: Facsimile des Erstdrucks der Musik*, ed. Adolf Sandberger (Augsburg, 1927), introduction, p. 4, and also several reviews of the 1913 performance.

32 Quoted from *Carl Orff: das Bühnenwerk*, an exhibition catalogue (Munich, 1970), p. 31.

33 Translation from Andreas Liess, *Carl Orff*, trans. Adelheid and Herbert Parkin (London, 1966), pp. 77–8.

34 Those in Monteverdi's Act IV are described in Glover, 'The Metamorphoses of "Orfeo" ', pp. 137–8.

35 One of the scene designs representing the Underworld (Act II in this production) is reproduced in the Roman newspaper *La tribuna* (28 December 1934).

36 Quoted in Elsa Respighi, *Ottorino Respighi: dati biografici ordinati* (Milan, 1954), pp. 295ff. I am most grateful to John C. G. Waterhouse for providing me with copies of this volume and other bibliographical material and for helpful discussions on the background to the Italian editions discussed in the present survey.

37 See Fiamma Nicolodi, *Gusti*, pp. 131–7, for an account of this version, including five music examples. This fascinating book contains extended discussions of twentieth-century Italian attitudes to the Italian musical heritage. See also the same author's 'Repêchage nell'antico: il melodramma del '600–700 nelle mani dei primi "restauratori" ', *Antologia Vieusseux*, no. 55, xiv/3 (July 1979), pp. 2–18.

38 Quoted in Elsa Respighi, *Ottorino Respighi*, p. 299. Also on Respighi's version, see Leonardo Bragaglia and Elsa Respighi, *Il teatro di Respighi: opere, balli e balletti* (Rome, 1978), pp. 167–77.

39 John C. G. Waterhouse, *The New Grove*, xv, 758.

40 See Bragaglia and Respighi, *Il teatro di Respighi*, pp. 172–4.

41 They are substantially reprinted, together with reviews, in Liliana Pannella, *Valentino Bucchi: anticonformismo e politica musicale italiana* (Florence, 1976), pp. 203–11.

42 See G. Francesco Malipiero, 'Claudio Monteverdi. Commiato', in *Il filo d'Arianna: saggi e fantasie* (Turin, 1966), p. 96; also Francesco Degrada, 'Gian Francesco Malipiero e la tradizione musicale italiana', *Testimonianze, studi e ricerche in onore di Guido M. Gatti (1892–1973)* (Bologna, 1973), pp. 412–32.

43 Malipiero, 'Claudio Monteverdi. Commiato', p. 99. See also Guglielmo Barblan, 'Malipiero e Monteverdi', *L'approdo musicale*, iii (1960), 126.

44 Malipiero, 'Claudio Monteverdi. Commiato', pp. 98–9.

45 See, for example, Nicolodi, 'Repêchage', p. 3.

46 Cf. note 31 above.

47 'Malipiero e Monteverdi', loc. cit.

48 'Notes on Monteverde's "Orfeo" ', *Musical Times*, lxv (1924), 509–11.

49 Gerald Abraham, 'Jack Allan Westrup 1904–1975', *Proceedings of the British Academy*, lxiii (1977), 473. The circumstances that gave rise to these performances are described in Robert Ponsonby and Richard Kent, *The Oxford University Opera Club: a short history (1925–1950)* (Oxford, 1950), p. 5, quoted in Eric Walter White, 'A Note on Opera at Oxford', in F. W. Sternfeld, Nigel Fortune and Edward Olleson, eds., *Essays on Opera and English Music in Honour of Sir Jack Westrup* (Oxford, 1975), p. 171.

50 'Notes', p. 509.

51 Westrup, 'Monteverde's "Orfeo" '. Further on Westrup's version of *Orfeo*, see also his article 'Monteverdi in Inghilterra', *Pan: rassegna di lettere, arte e musica*, iii (1935), 442–6, especially 443–4.

52 The English translation used for this performance, by Robert L. Stuart, is reproduced in the booklet accompanying the recording of *Orfeo* conducted by Jürgen Jürgens (see Discography, 1974).

53 'Vi ricorda o bosch'ombrosi', No. 1 in *Songs and Duets from the Works of Claudio Monteverde*, arr. and ed. J. A. Westrup (London, 1929).

54 'Zur Bearbeitung von Monteverdis "Orfeo" ', *Schweizerische Musikzeitung*, lxxvi (1936), 37–42, 74–80, especially the latter sequence of pages; a version of pp. 76–9 appears in Redlich, *Claudio Monteverdi*, trans. Kathleen Dale, pp. 160–3.

55 Further on this edition and its background, see Andres Briner, *Paul Hindemith* (Zurich and Mainz, 1971), pp. 160–62. The reviewer quoted was Christopher Raeburn: see *Opera*, v (1954), 566. I am grateful to Stephen Hinton and to Giselher Schubert of the Paul-Hindemith-Institut, Frankfurt-am-Main, for facilitating my scrutiny of this edition and to Luther Noss for helpful information about the circumstances attending its preparation at Yale.

56 De' Paoli, *Claudio Monteverdi*; Redlich, *Claudio Monteverdi*; Schrade, *Monteverdi*.

57 Abert, *Claudio Monteverdi*; Grout, *A Short History*; Kerman, *Opera as Drama*.

58 The use of *periaktoi* is explained in Pirrotta and Povoledo, *Music and Theatre*, pp. 358–9.

59 Berio's version may be an exception, especially if it is set against an 'authentic' edition, as it was, with Norrington's second version, at the 1984 Maggio Musicale.

Chapter 6. A review of Vincent d'Indy's performance (Paris 1904)

1 'L'opéra avant l'opéra', *Revue de Paris*, 1 February 1904.
2 'We hear', said Artusi, 'a mixture of sounds, a variety of voices, a rumbling harmony which the senses can scarcely tolerate. One voice sings a fast movement, another a slow; one voice utters one syllable, another a different one; one voice rises to the heights, while another descends to the depths; and as if that were not enough, a third is neither low nor high; one voice sings the harmonic division of the octave [i.e. the authentic form of the mode], another the arithmetic [the plagal form]. With the best will in the world, how can the mind possibly hope to appreciate such a whirlwind of impressions?' [Giovanni Maria Artusi, *L'Artusi, overo Delle imperfettioni della moderna musica* (Venice, 1600), ff. 14ᵛ–15.]
3 The orchestra at the *Schola* consisted of two small flutes, two oboes, two trumpets (in D and C), five trombones, one harp–lute, one chromatic harp, one harpsichord, a quartet of strings and an organ.
4 Apart from Robert Eitner's edition it is unclear which other versions of the work Rolland can have been referring to at this date. [Editor]

Chapter 8. Solving the musical problems

1 Oxford University Opera Club, February 1975.
2 See the list in Appendix 2.
3 'Duoi Organi di legno, & duoi Chitaroni concertorno [*sic*] questo Canto sonando l'uno nel angolo sinistro de la Sena, l'altro nel destro.' Monteverdi left similar instructions for the placing of the continuo instruments in his ballet *Tirsi e Clori* (1615; published 1619). In a letter dated 21 November 1615, to Annibale Iberti in Mantua, he wrote: 'I would think it proper to perform it in a half-moon, at whose corners should be placed a theorbo and a harpsichord, one each side.' See Monteverdi, *The Letters*, trans. Denis Stevens, pp. 107–8.
   In this chapter I have used the original Italian names of the characters, for ease of reference to the score.
4 In the preface to the opera *Dafne*, performed at Mantua the year after *Orfeo*, the composer Marco da Gagliano gives instructions for a similar call to attention: 'Before the curtain is raised, in order to gain the attention of the audience, a sinfonia is played.'
5 I am interested by the theory that this statement of the sinfonia, as well as its repetition on p. 103 of the score, should be played by strings (see above, p. 69). Nevertheless, I hold to my opinion that Monteverdi's rubric (p. 103) indicates a change of scoring.
6 In a letter written nine years after *Orfeo*, Monteverdi referred to the 'righteous prayer' which was for him the highlight of the piece, just as a 'just lament' had been of *Arianna*. See above, p. 77, and Monteverdi, *The Letters*, trans. Denis Stevens, p. 117.
7 Two other long monologues in Monteverdi's later operas also divide into neat, logical sections, and so assist the editor: Penelope's 'Di

misera Regina' in *Il ritorno d'Ulisse in patria*, I.1, and Ottavia's 'Disprezzata Regina' in *L'incoronazione di Poppea*, I.5.

8 This solution was adopted, with great success, by both Norrington for Kent Opera and Gardiner for the English National Opera.

9 See *La Dafne di Marco da Gagliano*, transcribed and edited, with a translation of the composer's preface, by James Erber, pp. iii–iv.

10 If a performance is envisaged with an exit to the temple in Act I (see above, pp. 52–3), then, obviously, the soprano line on p. 34 must be allocated to another singer.

11 Marked 'Choro', but in fact a duet.

12 On the other hand, there may have been occasions when editors have been tempted to re-bar where no re-barring is necessary. In Denis Stevens's edition of the opera (London: Novello, 1967; corrected edn, 1968), for example, the Act I chorus 'Qui miri il sole' (Malipiero edn, p. 16, Stevens edn, p. 24) has been barred in 3/2 instead of 6/4. This makes nonsense of the text.

13 English translation here by Anne Ridler.

14 This contrasts vividly with the practice evolved some sixty years later in early French opera, whereby each stress of each word was measured meticulously, resulting in an apparently complicated succession of 4/4, 3/4 and 2/2 bars. The outcome, in fact, sounds the same, even if the performer is allowed less freedom.

Bibliography

For biographical information on Monteverdi and general discussions of his music see, in particular, Arnold, *Monteverdi*, and Schrade, *Monteverdi, Creator of Modern Music*. Important, though in some respects controversial, interpretations of *Orfeo* and the Orpheus myth will be found in Donington, 'Monteverdi's First Opera', in the same author's *The Rise of Opera*, and in Drummond, *Opera in Perspective*. Gary Tomlinson's 'Madrigal, Monody' contains very perceptive analysis of the musical language of Monteverdi's early operas. For a discussion of the creation and early development of opera which takes account of recent research, see Pirrotta, 'Early Opera and Aria' in Pirrotta and Povoledo, *Music and Theatre*. Scenic and dramatic aspects of the *intermedio* tradition are covered in Nagler, *Theatre Festivals* and Strong, *Splendour at Court* as well as in Pirrotta and Povoledo, *Music and Theatre*; the orchestras used in *intermedi* are discussed in Brown, *Sixteenth-Century Instrumentation*. Reviews of the performances discussed in Chapter 5 have, in general, been omitted from the Bibliography, though references to some of the less easily traceable reviews of the early French and German performances are given.

Abert, Anna Amalie, *Claudio Monteverdi und das musikalische Drama* (Lippstadt, 1954).
Apel, Willi, 'Anent a Ritornello in Monteverdi's Orfeo', *Musica Disciplina*, v (1951), 213–22.
Arnold, Denis, *Monteverdi* (London, 1963; 2nd edn, 1975).
Beat, Janet E., 'Monteverdi and the Opera Orchestra of his Time', *The Monteverdi Companion*, ed. Denis Arnold and Nigel Fortune (London, 1968), pp. 277–301.
Bertolotti, Antonio, *Musici alla corte dei Gonzaga in Mantova del secolo XV al XVIII* (Milan, 1890/R1969).
Boyden, David D., 'Monteverdi's *violini piccoli alla francese* and *viole da brazzo*', *Annales musicologiques*, vi (1958–63), 387–401.
Brown, Howard Mayer, *Sixteenth-Century Instrumentation: the Music for the Florentine Intermedii* (*Musicological Studies and Documents*, xxx), ([Rome], 1973).
———, 'How Opera Began: an Introduction to Jacopo Peri's *Euridice*', *The Late Italian Renaissance 1525–1630*, ed. Eric Cochrane (London, 1970), pp. 401–43.
Budden, Julian, 'Orpheus, or the Sound of Music', *Opera*, xviii (1967), 623–30.

Bussi, Francesco, 'Amilcare Zanella musicista piacentino (1873–1949)', *Studi storici in onore di Emilio Nasalli Rocca* (Piacenza, 1971), 83–121.

Castéra, René de, 'L'Orfeo de Monteverdi', *Guide musical*, l (1904), 286–8 [review of 1904 Paris performance].

Cesari, Gaetano, 'L' "Orfeo" di Cl. Monteverdi all' "Associazione di Amici della Musica" di Milano', *Rivista musicale italiana*, xvii (1910), 132–78.

Collaer, Paul, 'Notes concernant l'instrumentation de l'*Orfeo* de Claudio Monteverdi', *Claudio Monteverdi e il suo tempo*, ed. Raffaello Monterosso (Verona, 1969), pp. 69–73.

——, 'L'orchestra di Claudio Monteverdi', *Musica*, ii (Florence, 1943), 86ff.

Dante, *The Divine Comedy, 1: Inferno*, trans. John D. Sinclair (New York, 1939).

Davari, Stefano, 'La musica a Mantova: notizie biografiche de maestri di musica, cantori e suonatori presso la corte di Mantova nei secoli XV, XVI, XVII, tratte dei documenti dell'Archivio Storico Gonzaga', *Rivista storica mantovana*, i (1884), 53ff; ed., with appendices, by Gherardo Ghirardini (Mantua, 1975).

——, *Notizie biografiche dell distinto maestro Claudio Monteverdi* (Mantua, 1884).

De' Paoli, Domenico, *Claudio Monteverdi* (Milan, 1945).

——, *Claudio Monteverdi* (Milan, 1979).

——, ' "Orfeo" and "Pelléas" ', *Music and Letters*, xx (1939), 381–98.

——, 'A Few Remarks on "Orfeo" by Claudio Monteverdi', *The Chesterian*, xx (1938–9), 61–7.

Dent, Edward, J., *Opera* (Harmondsworth, 1940; rev. edn, 1949).

Dioli, Arrigo, and M. Fernando Nobili, *La vita e l'arte di Amilcare Zanella* (Bergamo, 1941).

Doni, Giovanni Battista, *De' trattati di musica ... tomo secondo*, ed. Anton Francesco Gori (Florence, 1763), p. 104; this page, from the *Trattato della musica scenica*, which includes Doni's only comment on *Orfeo*, is reprinted in Angelo Solerti, *Le origini del melodramma* (Turin, 1903/R1969), p. 221.

Donington, Robert, 'Monteverdi's First Opera', *The Monteverdi Companion*, ed. Denis Arnold and Nigel Fortune (London, 1968), pp. 257–76.

——, *The Rise of Opera* (London and Boston, 1981).

Drummond, John D., *Opera in Perspective* (London, 1980).

Epstein, Peter, 'Zur Rhythmisierung eines Ritornells von Monteverdi', *Archiv für Musikwissenschaft*, viii (1926), 416–19.

Fenlon, Iain, 'Monteverdi's Mantuan *Orfeo*: Some New Documentation', *Early Music*, xii (1984), 163–72.

——, 'Monteverdi's Mantuan Stage Works', *The New Monteverdi Companion*, ed. Denis Arnold and Nigel Fortune (London, 1985), pp. 251–87.

——, *Music and Patronage in Sixteenth-Century Mantua* (2 vols., Cambridge, 1980–2).

Freund, Erich, 'Claudio Monteverdi's "Orfeo": Deutsche Uraufführung in Breslau', *Die Musik*, Jg. 12, vol. xlviii (1912–13), 26–7 [review of 1913 Breslau performance].

Frobenius, Wolf, 'Zur Notation eines Ritornells in Monteverdis "L'Orfeo"', *Archiv für Musikwissenschaft*, xxviii (1971), 201ff.

Gagliano, Marco da, *La Dafne*, ed. James Erber (London, 1978).

Glover, Jane, 'The Metamorphoses of "Orfeo"', *The Musical Times*, cxvi (1975), 135–9.

Grout, Donald Jay, *A Short History of Opera* (2 vols., New York, 1947; 2nd edn, 1965).

——, 'The Chorus in Early Opera', *Festschrift Friedrich Blume zum 70. Geburtstag*, ed. A. A. Abert and W. Pfannkuch (Kassel, 1963), pp. 151–61.

The New Grove Dictionary of Music and Musicians, ed. Stanley Sadie (20 vols., London, 1980).

Guérillot, F., 'L'Orfeo de Monteverde', *S[ociété] I[nternationale de] M[usique] Revue musicale mensuelle*, vii (1911), 77–8 [review of 1911 Paris performance].

Hanning, Barbara Russano, *Of Poetry and Music's Power. Humanism and the Creation of Opera* (Ann Arbor, 1980).

Harnoncourt, Nikolaus, 'Werk und Aufführung bei Monteverdi', *Österreichische Musikzeitung*, xxxiii (1978), 193–9.

Hell, Helmut, 'Zu Rhythmus und Notierung des *"Vi ricorda"* in Claudio Monteverdi's *Orfeo*', *Analecta musicologica*, xv (1975), 87–157.

Heuss, Alfred, 'Die Instrumental-Stücke des "Orfeo"', *Sammelbände der internationalen Musikgesellschaft*, iv (1902–3), 175–224.

Hirst, David L., *Tragicomedy* (London, 1984).

Howes, Frank, 'Notes on Monteverde's "Orfeo"', *The Musical Times*, lxv (1924), 509–11.

Jung, Hermann, *Die Pastorale: Studien zur Geschichte eines musikalischen Topos* (Berne and Munich, 1980).

Jürgens, Jürgen, 'Urtext und Aufführungspraxis bei Monteverdis *Orfeo* und *Marien-Vesper*', *Claudio Monteverdi e il suo tempo*, ed. Raffaello Monterosso (Verona, 1969), pp. 269–99.

Kerman, Joseph, *Opera as Drama* (London and New York, 1956) ['Orpheus: the neoclassic vision' repr., slightly revised by the author and omitting the complementary discussion of Gluck's *Orfeo ed Euridice*, as Chapter 7 in this book].

Lemprière's Classical Dictionary of Proper Names mentioned in Ancient Authors (3rd edn, London, 1984).

Leopold, Silke, 'Die Hierarchie Arkadiens: soziale Strukturen in den frühen Pastoralopern und ihre Ausdrucksformen', *Schweizer Jahrbuch für Musikwissenschaft*, new series, i (1981), 71ff.

——, *Claudio Monteverdi und seine Zeit* (Regensburg, 1982).

——, 'Orpheus in Mantua – und anderswo', *Concerto*, i (1983), 35–42.

Monteverdi, Claudio, *Claudio Monteverdi: lettere, dediche e prefazioni*, ed. Domenico de' Paoli (Rome, 1973).

——, *The Letters of Claudio Monteverdi*, trans. and introduced by Denis Stevens (London and New York, 1980).

Nagler, Alois M., *Theatre Festivals of the Medici, 1539–1637* (New Haven, 1964).

Neufeldt, Ernst, 'Monteverdi's "Orfeo" in Breslau', *Signale für die musikalische Welt*, lxxi (1913), 1090–3 [review of 1913 Breslau performance].

Nicolodi, Fiamma, *Gusti e tendenze del novecento musicale in Italia* (Florence, 1982).

Ovid, *Metamorphoses* (Loeb Classical Library), trans. Frank Justus Miller (2 vols., London, 1916).

——, *Le metamorfosi di Ovidio, ridotte da Giovanni Andrea dell'Anguillara . . . con l'annotationi di M. Gioseppe Horologgi* (7th edn, Venice, 1581).

——, *Le trasformazioni di M. Lodovico Dolce* (6th edn, Venice, 1561).

Palisca, Claude V., *Baroque Music* (2nd edn, Englewood Cliffs, N.J., 1981).

——, 'The "Camerata Fiorentina": a Reappraisal', *Studi musicali*, i (1972), 203–36.

Parry, C. Hubert H., 'The Significance of Monteverde', *Proceedings of the Musical Association*, xlii (1915–16), 51–67.

Pirrotta, Nino, 'Monteverdi e i problemi dell'opera', *Studi sul teatro veneto fra Rinascimento ed età barocca*, ed. Maria Teresa Muraro (Florence, 1971), pp. 321–43; English translation in Pirrotta, *Music and Culture in Italy from the Middle Ages to the Baroque* (Cambridge, Mass., 1984), pp. 235–53.

——, 'Teatro, scene e musica nelle opere di Monteverdi', *Claudio Monteverdi e il suo tempo*, ed. Raffaello Monterosso (Verona, 1969), pp. 45–64; English translation in Pirrotta, *Music and Culture in Italy from the Middle Ages to the Baroque* (Cambridge, Mass., 1984), pp. 254–70.

——, and Elena Povoledo, *Music and Theatre from Poliziano to Monteverdi* (Cambridge, 1982): revised English version, trans. Karen Eales, of *Li due Orfei* (Turin, 1969; 2nd edn, 1975).

Porter, William V., 'Peri and Corsi's "Dafne": Some New Discoveries and Observations', *Journal of the American Musicological Society*, xviii (1965), 170–96.

Prunières, Henry, *Monteverdi, his Life and Work* (London, 1926/R1972): English translation, by Marie D. Mackie, of *La vie et l'oeuvre de C. Monteverdi* (Paris, 1924).

Redlich, Hans F., 'Zur Bearbeitung von Monteverdis "Orfeo"', *Schweizerische Musikzeitung*, lxxvi (1936).

——, *Claudio Monteverdi: Life and Works* (London, 1952): revised English version, trans. Kathleen Dale, of *Claudio Monteverdi: Leben und Werk* (Olten, 1949).

Riesenfeld, Paul, 'L'Orfeo', *Allgemeine Musik-Zeitung*, xl (1913), 997–8 [review of 1913 Breslau performance].

Robinson, Michael F., *Opera before Mozart* (London, 1966).

Rogers, Nigel, ' "Orfeo" aus der Sicht des Interpreten', *Concerto*, i (1983), 43–4.

Rolland, Romain, 'Chronique musicale', *La revue d'art dramatique et musical*, xix (1904), supplement, pp. 49–54 [partly repr. and trans. as Chapter 6 in this book].

Ruthven, K. K., *Myth* (London, 1976).

Sartori, Claudio, 'Monteverdiana', *Musical Quarterly*, xxxviii (1952), 399–413.

Schneider, Louis, *Un précurseur de la musique italienne aux XVIe et XVIIe siècles: Claudio Monteverdi: l'homme et son temps* (Paris, 1921).

Schrade, Leo, *Monteverdi, Creator of Modern Music* (London, 1950/R1964).

Solerti, Angelo, *Gli albori del melodramma*, 3 vols. (Milan, 1904–5/R1969); vol. iii includes a transcription of the libretto of *Orfeo*.

Sternfeld, Frederick W., 'Aspects of Echo Music in the Renaissance', *Studi musicali*, ix (1980), 45–57.

——, 'The Birth of Opera: Ovid, Poliziano, and the *lieto fine*', *Analecta musicologica*, xix (1979), 30–51.

Stevens, Denis, *Monteverdi: Sacred, Secular and Occasional Music* (Rutherford, N.J., 1978).

Strong, Roy, *Splendour at Court* (London, 1973).

Tiersot, Julien, 'L'Orfeo de Monteverde', *Le Ménestrel*, lxx (1904), 75–6 [review of 1904 Paris performance].

Tomlinson, Gary, 'Madrigal, Monody, and Monteverdi's "via naturale alle immitatione"', *Journal of the American Musicological Society*, xxxiv (1981), 60–108.

Trevor, Claude, 'Claudio Monteverdi (1567–1643)', *Monthly Musical Record*, xl (1910), 149–51.

Virgil, *Eclogues, Georgics, Aeneid I–VI* (Loeb Classical Library), trans. H. Rushton Fairclough (rev. edn, London, 1935).

Walker, Thomas, and Edward H. Tarr, '"Bellici carmi, festivo fragor": Die Verwendung der Trompete in der italienischen Oper des 17. Jahrhunderts', *Hamburger Jahrbuch für Musikwissenschaft*, iii (1978), 143–203.

Westerlund, Gunnar, and Eric Hughes, *Music of Claudio Monteverdi: a Discography* (London, 1972).

Westrup, Jack A., 'The Continuo in Monteverdi', *Claudio Monteverdi e il suo tempo*, ed. Raffaello Monterosso (Verona, 1969), pp. 497–502.

——, 'Monteverde's "Orfeo"', *The Musical Times*, lxvi (1925), 1096–1100.

——, 'Two First Performances: Monteverdi's "Orfeo" and Mozart's "La Clemenza di Tito"', *Music and Letters*, xxxix (1958), 327–35.

Ziegler, Konrat, 'Orpheus', *Paulys Real-Encyclopädie der classischen Altertumswissenschaft . . . Neue Bearbeitung begonnen von Georg Wissowa* (34 vols., Munich, 1894–1972), xviii, part 1 (1939), cols. 1200–1417.

——, 'Orpheus in Renaissance und Neuzeit', *Festschrift Otto Schmitt* (Stuttgart, 1951), pp. 239–56.

Discography

MALCOLM WALKER

Only 'complete' recordings of the opera are listed in this discography. (For the different editions of *Orfeo* see Chapter 5 and Appendix 2.) For a list of recorded excerpts, dating from before 1919 to 1970, see Westerlund and Hughes, *Music of Claudio Monteverdi: a Discography*.

O Orfeo; *E* Euridice; *LM* La Musica; *M* Messaggera; *A* Apollo; *LS* La Speranza; *P* Proserpina; *Pl* Plutone; *C* Caronte; ⓜ = mono recording

1939 [Benvenuti's first version]
De Franceschi *O*; Vivante *E*; Lombardi *LM*; Mannacchini *A*; Nicolai *LS*; Palombini *P*; Marone *Pl*, *C* / chorus and orchestra / Calusio
> HMV (Voce del padrone) ⓜ QALP 10364/5
> (= Odeon ⓜ QALP 10364/5)
> from Musiche italiane antiche ⓜ 014/25
> (= HMV ⓜ DB 5370/81)
> EMI ⓜ 3C 153 18406–7M

1951 Meili *O*; Trötschel *E*; Fleischer *LM*; Lammers *M*, *LS*, *P*; Krebs *A*; Härtel *Pl*, *C* / Berlin Radio Vocal Ensemble and Chamber Orch / Koch
> Discophiles Français ⓜ DF42–44
> (= Haydn Society set 3001)
> Vox ⓜ VBX21
> (= DL 6440)
> (= Eterna 820 136/8)

1955 [Wenzinger's edition]
Krebs *O*; Mack-Cosack *E*; Guilleaume *LM*, *P*; Deroubaix *M*, *LS*; Wunderlich *A*; Günter *Pl*; Roth-Ehrang *C* / Chorus of the Staatliche Hochschule für Musik, Hamburg, 1955 Hitzacker Festival Orch / Wenzinger
> DG ⓜ 2708 001
> DG ⓜ APM 14057–8
> ARC ⓜ ARC 3035–6

1967 [Bucchi's edition]
Cited in L. Pannella, *Valentino Bucchi* (Florence, 1976), p. 210 and n. 103. No further details are available of this recording.
> RAI TOM 11325–8 (2 discs)

1967 [Tarr's edition]
Tappy *O*; M. Schwartz *E*; W. Staempfli *LM*; Sarti *M*; Altmeyer *A*;
Conrad *LS*; Bise *P*; J. Staempfli *Pl*; Loup *C* / Lausanne Complesso
Strumentale / Corboz
Erato STU 70440–2
HMV SME 95038–40
Musical Heritage Society 939–41
(= World Record Club SOC 237–39)
RCS (US) ARL3 2536

1969 [Harnoncourt's edition]
Kosma *O*; Hansmann *E*, *LM*; Berberian *M*, *LS*; Van Egmond *A*;
Katanosaka *P*; Villisech *Pl*; Simkowsky *C* / Munich Cappella
Antiqua Chorus, Vienna Concentus Musicus / Harnoncourt
Telefunken FK6 35020
SKH 21(1–3)
JY6 35376

1974 [Jürgens's edition]
Rogers *O*; Petrescu *E*, *LM*; Reynolds *M*, *P*; Partridge *A*; Bowman
LS; Dean *Pl*; Malta *C* / Hamburg Monteverdi Chorus, Hamburg
Camerata Accademica / Jürgens
DG 2728 018

1975 [Carl Orff, *Orpheus*, (*Lamenti*): in German]
Orff *Der Sprecher*; Prey *Orpheus*; Popp *Euridike*; Wagemann *Die
Botin*; Ridderbusch *Der Wächter der Toten* / Chorus of Bayerischer
Rundfunk, Münchner Rundfunk Orch / Eichhorn
BASF (Acanta) 44 22458–9

1981 [Version by Siegfried Heinrich attempting a reconstruction of the
original ending, using music from Monteverdi's ballet *Tirsi e Clori*
(pub. 1619)]
Seipp *O*; Liebermann *E*; Bühler *LM*, *LS*; Blanke-Roeser *M*; Spaett
A; Travis *P*; Hauptmann *Pl*; Bliesch *C* / Frankfurt Madrigal
Ensemble, Bad Hersfeld Festival 1980 Choir and Orch, Early Music
Studio of the Hesse Chamber Orch / Heinrich
TOL (Jubilate) JU 85810–12

1981 [Harnoncourt's Zurich edition]
Huttenlocher *O*; Yakar *E*, *LS*; Schmidt *LM*, *M*; Hermann *A*;
Linos *P*; Gröschel *Pl*; Franzen *C* / Chorus and instrumental
ensemble of the Zurich Opera / Harnoncourt
Telefunken EK6 35591

1984 [Nigel Rogers's edition]
Rogers *O*; Kwella *E*; Kirkby *LM*; Laurens *M*; Bolognesi *A*; Denley
LS; Smith *P*; Varcoe Pl; Thomas *C* / Chiaroscuro, London Cornett
and Sackbut Ensemble, London Baroque / Rogers and Medlam
EMI EX 270131-3 (records)
EX 270131-5 (cassettes)

Index